FIFTY YEARS IN THE FURNACE

Autobiography of a *nonconformist*

C. V. Myers

Falcon Press
Spokane, Washington

Library of Congress Catalog No. 89-23307

Library of Congress Catalog No. 89-23307

ISBN 0-9614883-1-X

Published by Falcon Press, P.O. Box 18586,
Spokane, Washington 99208

PRINTED IN THE UNITED STATES OF AMERICA

TO ALL NONCONFORMISTS

With the insight to see the Truth under camouflage,
With the courage to shout the Truth against the crowd,
With the nerve to challenge the bureaucrats
When their voices get too loud.

For you are the watchdogs of freedom!

TABLE OF CONTENTS

BOOK THREE
LIGHTNING

Other books by C.V. Myers:

Oil to Alaska, *Exposition, Inc. Press,* 1955

Philosophy of Investment, *MFR Publications Ltd.,* 1968

The Coming Deflation, *Arlington House Publishers,* 1976

Unbridled Bureaucracy in Canada, *Falcon Press,* 1979

Money & Energy, *Soundview Books,* 1980

World Rollover, *Falcon Press,* 1985

FIFTY YEARS IN THE FURNACE

Autobiography of a *nonconformist*

PREFACE

The first question that comes to mind in the writing of my autobiography is: Why do I think my life story is worth telling? I have never won a Pulitzer prize, a medal of honor. I have never even won a foot race.

The second question that comes up is even harder to answer: Why do I think people will be interested in me? I am not a celebrity, have never even been the friend of a celebrity. I have never even slept with a movie star. Darn it!

Still, I want very much to tell the story because I'm convinced that my life contains an interesting one - famous or not. After all, Big Names are, when you get right to the bottom of it, ordinary people, moved by the same emotions, beset by the same fears, moved forward by similar ambitions, gratified by the same kinds of appetites, appreciative of sincerity, repelled by patronage.

I once saw Orson Welles in the lobby of The Desert Inn in Las Vegas where he was performing. I had long ago made up my mind that if I ever had the chance I would tell him how much I admired his performance in *Citizen Kane*. Unexpectedly, and all of a sudden, Welles appeared, coming directly toward me.

I started to approach him. In that instant Welles actually looked scared, apprehensive.

I said simply: "I'm sorry to interrupt you, Mr. Welles, but fifteen years ago I saw you in *Citizen Kane* and I promised myself that if ever I had the chance I would tell you how powerful it was; the best picture I have ever seen, before or since."

Welles' expression changed completely. "Thank you!" His smile was spontaneous, almost like the smile of a friend. "Thank you," he repeated and walked on.

I felt good. Imagine, the Great Welles so easily softened, even though it must have been an unusual compliment for his picture to be remembered so long. I'm sure the Big Names are not much different from you and me, and you and I are not very different from one another. Realizing our kinship, I am comfortable in telling you the story, and I'm confident that you will recognize a lot of our common ground.

But a lot happened before all that and all along there were big flukes that made big changes in my life.

I have cut some mustard in my time. I foretold the defeat of the U.S. Treasury when it could no longer hold the price of silver. My subscribers mostly missed it because my letter was new then and they didn't believe me. But the next time when I firmly declared that the U.S. would default on U.S. gold obligations and that the gold price would soar, they did believe me. I made millionaires out of many of them; they told me so in their letters. I preserved or created future security for many others. In looking back over all of it, what comes out stronger to me than anything else is the truth of the old adage: "When you make your bed, you lie in it."

I did smart things and dumb things. I was sometimes courageous and sometimes foolishly timid: often too daring. But it's clear in retrospect that for whatever I did there was always an inevitable consequence. What happened to me always arose out of what I had done. Today is the result of yesterday. Tomorrow will be the result of today.

One thing of interest in my story is that it starts so long ago. My early years were lived within a social structure so different that it's hard for the kids of today to believe that conditions ever could have been so primitive, and just as hard for people of the latter twentieth century to envision the social order as we approach the last decade. And it's hard for the current population to accredit the reality of such a past.

For instance when I was born a doctor had to ride forty miles on horseback to save my mother's life. I first learned about the wonderful automobile when I was about five years old, experienced the marvel of the telephone when I was seven and the impossible concept of the radio when I was twelve.

I was sent to college a thousand miles from home and became the only college graduate within thousands and thousands of square miles of the Western Plains at that time.

I navigated the Depression which in our case lasted from 1929 to about 1939. I suffered the despair of joblessness; **for ten years** following my graduation I could not get my feet on the ground.

I thought there would never be any hope for me to own a car of my own. But I learned that things do change; bad eventually gets better, good can easily get worse. Going forward these conditions both seem to consume a lot of time; looking backward it's not nearly so long.

From writer I graduated to publisher and took on the biggest trade organizations in Canada and beat them all, selling out at the end of it for a small fortune I could never have dreamed of.

By this time I was in the furnace and I didn't know it. I had escaped going broke by only a hair. Now I commenced to write a financial advisory letter in 1967. That's where the furnace was fanned and the fire hasn't died out yet.

As a financial analyst I advised my subscribers to buy gold. This was in direct defiance of the United States government, which forbade citizens to own gold. But I was in Canada. I told them when I was in the U.S. I would obey U.S. laws but when I was in Canada I would obey only Canadian laws. I sold Americans some millions of dollars worth of gold and stored it anonymously for them in Canada.

Then one day the Canada Revenue moved in on what was the biggest raid ever conducted. They used twenty-five men to rifle my home, my offices, my banks, my auditors.

Now I was in the furnace all right and somebody had just slammed the door. Before it was all over I would finally come to terms with incarceration, escape, a life of exile in the United States, away from all friends and family, deportation orders and even another stint in jail, with my wife dying. Indescribable depression dogged my days and nights.

I fought the bureaucracies on both sides of the forty-ninth parallel. I appeared three times on the *Merv Griffin Show; Fifth Estate* (a Canada equivalent of *60 Minutes*) devoted a whole section to me, and I wrote three books.

People sometimes say to me: "How did you do it? I couldn't have made it through."

I respond, "Of course you would have made it through. Anybody would have made it through for the simple reason he has to; there is no other choice." My dad once told me a story that proves it.

A lad came running to his boss, "Boss, I just saw a frog down at the well and he jumped ten feet."

The farmer replied, "Nonsense, no frog can jump ten feet."

"Well," said the lad, "down there in this old well there is a big rattlesnake and this frog **had to** jump ten feet!"

You can influence what will happen tomorrow by the wisdom you exercise today. For instance this was a stupid frog. It was very careless of him to fall into the pit with a rattlesnake on the bottom. Watch where you're going.

But regardless of mistakes, it always remains true: Make your bed and lie in it. As ye sow, so shall ye also reap. Rattlesnakes eat frogs.

My story will tell you about a few of them.

Introduction

DESTINY

Can the course of one's life be totally altered by a triviality? Definitely yes.

In my case a simple coffee break set off emanations that embraced half a century. By that forbidden action I challenged America's most powerful bureaucracy during World War II. That was the U.S. Army Corps. of Engineers. It happened simply, if not innocently.

The U.S. Army was engaged in the biggest construction effort ever undertaken by man, although to this day it is little known, almost a forgotten incident.

The Japanese had sunk the American fleet at Pearl Harbor. Japan was suddenly the top naval power in the Pacific. They had landed in the Aleutian Islands of Alaska. And an invasion from Japanese bases in Alaska was feared. The Aleutian Islands were viewed as stepping-stones to the continent.

In an almost knee-jerk reaction the U.S. went to work on the Alaska Highway, a 2,000 mile road starting at Edmonton and forging northwest to Fairbanks where new air bases sprang up almost overnight.

There was a serious hole in the defense plan - no oil, either to supply American planes, or to fuel the naval ships. And there was no sign of any oil in Alaska's remote sediments.

But there was oil in northern Canada, in a place called Norman Wells, at the mouth of the mighty MacKenzie River on the rim of the Arctic Circle. The most fantastic plan was quickly hatched, given top priority, and a military classification of top secret.

An oil pipeline would be built from Norman Wells across the unexplored MacKenzie Mountains to Skagway, Alaska, where the Army would immediately build a refinery to process the crude oil from Norman Wells as fast as human effort could get it there. No oil, no fighting force, a Japanese invasion of the United States!

This top secret project was called "CANOL" after Canadian Oil. The jumping off place for the pipeline was Norman Wells but the jumping off place to get to Norman Wells was Edmonton, Alberta, Canada, where arrangements were made to transfer thousands of men, their housing, their fuel, their medical supplies and also their pipe, across 2000 miles of barren wasteland without a rail point, a town, a landing field, or even a road. The only means of transportation was down the MacKenzie River to the Arctic Circle; but the river lay frozen the better half of the year and in 1942 it froze early.

Edmonton was teeming with Americans; accents from Texas to Georgia to California and the Midwest were common on the streets.

I stumbled into this drama in the deep January freeze of 1942 and from this happenstance the tree of my career took root.

I say "stumbled" advisedly. Whoever looks back on his own history and the history of civilization generally comes to wonder how much has been fashioned by intelligent decision and how much by sheer chance. The records are rich with examples of success resulting from mistakes, and defeat arising out of bad luck. Generals have committed blunders which by every measure of common sense should have resulted in the destruction of their armies, but which by a whiff of circumstance changed into undeserved victory, resulting in long enduring changes by which millions have lived, or contrariwise, been obliterated.

What if Abraham Lincoln had missed getting the fatal tickets to the theater? Would he have enacted his plan to send the slaves back to Africa, and if so how would our country differ today? Just by missing those tickets.

What about the love letter that was unfortunately burned in the mail fire and never received? What about the telegram entrusted to a friend but never sent? Has irascible destiny divined our intentions, and then perversely thwarted them?

Should we reason we are controlled by the stars? Is there a luck so determined that it can either make us or break us?

I knew a man who did his damnedest (unwittingly) to avoid becoming rich. This man was a lawyer who, prior to the big oil discovery at Leduc, Alberta, found himself the owner of a very large tract of mineral rights in lieu of a legal bill he couldn't collect. A modest amount of gravel on the land was the sole claim to value. When Eric Harvey tried to realize on the property he found no market for the gravel. So he filed the title away at the back of his cabinet.

Then came Leduc and the great land rush in Northern Alberta led by Imperial Oil, the biggest oil company in Canada.

Imperial Oil, on advice of its geologists, made the decision to buy available mineral rights in the Redwater area, part of a general land acquisition scheme. Their boundary was arbitrary, existing for no reason other than in totality wildcat purchases had to stop somewhere. The Eric Harvey land bordered the Imperial lease block. Imperial was adamant against Harvey's pleadings to include his property in their block. He brought the price so low it couldn't have mattered a sou to big Imperial Oil. But a corporate decision had been made. The boundary was the boundary.

Sometime later Imperial drilled an exploratory well on the Redwater lease block and they struck oil far richer than the biggest oil flows at the by now famous Leduc Oil Field. Other wells soon showed that Harvey was the owner of three full sections, almost 2,000 acres, in the heart of what later would become the richest oil field in Canada, namely sections 21, 31 and 17, in Township 57, Range 21, W4th. Imperial Oil now had to buy leases on **proven** property. Harvey reaped 98 prolific oil wells while much of Imperial's land turned out to be moose pasture. Harvey became one of the wealthiest men in Canada, despite his determined efforts to avoid it.

Similarly, it seems to me that I stumbled into my future when I opened the door of the big California redwood building that housed the secret project of the U.S. government in that chilly

January 1942.

I was thirty years old. It was the unsuspected beginning of half a century in the furnace. Fifty years hasn't yet quite expired but then neither am I yet completely out of the furnace.

BOOK ONE

CRADLE

Chapter One

A CUP OF COFFEE

The top secret project under the code name CANOL was carried out under the auspices of three of the biggest U.S. construction companies, the Bechtel Company, the Callahan Construction Company and the Price Pipeline Company. These private companies were working for the U.S. government on what was known as a cost-plus basis. That is, the contractors' fee was 10 percent of the total cost of everything spent on the project. That required a watchdog and the watchdog was the U.S. Army Corps of Engineers. The engineers had no power to tell the contractor what to do or how to do it, or whom to hire or whom to fire, but every dollar the contractors spent had to have prior approval by the engineers before the contractor could be paid. A veritable stream of paper went back and forth. The bureaucratic organization controlled the purse strings.

This would vitally affect the ramifications of the clandestine cup of coffee I was soon to drink.

I worked very hard at my job and I was soon in the position of expediting all of the personnel used on the project from Edmonton, 2,000 miles north, through these dreary, frozen, barren wastes.

The Bechtel Engineers would order something like: 100 carpenters, 30 cooks, 20 accountants, two dozen bulldozer operators, and so on down the line. It was my job to get them there. Sometimes I worked long hours after everyone else had left the office, and sometimes I came in early. I never missed an objective. I worked right out of the office of project manager J.P. Shirley, Jr. I know my effort was appreciated because on the Christmas of

1942 I was given a bonus that amounted to about $5,000 in today's money.

Along the early part of 1943 the U.S. Army Corps of Engineers got the idea that too much time was being spent by employees drinking coffee. We had a huge office building there with several hundred employees and at coffee time they would pour out of the California redwood building and across the street. The engineers said the privilege was being abused and they declared that there would be no more coffee breaks for employees, or at least the U.S. government would not pay the contractors for the time consumed. No more coffee!

I still had the simple fairness approach of a boy off the farm. I felt this restraint on the part of the engineers was an insult to my total dedication. I gave many hours beyond my duty and they weren't going to give me fifteen minutes?

On the first restricted morning at ten o'clock I approached, as usual, the wide exit. Immediately a guard threw himself between me and the exit (guards invariably do that). "You can't go out," he announced.

I said, "You may be able to keep me out of this building, but you certainly can't keep me in." I pushed him out of the way and I went out and had the fateful "CUP OF COFFEE."

Upon returning the guard was there to block my entry. I told him that I was employed by the contractor, and the Army Corps of Engineers had no power to keep me out.

Now guards have no reason for existence other than to enforce the bureaucratic rulings on top. This guard became very red in the face, as I pushed him out of the way and entered the building.

I did this again the next day.

On the third day J. P. Shirley, Jr. called me into his office; "What the hell is going on with you and the engineers on the coffee business?" he said.

I told him I felt that my long hours outweighed this triviality. Shirley said, "I agree with you. But you're causing me a hell of a lot of trouble and I want you to stop it!"

So I did. Nothing more was heard about the incident. But

later as the project wound down, time came to get the men out of CANOL. Since I had expedited them in, Shirely thought I was the man to expedite them out and he wanted to send me up to do it. But he had to have travel authority from the Army Engineers. They refused. They replied in writing; "This man is a non-conformist!"

J. P. Shirley responded; "Either approve his travel authority or give me orders to fire him."

Well, of course, they would be exceeding their authority to order any hiring or firing. True to the mentality of bureaucrats everywhere, they did nothing. After some consecutive days I asked Shirley what I should do and he said simply, "Sit there." That I did.

Then I learned that with the Japanese threat receding swiftly, the "classified" status of CANOL had been removed. Anyone was now free to write about the project.

I had access to photographs from the entire project including the ice regions of the Great Northern Lakes and the caterpillar trains across the tundra. I began putting the material together in a small book. It was only about 30 pages, but it gave the story of the Canol project with very dramatic pictures, and I felt it would sell; no one else had the story. I took what money I had in the bank and the little I had in insurance, and published the book myself. By the time of the great exodus I had it done. I got it out quickly to the newsstands in Edmonton, and right away it began to sell. In less than two weeks, as men swarmed in out of the north, I had sold three thousand books at a dollar a copy. Paul Grafe, President of the Callahan Construction Company, bought a thousand copies to give to his friends.

That was the turning point in my career. It set the stage for the rest of my life. It all revolved around that cup of coffee without which I would have gone to CANOL, I would never have written the booklet, and probably would never have gotten a job as journalist, in which case I would never have, as we shall see later, antagonized the U.S. and Canadian governments, would there-fore have avoided incarceration, escape, exile and the threat of deportation from the U.S.

My fifty years in the furnace had commenced.

Chapter Two

IN THE BEGINNING

In the beginning there was a lonely little shack upon the flat and endless Canadian plains with never a tree or even a shrub - only a sea of grass, grass, grass. They called it buffalo grass.

And in this little shack there lived a man called Amil and a woman, Lena, and one small boy-child. The woman was young, very pretty, with lively blue eyes. She was tiny with flaxen hair the color of burnished straw in the sun. The man, her husband, was the picture of endurance. Heavy set, medium height, square jawed, unshaven; carrying a heavy load, he leaned forward into the strong wind out of the west, or in the wintertime against the driven snow from the north that sometimes lasted days on end. The boy was a towheaded three-year-old who played outside, around the shack.

In the beginning the greatest hazard to existence was the fierce winters when weather unleashed its frightful blizzards against the tiny fortresses of homesteaders standing fully exposed on a wide plain of the Canadian Northwest. And in the single boarded shack the coal stove was kept stoked to full power to combat the 40-below-zero temperatures that sometimes lasted for days on end; the room stayed warm in the center but not so warm around the perimeters, at the door and the two windows, where sometimes the fine snow was driven between the cracks. The cold was so fierce that the hoarfrost often built up half an inch thick on the window panes, blocking out the light. Here the boy would amuse himself by creating crude drawings with a knife or a fork through the thick frost on the window.

The sun lagged in the mornings and often would not rise until

Sweep of the prairies. Originally the 12' X 12' shack where the house is, was the sole man-made feature.

Standing at the southwest corner of the original shack, 1988. It had been raised to sit on a foundation.

Two teams in tandem, four horses each, starting the day on an
8-foot disk. Photographer clearly preferred horses to driver,
which was me.

Amil, Lena and me at the age of three or four.

10 o'clock and it disappeared in the early afternoons, sometimes by 4:30 and the lonely evenings and nights stretched out endlessly. There was little room to move around in the shelter of the house for it was only twelve feet long and twelve feet wide, big enough only to hold a bed, a stove, a dresser and a small wash tub. Other clothes could be hung from hooks on the walls where sometimes, if they had been washed, they would be found frozen stiff in the mornings. The fire demanded constant attention; when it went low the water froze in the water pail on the wash stand, and the breaths of all three became visible vapors.

The food, such as it was, sow belly and beans, had to be stored in the dirt basement under the house before winter came. In a small shed 50 yards beyond the house one lucky cow, two horses and some chickens found their winter shelter. From the cow came the milk and the cream each day, from the chickens the eggs and sometimes the meat. The water carried to the livestock had to be brought out quickly so that it didn't freeze before they had time to drink it. When the storm finally abated the horses, relieved from dark confinement, ran breakneck into the pasture putting on an exhibition of bucking and wheeling to burn off the excess energy. The boy too, fretting and fussing at the seemingly endless confinement, welcomed the freedom that came with the breaking of the sun with shrieks of glee. Even so the waist high snow drifts in the yard demanded constant vigilance since the child might easily disappear in one of the drifts, never to be found.

It was a 40 mile journey to Stavely, the nearest town and point of rail. In the town there dwelt a doctor, but only the most life-threatening illness could bring him out to a home. It took a horseman most of the day to ride to the town to tell the doctor. The doctor took most of a day to get there, then still had a seven hour ride back. Meanwhile many other urgent patients could be in trouble. Not only that but the unpredictable winter storms could come without notice and a man or his horse could be lost in the 40 mile trip to the town of Stavely. If he didn't get back the woman would not know for days, for there was no such thing as a telephone, and it was not likely that any messenger would venture the trail until the storm had blown itself out.

One day this man began to complain of a toothache. As the days passed on the winter storm grew worse. By night the pain was getting unbearable. It was in fact an abscessed tooth, to which there is no remedy but removal. The couple hung on hoping for the weather to break. It did not break. When at last the pain became too much for either of them to stand, as if by mutual understanding and without words, the woman started to prepare for the operation. She boiled a can opener and a pair of pliers thoroughly in a cooking pot. She took out a much prized partial bottle of whiskey to dull the pain that would come with this operation. She used the can opener to dig in under the tooth and the pliers to wiggle it as it got looser. Constant pressure and constant wiggling brought it thankfully from its socket and out of the ravaged mouth. By the use of some peroxide and more whiskey infection was avoided. The man was free. When the storm continued even worse that night they were both thankful that it had been done.

* * * *

In contrast, the progress of the twentieth century is most distinctly expressed in a single experience of mine. In New York in 1987 I bought a ticket on the Concorde. I landed in Paris in less time than it took us in my boyhood to travel the twenty miles to Vulcan - the nearest town - and back. That is an illustration of the advance not only in travel but in almost every other aspect of life.

We didn't know when we bought a brand new buggy in 1916 that within another year we would have a new Ford car. The buggy by itself was a luxury that we had hardly dare dream of. Prior to that it was horseback or the slow lumber wagon. I remember still as a four-year-old child standing in the shed where the shiny new leather buggy was being made ready to hitch our horse to. It had a fine upholstered seat. The rear end of it was a built-in box where you could carry groceries or anything else you had a mind to buy in town. The front of it was a fancy dash with brass finish and it was even equipped with a couple of kerosene lamps at the side. This seemed to be for fancy city folk because we never had occasion to use the kerosene lamps.

On our way home that fall day of 1916 we even put up the

Eisenglass curtains to keep the wind out. Some style. We made the twenty miles home in about an hour and a half. A new world was opening up to us.

So many things happened in the ten years following the outbreak of war in 1914 it's hard to keep them straight in one's mind. Between the ages of two and fourteen my world took its first big leap.

We had a big crop in 1915 and a bumper crop of over sixty bushels to the acre in 1916.

At the end of 1916 we bought another place with a house and barn on it, enlarging our land holdings to 900 acres. My dad needed help with all that work. My mother's brother, Carl, who was out of work, came up from Denver with his family to rent the new place.

My mother had contracted pneumonia late in 1915 and nearly died. I recall being brought into her bedroom and standing beside her bed with my three-year-old head not much higher than the mattress and being asked to tell my mother good-bye. I didn't have the faintest idea of what it meant. I thought she was going to a neighbor's place. She recovered by benefit of about the only remedy that medicine could advise at that time. That was to keep the windows wide open and get lots of fresh air.

The next year a wave of typhoid fever hit the country and my dad nearly died. By now they had a hospital in Calgary and a train to get there through Vulcan. My father was so seriously ill that my mother had to travel with him on the train to take him to the hospital. She left me with an English-speaking family who lived less than a mile from our place. The biggest effect it had on me was to terminate a growing familiarity with the German language.

My parents had spoken nothing to me but German with the idea that I would learn English anyway when I went to school and I would be also equipped with a second language. I haven't the slightest memory of whatever could have happened, but they told me in later years that when they got back from Calgary and commenced to speak German to me I would not answer. I had spoken my last German word. From that moment on I would only speak English.

A psychiatrist has suggested to me that this may have been a trauma for me, being deserted in my young mind by both my mother and my father, my home being taken from me, and planted with people who I couldn't talk to and who couldn't talk to me. At three years old that would be quite a shock, I guess, but I've had some shocks since then that could come close to it.

The part of my life that I remember most vividly centered around the age of four to seven when we bought our first car.

In those years we lived, in the long winter evenings, by the dim light of an oil lamp. We had two of them, for now our house was a little bigger than it had been earlier. The bowls had to be kept filled and the wicks trimmed. Otherwise the carbon from the flame would deposit on the chimneys and block out nearly all the light. My dad and my mother spent long winter evenings reading to one another from popular books of the day by Zane Grey and Edgar Rice Burroughs. I remember *Riders of the Purple Sage* and *The Winning of Barbara Worth*. I didn't understand much of it, but I liked to hear it anyway. The time hung very heavy.

I don't know what the younger generation of today would do with such evenings. Some would probably go out and rape somebody or get high on cocaine. There was no crime, though, in those days. I never heard of crime and then only one when I was about 13. And it was the talk of the country until the culprit was hanged.

A young man, known to me only as the Dorch kid, had been working for a fairly well-to-do farmer about ten miles west of us near the town of Vulcan. The harvest was over and Dorch was let go. One night with his brother he drove into the farmer's yard after midnight and banged at the door. The farmer lit the lamp upstairs and appeared at the window to see what was wanted. Dorch asked him if he would come down and lend him a pail of gas. When the farmer, still in his nightgown, bent over to get a wrench to open the drum, Dorch brought out a shotgun and blew his head off.

The story around the country, that I hardly understood, was that Dorch had a great liking for the farmer's wife. I didn't see anything wrong with liking the farmer's wife, but of course I didn't know the end product of "liking." Anyway, the mounted police were called. They came at daybreak and were able to follow Dorch's tracks; there was only dirt road in those days. By ten o'clock they found him in the pool hall as it opened and they arrested him. Within a few weeks he was tried and sentenced to hang. In less than three months after the trial we learned that Dorch had been hanged at the Lethbridge jail. The country was in shock for a year, and I never heard of another crime for another seven or eight years, until in the early Depression when some vagrant, having engaged a taxi to take him out of town, murdered the taxi driver and took the taxi.

We never locked our doors and we never lost anything more than a barrel of gas. It was just the thing to do in those days to leave the doors open in case some traveller got stranded and couldn't make it home, needed a meal and feed for his horses. Policemen then must have been lonelier than the Maytag men of today.

Without being aware of it we have undergone a social revolution in the last half century. But we still have a way to go; now most of us live within blocks of a hospital but hardly anyone can afford it.

Chapter Three

DOCTOR ON HORSEBACK

Luckily, I was born in June. Otherwise I would never have arrived and my mother would never have survived. The ordeal of my birth was something that was rarely talked about in our home and I only heard minor details fleetingly years later.

I was aware that my mother thought I was a child of destiny because of the unlikelihood that I could be born alive.

Labor had commenced about six o'clock in the morning with a neighbor lady in attendance to supervise my emergence as the latest member of the human race. I don't know the details but I do know that after about eight hours of labor a state of alarm had spread to all the neighbors and a full-fledged crisis of life or death was at hand. A number of neighbor ladies consulted in great urgency. Not one among them had enough skill as a midwife to bring this birth about. The whole community was in an uproar. A woman was about to die here and absolutely **no one** could lift a finger to save her, although life was still strong within her. They just had to get a doctor. A young neighbor, Art Fitzpatrick, about 24 years of age, now long since passed away, volunteered to make the 40-mile dash to Stavely to get the doctor to save my mother's life. Art galloped out of the yard and the women returned to give what small comfort and compassion they could to my suffering mother. I once heard my dad say there could never come a time in all his life, no matter how bad, to match those next many hours.

Art rode into Stavely with the horse covered with foam and dripping wet. He got the message immediately to the doctor and explained what he could while walking off the horse because he dare not let him stop for a moment until he had cooled out. The doctor - no one seems to remember his name - saddled a fresh horse immediately and with the essential tools in his medical kit took off across the prairie, following the wagon trail east over the miles and miles, down the river banks of the Little Bow now at its lowest ebb - because there had been no rain - up the other side and into the last stretch, eight miles still from the Myers' homeshack. His patient by now neared total exhaustion. Through the pain, the suffering, and the strain, my mother was barely conscious. No one could know if Art had actually reached the doctor or if the doctor would be present and available. Time rolled on. After eight hours they began to fear the doctor would be too late. They couldn't possibly expect his arrival in less than 12 hours from the time Art had left. They kept coming out to look down the trail, but there was nothing to be seen. At the height of despair someone shouted, "Here he is!" About a mile away over the high ground the mounted doctor came into view.

People were shouting and cheering as the doctor slid from the saddle, the sweat streaming off his horse. Neighbor men kept the horse walking for the next three hours cooling him off to save his life while the doctor attempted the rescue of the patient, by now almost totally drained of strength.

Decades later, after my mother had passed away, I heard a horror story of how she had been strung up in stirrups attached to the rafters in the barn to allow the birth to happen.

Small wonder she attributed my birth to God's intervention. She thought God must have a personal interest in me. My mother had deep religious beliefs and that conviction never left her. She told me once afterward that she had had a vision that my name would be known far and wide. I'm glad it was not revealed to her just how, because in Canada it became known throughout the country through the notoriety of a tax case that, before it was finished, saw me in exile in a foreign country and the Canadian tax authorities confounded, impotent, and despised because of conduct that became widely recognized as vicious, personally vindictive and oppressive, employing eventually even double jeopardy to try to win a point. My mother's vision would have been a nightmare instead. If God had an interest in me He was most inefficient in the way He handled it.

I've been told that it took some time for my head to come back into proper shape after that difficult birth. My mother was never able to prove God's intervention but I can prove the doctor's by a fairly deep scar on either side of my forehead reaching well up beyond the hairline, results of a torn scalp. I'm afraid my friends, when they learn of this, are going to say, "I wondered what's been the matter with you all along; now I know."

* * * *

Well, that was kind of a rough start. It seems to me a person is entitled to a better welcome into the world, but my biggest sympathy goes out to my mother. She vowed never again to bear a child outside the hospital and both my sister Ruth, born five years later, and my brother Richard, born 15 years later, were delivered in the Holy Cross Hospital in Calgary, a city that has grown from five or ten thousand people at that time to more than a half of a million people now.

It's sobering to think that all of the adults of that time in that city are now long since buried, as are their contemporaries all over the world, and that in another 70 or 80 years all of the adults alive today will have turned this planet over to a new bunch who will have their turn at mismanagement.

At any rate, my turn at life came on June 15, 1912, two weeks after my mother's 24th birthday at about five o'clock in the afternoon. I don't know how the doctor got home or what horse he used, but it must have been a borrowed horse for the two that had been used in this operation would have been too tired to handle another 40-mile ride. I presume that the neighbors went home soon after the triumphant birth as I, with a totally exhausted father and mother, began my first day of life. I hope that the good doctor lost no time in making it back to Stavely for the heavy clouds which began to darken the skies about the time I was delivered thickened and by ten o'clock they opened on the parched land and the dying crops with yellow stems barely clinging to life. The downpour started by midnight and it lasted for three days and three nights and never had that farm country got such a shot in the arm in one sustained spell, before or since.

Although I could not be a witness, I know the story through its repetition, as well as if I had been exposed in my cradle to this blessing. The crop that looked like it didn't have a chance on June 15 became the bumper crop of record.

At 60 bushels to the acre our quarter section yielded 9,600 bushels which, measured in 1912 dollars, must have looked like a fortune to these dry land homesteaders who'd barely had enough money to survive through the previous winter. I was born into a greater prosperity than I would see again in the first 50 years of my life.

From the moment of my birth my mother was convinced that she had conceived a genius. She often confided with my father her fear that I was, she said, "too smart to live."

Maybe I proved her wrong because I did live. But always I was under her spell. My sister, five years younger and a social worker in New York, told me many decades later that Sigmund Freud had declared: "The first born has no choice but to fulfill the dreams of the mother."

I do believe that I was doomed to try. I can never remember a time of any doubt that my schooling would continue into the indefinite future. While my classmates in the country school all looked jubilantly forward to getting out of school on the day that they would finish grade eight, which was compulsory, no such thought ever occurred to me. My future seemed cast in a mold, a mold that called for the highest education, even university, although I doubt that any university existed within 1500 miles of our homestead at that time. No alternative could be possible.

Both my mother and my father came from German working class stock. My mother's father was a basket weaver in the town of Oberweidt, Germany and my dad's father was a steelworker in Switzerland. In Europe they both lived on the edge of hunger because back in the later part of the nineteenth century common people had only one motivation - food enough to sustain life, and a dry, warm shelter to stay in. There were no extras. This was the concept that my parents brought with them to the new world. As long as we had a home, a roof that didn't leak, a stove and the coal to fuel it, and enough to eat, we were well off. A fortune of

$15,000 in one year? Unbelievable right up to the moment the harvest came and the golden grain rolled down the spout into the granary.

Thereafter for many years the local reference point became June 15, doctor on horseback, and the deluge.

Chapter Four

HARVEST

Actually, I was a late comer. The 1912 crop was our fourth crop. The year 1908 was spent preparing the raw land. First of all it had to be plowed. That had taken my dad nearly all summer with his four horses and his two-furrow Sulky plow with a 28 inch bite. Big tractors of today will plow a swathe 40 feet wide, will do more in half a day than my father did in all the summer of 1908.

After the land was plowed it had to be disked, cultivated, harrowed, or in some way worked up to make a reasonable seed bed. In 1909 and the year preceding my father had had to work up other people's land to buy the necessities preceding our 1910 crop.

As soon as the wheat was ripe my father would start out with a horsedrawn binder eight feet wide to cut the 160 acres - to cut it and bind it into bundles tied automatically by the knotter with twine, kicked out onto a dump basket which could hold about eight bundles. Every eight bundles he would dump the basket and as he went round and round the field, these lines of dumped baskets began to grow so that each of these lines became what was known as a windrow. When the wheat shockers came in each would start at the beginning of a windrow and stook to the middle of the field which would be about a quarter of a mile.

The summer I was thirteen I joined the men. The summer was hot. The bundles were heavy. Sweat flowed profusely. The stooking started exactly at 7:00 A.M. following our breakfast from 6:00 A.M. to 7:00 A.M. It lasted until 12:00 noon when we broke for an hour at lunch - we called it dinner. It had to be a hearty meal. And then we stooked again from 1:00 P.M. until 6:00 P.M. when we would stop for supper off my mother's coal stove, including home made bread, everything produced there on the farm.

That was only the beginning of a long hard road to market and money and payment for the wheat. After all the wheat had been stooked, the thrashing machine would make a dramatic entrance to our farm. The thrasher was one of the local farmers who had managed to get together the capital to buy a machine. This thrasher consumed the bundles in flying knives and beaters so that the crushed straw came flowing out one spout and the golden grain down another spout into the granary. The granaries were usually twelve feet square and seven feet high. They would hold about a thousand bushels and each granary when full would have beside it a large straw stack from which the straw could be forked into hay wagons at the end of the season and taken into the farm for the stock during the winter.

Some farmers burned their straw stacks in the fall after the grain was out and the granaries were moved, but we never did. My mother used to say, "You never know what next year will bring, maybe we won't have a crop at all. Let's save the straw stacks." So whenever we burned straw stacks they were at least two years old.

When the thrashers left that was like declaring victory. The hustle and bustle suddenly stopped. Peace and quiet set in over our vegetable garden where the thrashers helped themselves to all the potatoes and vegetables they needed for their crew of at least a dozen men. This was understood practice.

When the crew left they made quite a procession. The bundle wagons, as they emptied their last loads into the separator, started off down the road to the next farm, followed by the cook car, followed by the bunk car where the men slept, and finally followed by the flunky wagons and then the steam engine pulling the separator. There was the sigh of relief. We knew our crop was safe. Our livelihood had been saved, all we needed to do was get it to rail.

The nearest market was of course, at Stavely where my dad had first set foot when he came to the country. My parents had two wagons each holding about sixty bushels, each drawn by a team of horses. Fairly early before I had come onto the scene, they had obtained four horses. My father drove one team of two and my mother drove the gentler team. To get to Stavely by dark they had to leave in the morning no later than six o'clock. They had absolutely to be up in the five o'clock darkness. The night before the wagons would have to be filled. That meant backing them up to the granaries and with a scoop shovel lifting about thirty-six hundred pounds from the granary into each wagon. This was about the hardest job that I would ever experience which I did a-plenty in later years.

Now when the wagons were full, the horses would be unhitched, put in the barn and bedded down. And my parents would go to bed as early as possible for the big trip the following day.

No ordinary horses walk four miles an hour over the course of several hours, especially if they are drawing a heavy load. It was more likely about three miles an hour. This trip to Stavely therefore would take twelve to thirteen hours. In October, the sun began to set early and rise late and it was often cold. My parents, bundled up, hitched up their horses in the cold darkness, climbed onto their wagons with the prepared lunch, and if they got away about six o'clock in the morning they would reach Stavely in the six or seven o'clock darkness of the evening. Then there was the job of getting the wheat off the wagons.

At first it had to be shoveled off; later on when elevators became common the wagons were drawn over a hydraulic hoist, lifted; the end gate in the back was opened and, lo and behold the wheat flowed freely out!

The next day meant another early rising in order to make the distance from Stavely back to the farm again and another re-shoveling of the grain to fill the wagons for another twelve hour drive to Stavely the following day. But it was all joyous work for what was in the wagons was real money. A handful of red hard grain was like holding gold. It was all of the grade known as Northern Canadian Number One Hard, the best wheat in all the world.

If you had a thirty bushel to the acre crop, 160 acres would yield 4800 bushels. Two wagons would deliver 120 bushels a trip.

At two days a trip the forty trips would take eighty days - nearly three months, right up to the time of the harsh winter. But a sixty bushel crop, that was another matter. The crop of 1912 after the downpour of June could not have been handled.

Fortunately, the town of Vulcan was also born in 1912 and by the fall of that year, one of those tall elevators that so commonly dot the Canadian prairie was erected to take the grain. Vulcan was only twenty miles away.

Now a return trip to town could be made in a single day. At thrashing time my father bought a brand new tank wagon that would hold 120 bushels, pulled with four horses in tandem. And my mother didn't have to make the trip any more, which was a lucky break because there was no way she could have handled the two day trip to Stavely and looked after me as well. There were few babysitters on those homesteaded plains.

So there you see my origins, and my parents establishing themselves on the Canadian plains. How did it happen that they were there?

Chapter Five

BEFORE THE BEGINNING
100 YEARS AGO

The town of Vulcan and I were newcomers in the year of 1912; my mother and father were newcomers in the year 1908; my father and his father were newcomers to the Oklahoma Indian Territory known as the Cherokee Strip in 1893 when my father was a boy of 12. This was the last free land to be opened up to white settlers in the United States. The Indians had been cleared out of it; all subdivisions had been marked within the territory, a homesteader could claim as much as 160 acres. These subdivisions were all staked by the government and they were offered on a first come - first served basis.

To give all an equal chance the settlers were to start at the crack of a gun fired on the frontier line. My father described that line to me when I was a boy.

He said, "There were wagons just about as far as you could see and there were buggies, and there were men on horseback and there was some covered wagons with families. We were all drawn up to a line on a level flat stretch of land and when the gun was fired we all started out.

"Us guys with wagons was the slowest compared with them on horseback or in buggies but we thought there would be enough land for everyone, so we had been told.

"Our horses were not the fastest walkers but we drove steady all day until about sunset we came to a little stream. And just on the edge of a stream on a bluff that was uphill from the stream there was surveyor's markings that showed some unclaimed land. What we had to do was drive in our stakes to mark the land as ours.

"Our horses were tired and thirsty and hungry. And so we

27

took the wagon down to the water, unhitched the horses, took them for a drink and we was tying them up to have a feed on the oat bundles we had brought along when all of a sudden we heard this loud voice."

My father told me:

"I looked up and I saw a man on a horse, in a black jacket, and black hat and also about thirty feet away. He was pointing a gun at us.

"The man says, 'You fellers better move on.'"

"'But we've just come up on this land and we're ready to drive our stakes. We're just watering," my dad's dad said to him. The man said, "You're too late. Hitch up and move on."

My dad told me the voice was very rough. His father was no gunslinger. There was no choice.

So they took the partly fed horses and hitched them up again and drove off into the night and on the following morning they found a place that was available for claiming. It was not a very good place. The soil was poor. There was no water on the place but at least it was level and no trees to be cleared.

They had passed many claimed tracts of land in their days' journey and some of these tracts had been staked before the firing of the official gun. People had sneaked in, driven in stakes, and unless they had been caught who was to say the stakes hadn't been driven earlier? These people were called "Sooners" and that is the origin of the slang term "Sooner" in Oklahoma.

As my grandfather drove, my father had huddled under the straw of the wagon during the chilly night and in the morning he was tired and cramped but more hungry than tired. They had enough grub to cook a meager breakfast. Then my grandfather Gustav Meier staked this land as "Our home, son. Our home in the United States of America," he said in broken English with pride.

It did not turn out to be any swell home. The only kind of a house they could afford was the one that would rise out of the land itself; a sod house. They cut sod in squares of about four inches deep and they built a small house out of this sod which would, they hoped, be large enough to house my dad's mother and the other three children when they arrived.

Grandfather's family worked the soil, they did the best they could. They had a few cows and they had purchased a bull for a very low price. The reason for the low price was because the bull was known to have attacked people.

Years later when I was trying to get information to justify my entry into the United States on the basis of my father's citizenship in the Oklahoma strip, I learned from an old neighbor of the Gustav Meier family that my father's younger brothers Fred and Bob had taken turns at teasing the bull in his corral when my grandfather was absent.

"There's no doubt," said old Myerson, "Those boys teased the bull. That could have been the cause of what happened."

What happened was dire. Gustav returned home one day just in time to see the horned bull attack my uncle Bob, who was putting feed into the corral. Infuriated, my grandfather grabbed a club, leaped the fence (he was only 45 years of age then), hot after the bull.

The bull was faster. From a side attack he hurled himself into the body of Gustav who fell bleeding. At that moment, the dog - my dad told me - jumped into the corral and chased the bull off, as they dragged my mortally gored grandfather out of the corral and into a wagon to be taken to a doctor somewhere - that was beyond my father's memory. In any case Gustav died before he ever saw a doctor and the young mother Selina (44) was left to bring up four children on a meager patch of poor land in the Indian Territory of the Oklahoma strip so well known in history.

My father was 16 years old at the time, second in line to his elder brother, Gustav Meier, Jr. But Gustav Jr. was away in Colorado making a living for a family he was starting himself. The job of feeding the younger children and my grandmother fell on the shoulders of my father.

The records show that my grandmother filed for the homestead in her own name after my grandfather's death. That document resides in the archives of the State of Oklahoma. And it proves something important because my grandmother would not have been allowed to file for a homestead unless she had also been a citizen. But there was no existing record of her citizenship.

The courthouse at Chase, Oklahoma, where all the early records had been kept, was burned. Records lost forever. No doubt my grandmother's application for citizenship and the issue of citizenship was among those papers.

When I later attempted to establish American citizenship on the basis that my father was a citizen, I ran into the same dead end. There was no record. Unless my father's citizenship became recognized I had no claim.

If the **known** citizenship registration of my grandmother was beyond doubt by virtue of her homestead and if her papers had obviously been lost in the court house fire, then wasn't it likely that my father's citizenship records were lost there with them? And how could anyone say that Emil Meier was never a citizen? Government agencies are not notably logical. U.S. Immigration simply declared our case as inadequate and closed the book.

The matter may be premature in this part of my story, but it shows how the events that took place in the Cherokee Strip 100 years ago surfaced again in the late part of this century and became a matter of utmost importance to my survival. I shall deal with the continuation in proper sequence.

Chapter Six

BASIC LESSONS

Our most important learning does not come from books. It comes, in fact, before we have ever learned to read. Our lives are not the manifestations of our knowledge - of what we know. They are the manifestations of what we believe. These fundamental concepts come to us passively through what we witness in our earliest years. These concepts, although we are hardly aware of them, take shape in our subconscious mind and they build a gridwork, or a mold, which in adult life will motivate us, restrain us, inspire us, or shame us.

I know my conscience is rooted in the deep past. It does not spring from what I was taught in Sunday school, but from the attitudes and the examples that made impressions on me as my early life advanced.

We learn through experience that reality is unalterable. The child does not know what hot is until he touches the stove. He does not know the meaning of hunger until he goes without food. He does not know what a spanking is until he gets one. He does not understand entrapment until he gets into a box, sometimes of his own making. If he doesn't have bad experiences early in life he will have to learn from other experiences later on.

On the pioneer farm we took life as it came. Children could not be protected from everything. Nor was there any such effort to protect them.

I find near the end of my seventh decade that most of my fundamental beliefs rose out of the first five years of my life. My attitudes developed from what happened to me and to what I saw happen around me.

I remember many stories of the first World War and I was told many others as our little homestead shack weathered well the storm of the second decade of the century. Highest in effectiveness are those events that happened observably around me and those that happened to me directly.

I was impressed with the cold impersonality of the law by what happened to Jack Albert, a neighbor who lived two and a half miles north of us. During one of those early winters he had run out of food for his family and with no other purpose than simple survival, he had killed a steer belonging to a very large absentee rancher.

In those days the cattle of Pat Burns roamed the southern plains at will. You had to build fences to keep them out of your crops. The onus was not on the owner of the cattle; the onus was on the owner of the land. I heard my dad tell of how a herd of wild cattle had converged upon him with his four-horse outfit in the field, so close that he became alarmed, which was unusual for him. At that point he threw a mackinaw over his head and shoulders and charged the cattle. They took off at a high rate, frightened to death at the apparition.

But the neighbor I speak of had committed the crime of rustling. It wasn't rustling as it was normally known because it concerned only one critter taken in the throes of hunger.

The kill took place in the desolate valley about a mile east of his home. It was known as Snake Valley and later became the reservoir that was known as Lake McGregor. At that time it consisted of rocks and some dried-out fall grass. Mr. Albert gutted the critter there on the ground, leaving its entrails, and by horse dragged it out of the valley up to his homestead and cut and quartered it.

One of the settlers had seen Pat Burns' scout riding west at a brisk pace. The settler knew Albert and he told him that he believed Jack Lucas must be going to High River to report to the Mounted Police.

The penalty was severe, a substantial term in jail. In a great hurry, Mr. Albert, his wife and his two children piled all of their moveable possessions into a wagon, hitched their horses and took off, abandoning their home and everything they had.

By the time the scout and the mounted policeman got back to the "rustler," their prey had the advantage of a two-day lead.

In those days, without telephone, much less radio, a chase would be hopeless. If the officer undertook to ride west toward Stavely, which was the most likely direction, the time involving another day would put Albert still further out of reach and still in an unknown direction.

Meanwhile, for poor Mr. Albert it was a major tragedy. No one in our country ever heard from him again.

It came closer to home than that. I learned in later years that we also had fallen upon hunger. We had consumed all the salted sowbelly that had been bought up in the fall months before. But the winter was longer than usual and we were hungry for fat and butter and meat. About all we had was flour, salt and pepper, yeast and the potatoes we had grown.

A mile north of us there lived a neighbor and friend of my father's, Porter Noyes. His family of a wife and two small children were in similar straits. My dad and Porter knew they had no choice. Together they cornered one of the roaming critters and butchered him on the plains. They were luckier than Mr. Albert, or smarter, for there was an old dug-out well and they poured the entrails and the hide into the well. As far as I know the hide still lies decaying in the dirt, maybe feeding a few remaining maggots this seventy years later.

No word ever got out about the fate of this steer. He became merely a statistic, if that. But my mother never got over the fear of the mounted police. Every time one made an appearance in the country my mother virtually trembled, thinking that somehow someone had stumbled on that ancient evidence in the old well. In later years occasionally I would go into the plains thirty to forty miles east of our farm and shoot an antelope. It wasn't always in season but there were very few hunters, and sporting rules fell into laxity from disuse. I can recall my mother being overjoyed at the first sight of the carcass and then becoming very nervous about the mounted police. She had never forgotten, and never forgot until her death, the episode with Pat Burns' steer.

Burns himself became a millionaire feeding his cattle freely off hundreds of thousands of acres in the western plain. Later on he became a senator of Canada, one of the highly respected elected officials in Ottawa.

My father often vowed that he would never leave his family to go to war unless our own country was threatened and then he vowed to be at the front of the line. I made a similarly and potentially dangerous determination; I would never go to fight in a foreign country, regardless of what the politicians in Ottawa ordered. It was lucky for me that my age and status was always a step ahead of conscription in the Second World War, thus allowing me to avoid an inevitable collision with authority. Unwittingly, I suppose, I had become an individualist and even maybe a nonconformist or potential rebel. When my wife lay dying seven decades later I came to her side regardless of the consequences, in spite of the fact that I knew I would probably be arrested and taken to jail. I guess I was bound to become that kind of a man unconsciously, as my beliefs and principles arose from what I observed.

But if Amil Myers had great strength he had also great compassion. He had anglicized his name long since when my "Uncle Gus" in Denver changed the family name from Meier to Myers. My father changed his name from Emil to Amil and from Meier to Myers, and that's the name he was known by throughout his life. He was a man loathe to use force, except in defense; a man with an aversion to whipping a child. He told me that his father had licked his children so severely that he vowed as a boy that if he ever had children of his own he wouldn't whip them.

He whipped me only once. I was about five years old. I think it was the crop of 1917. We had raised some good crops from 1912 and accumulated enough money to buy two more teams of horses, some additional farm machinery including a binder, truly the mechanical wonder of the day. But there was the odd bug in the binder and one of the bugs was in the knotter. As the heavy grain fell on the canvas and was elevated up to the binding platform a huge needle came up bringing the twine around the back of the grain and automatically tying it into a knot, and then the newly tied bundle fell neatly into the catcher. The catcher would hold about eight bundles, enough for a single stook and these bundles would be dumped regularly. On every round, the set of bundles would be dumped adjacent to the one of the round before. This resulted in a field with windrows, the center ones stretching about one quarter of a mile to the center of the field.

We had been granted ownership rights by the government to the "pre-emption" as it was called because we had successfully lived out the conditions on the homestead. Now we had two quarters of land. One quarter was summer-fallowed each year and kept clean all year and the second quarter was seeded in one piece.

Harvest time was high tension time around our house. My father, usually a quiet man, suddenly changed character. No one better cross my father or shirk his duty in harvest time. I was on the road allowance opposite the house, standing at the fence as my father's binder came clattering along and before it arrived opposite me. The swear words kept coming faster and thicker, the likes of which I had never heard, as my father kept jumping on the binder and off it, trying to adjust the knotter, watching three or four bundles come out tied, and the next one kicked out as a mass of tangled straw. The horses were throwing their heads against the horse flies, and occasionally kicking over a trace which had to be rehitched.

It was one of the hottest days I remember and I was leaning on the fence, a small boy, languid and lazy. Even the unheard of profanity did not arouse me until my father stopped his outfit and yelled at me, "Son, go to the shop and get me a ball of twine." He jumped off the binder, starting working once again with the binding machinery as I started off lazily toward the shop some 100 yards distance. Then the yell, the meaning of which was absolute, "Hurry up!"

But it was too hot, I kept stumbling along at a snail's pace until suddenly behind me I heard a swish of wind, turned my head only to see my father's arm reaching out for my collar. He put me over his knee and gave me the damndest spanking I ever had. When he turned me loose I took off, as the saying goes, "like a cut cat." I was up to the shop and back to the fence in a flash, a world record for the 100 yard dash if it had been clocked. I believe that licking taught me respect. My father's good nature was not to be taken for granted. To all things there are limits. And they stand like walls of stone.

The enforcement of these limits teaches respect and respect is an integral part of a strong and enduring love. Without respect love does not stand a chance of survival, whether it be between man and woman or child and parent. Respect is the antibody against contempt. Without respect, contempt tends to advance, maybe slowly at first but finally without restraint.

I will never be persuaded that corporal punishment is bad. It is in fact the most effective and therefore the most civilized punishment there is. If just and used moderately, it leaves the emotions unharmed. Its physical effect is transitory, yet its memory is enduring. But it is dangerous, for its use without intelligence and without restraint can leave permanent scars. Given in the heat of the moment it can be quickly forgiven. Given in cold deliberation it can sow seeds of enduring resentments and the results will be worse than no punishment at all.

My father did not think these things out. Dr. Spock had not yet written his catechism for children and my father could not have read it, if he had. And if he could have read it he wouldn't have. Bringing up children to him was not a subject for special study. Bringing up children was a natural function of life to be conducted with the same amount of common sense as the rest of life, even to the planting of the crops.

* * * *

So much happened between 1915 when I was three and 1926 when I went away to college that I can only touch on a few highlights that may help to trace the basic structure of those times.

The year of the bumper crop of all times was 1916. That year we built our big new red barn with a full high loft for hay and that year my father and mother and I went down to visit his folks near Enid, Oklahoma. We didn't live exactly in luxury but here was a poverty that I hadn't imagined. When my aunt asked me if I would have butter **or** jam on my bread, I was so surprised that I looked to my father for the answer. The answer was an unusually stern eye. I asked for only one, not both.

My father had told me that black people lived in the United States, something I found hard to picture. I wondered why they were black and what they were called. He said they were called niggers. He said their real name was Negroes but everybody called them niggers and they called one another niggers. He said there was nothing wrong with it; that's just what they were. They were different from white people and that's what they were called. He said they came from Africa and they had been slaves. It didn't occur to me to ask him why they weren't called blacks any more than why Chinese weren't called yellows. Chinese people were in our country by then opening up cafes in every little town.

For some reason I don't now understand I told my dad, "Well, the first nigger kid I see I'm going to go out and give him a whipping." Maybe for the simple reason that these people were different.

And I still remember walking down the cement sidewalk in Enid, and at a drug store, which I still see in my mind, in about the middle of the block, a black boy, about half again as big as I was, came sauntering out. My dad put his hand on my shoulder: I didn't see the twinkle in his eye but I'm sure it was there, "There's your chance. Go get him!"

Suddenly faced with the prospect of carrying out my threat I felt unsteady on my knees. My **imaginary** nigger kid was not nearly this big. By now I knew I had made a great mistake and I felt awful. I didn't know what was meant by "loss of face", but there was no way I was going out to tie into this kid. I shrank back ashamed. It was a lesson. Since then, to this day, I have never issued a challenge or made a boast regarding anyone or anything unless I've known the full truth about the object of the challenge.

I remember my grandmother Myers still in the rocking chair, an elderly lady with heavily swollen legs. I don't know what the illness was, they said it was "milkleg." At any rate I would not kiss my grandmother good-bye and I regretted soon after we returned to Canada to find out that she had died. I didn't know the meaning of death, but I knew I would never see my grandmother again.

I think it bothered my father that even though I was a small boy I had refused to kiss my grandmother good-bye, this mother of his who had been through so much hard times in the dirt floored sod house and saw her husband gored to death by a bull with the life ebbing out of him as they strove to reach a doctor. This mother of five who had held the family together through days of terrible poverty and who had had so little comfort and such little love in her lifetime.

The war was going full-tilt in Europe and my mother, a German to the core, kept on praising the Kaiser, even under some small danger of war time retribution. We had by this time a neighbor who lived only a quarter of a mile away, an Englishman to his core. And many were the volubly bitter arguments between my mother in favor of the Kaiser and the Englishman in favor of the King. I can remember him walking down the path from our house, so angry that he was kicking big rocks with the toes of his boots. Feelings ran high in those days.

A dyed-in-the-wool German had taken out a homestead about three miles from us. And he was always shooting off his mouth about the war. My dad tried to talk sense to him but he only laughed. Then one night a stranger came by on horseback and stopped at his place and asked for a night's lodging. Our German friend shouted in a jovial way in his broad accent, "Sure, by gott. Anybody but a gottdamn Englishman!"

I can well imagine Walter Gertz gave the special agent a very special account on who was entitled to win the war and who was going to win it. In any case, the very next morning Gertz disappeared from his homestead and we didn't see him until 1919 when he was released from a prison camp in the Argentine. He returned then with a German wife to take up residence once more in Canada.

The next year my sister Ruth was born as the war ended and the plague of influenza swept the country. All of us were sick in bed almost two weeks. It was the winter and the blizzards attacked our little home on the prairie in which we would have frozen to death had not my father summoned all the strength available to bring buckets of coal to the stove to keep the house warm. We had no food and no one strong enough to get up and prepare food. My mother was gravely ill. My sister had double pneumonia as well as influenza and came within an ace of dying.

The influenza was so contagious that no one dare come close to a person who had it. Very nearly all the countryside was down with influenza but we had a bachelor neighbor who for some reason escaped it. Each day he would come down the road allowance and drop off a pot of hot boiled chicken soup at about the spot where I received my first licking. My father was barely able to stumble out to the road and bring back the food for us and reheat it on the stove. Many people died. The doctor visited us once. By now he had a Tin Lizzy. A trip from Vulcan twenty miles out and back sometimes in snowbound roads almost took up a day itself. We survived but the cemeteries around the countryside got full and if you were to go down there years later to look at the small tombstones you would see the cemetery was full of children. Only the toughest survived.

But we were advancing into the modern age. I started school in 1918. It was only a mile away at the time but that school burned down and they built a new school two and a half miles away. In grade two I had to walk the five miles to school and back every day but we were getting modern. The telephone line was coming through. A machine with a big digger was coming down most of the road allowances.

We kids at school thought this was a great development and one of the greatest pieces of fun was for a kid to jump down the telephone hole and then get out again. I didn't realize that I was a little shorter than the kids I saw doing this trick and I was determined that I was going to try it. But I was not going to try it until I got away from the other kids so they wouldn't laugh at me if I couldn't get out. And I wasn't going to try it until I got near home. And that is what I did.

Somewhere about the place where I had received my first licking I looked down the telephone hole and decided now or never. So I jumped in. Then I found that my arms were short of the top of the hole by some seven or eight inches. I tried to jump. But there was no room to bend my knees to jump. I tried to jump with my toes but that would only take me up a few inches. I jumped and jumped but never could I reach the rim of the hole.

It was near five o'clock when I got in the hole, and when I discovered that I could not get out of the hole I began to yell for help. But no one could hear me. My mother in the house would not hear me. My father was working in the field. I had my first lesson in panic. And I learned for the first time in my life; never get into a hole until you know how deep it is.

About six o'clock my father unhitched his horses from the machinery, a team of six, I think, and unbridled them for a drink at the well. My telephone hole must have been about 60 yards up the hill from our watering trough. I heard some of the jangling of the traces and I began to yell and scream again. But my voice was muffled. I'm surprised he heard me. I've often wondered how this adventure would have ended had I chosen a hole somewhere along the country road. What searchers would think to look for a lost kid in a telephone hole?

Never in my life was I so thankful for the strong hands of my dad as when they reached down into that hole, grabbed me by the wrists and drew me into the sweet open air of liberty. My mother gave me a very strong lecture, but my dad said nothing. I guess he figured I had had enough punishment when I was down in the hole.

It taught me a valuable lesson, and all my life I've been careful never to get into a hole, financial or otherwise, unless first I knew how deep it was. Sometimes I misjudged.

Chapter Seven

THE PIONEER WOMAN

My father and my mother were both unusual people. My father was unusual in a very ordinary way. My mother was unusual in an extraordinary way.

My father came to the God-forsaken plains of Alberta from the God-forsaken Cherokee country of Oklahoma. My mother came to the God-forsaken plains of Alberta from the bright city lights of Denver, Colorado. My father was adapted to the pioneer kind of life. My mother hit it cold turkey. Early on her native self-reliance was put to the acid test.

Occasionally (before Vulcan became a town) the husband might have to make a trip to Stavely for repairs and that would nearly always mean an overnight stay. If the woman had fears she had to smother them. On one of those rare occasions when my mother was holding down the shack by herself, a band of roving Indians came idling into the yard late in the afternoon. They set up camp around our windmill about four hundred feet from the house, built their fires and generally settled in.

My mother was petrified, especially when they began coming in small groups to the door and asking for flour and sugar. She had to turn them down because she knew if she ever opened up to them there would be nothing left in the house. As darkness settled in she became very frightened. It wasn't like in later years when you could pick up the phone and call a neighbor. Neither dared she leave the house, nor would she have dared to try making it alone on foot to the nearest neighbor's place about a mile and a half away. The pleadings for flour and sugar became more persistent to the point where she dug in for a state of siege. She hauled one hundred pound sacks of flour, leaning them against the

41

door, along with a network of a dresser, chairs lodged against one another. No sleep at all that night.

She told me in later years that she had never been so relieved as when she looked out and saw the Indians packing up the following morning shortly after daybreak. By the time my father returned there was no sign of them.

The need for current supplies necessitated a number of trips to Stavely from spring through fall. There was neither room nor facility for long term storage. They had no refrigeration at all, not even an icebox. It was not possible to hold meat over for more than a couple of days in the spring and summer seasons. No drug store or grocery store was easily available. There was no ready made bread in those days and few, if any, canned goods.

The meaning was clear and stark. Our bread had to be baked. None of the myriad of cold cereals today were made in those times. There was no such thing as a "mix". You became your own mixer and thankful to have the ingredients.

Coal had to be brought in from out of doors in a coal bucket. Water had to be brought up a hill from a well some four hundred feet away, in pails weighing twenty to thirty pounds. Garbage consisted of few cardboard boxes and if there had been cardboard boxes they would probably have been saved for other purposes.

In the winter my father would keep the stove stoked with coal and the water pails full. But in the summer when he was busy on the land mother often found it necessary to handle the pails herself. The handles on the pail full of water cut into the hands.

The staple diet was sowbelly and beans because the sowbelly, a fat form of bacon, was salt cured and it would keep. The beans to go with it could be cooked. The bread could be made, and sometimes a cake. The latter was expensive because of the sugar and the icing.

My parents rendered the lard by using the fat from a butchered steer or pig. This was cooked down into a pretty good product. The fat not considered the best for lard, the trimming from the intestines and inner organs, was rendered down as a base for soap. After rendering, the fat was mixed with great amounts of lye and boiled for a long time in a big washtub on the stove, finally yielding strong but reasonably good yellow laundry soap which was cut into bars about half an inch thick and three-and-a-half by two-and-a-half inches.

Vegetables were available from only one source: my mother's garden. The garden was counted on to produce large quantities of beans which could be canned and kept in quart sealers after being boiled in a large round tub on the kitchen stove and then sealed with melted wax. Peas wouldn't keep but carrots would, and potatoes for the whole year could be stored in the cellar. My mother grew cabbage, cauliflower, carrots, turnips and delicious head lettuce that we feasted on all summer but was never seen from the time of first frost to the disappearance of the frost the next spring.

We could grow no fruit in that climate, so we relied on what was known as Saskatoons. These, a kind of a seedy blueberry, grew wild on bushes in the river valleys or in the foothills some fifty miles west. In August we would go on a berry picking trip that would last two or three days, sometimes with our neighbors, and come back with perhaps a couple of tubfulls of berries. The pickers carried a band around their waist threaded into the middle of a pail handle so they could use both hands for picking. My mother and another small lady up the road, Mrs. Fitz, were known as the champion berry pickers of the country. They would emerge from the bushes every once in a while beaming over their pails full to the brim of large plump berries.

Then came the job of cleaning the berries. As soon as we got back we tried to find a cool place to store the berries overnight. The cleaning began very early next morning. The berries all had to be washed and handled, the bad and wormy separated from the good, and then the canning process was ready to start. I have no idea how long it took my mother to can those berries, but I do know that the cupboards, that my dad built down in the cellar, were stocked with great numbers of quart sealers, which would have to last us for nearly a year to be used both as a dessert and filling for pies. I remember my mother complaining about the amount of sugar they took.

In the later years, particularly at harvest time, we might have as many as four or five men and my mother had to cook big hardy meals three times a day. Breakfast would usually include oatmeal plus bacon and eggs. Sorry, no orange juice. But sometimes at supper there would be Saskatoon pie.

My mother was very slight, no more than 5'1", but she could do the work of a horse, and she did. I remember seeing her night after night, following supper, hoeing away in the garden until darkness fell. I remember my dad yelling from the tool shop, where he was sharpening plow shares, "Lena, come on up now! I can't even see you down there anymore." Not til then would she come back to the house to finish the dishes and prepare for the morning.

My parents rose early with the sun, never later than five o'clock.

Beyond the cooking and the gardening my mother had to set aside a day for washing which was done in a large steel tub, with the aid of a corrugated washboard and using the laundry soap we had made.

About ten years later on we got a washing machine which could be operated by working a lever back and forth, about fifteen to twenty minutes per tubfull. All this took a lot of water and then of course all the clothes had to go back in the washing machine with new rinsing water to come out clean. Then they had to be wrung through the wringer which took a lot of elbow grease. Then they all had to be hung on the line to dry. Then came ironing the next day.

Another day was set aside for baking when she would make perhaps a dozen loaves of bread, enough to last through the coming week. She made also delicious crusty buns and sometimes cinnamon rolls as well.

We usually milked at least two cows. When I got to be about seven-or eight-years-old I helped my dad by milking one of the cows and later on I would milk both of the cows and run the milk through the separator. The skim milk would be fed to the pigs. Fresh milk would be kept aside for use and very thick wonderful cream was held separately.

Early on my mother urged my father to put up ice in the wintertime. We bought an icebox, and in the very bitter cold my dad with a team of horses would go down to Lake McGregor with a big long ice saw and with the help of another man saw huge blocks of ice sometimes two feet deep and perhaps two feet square. They were very heavy but they slid easily and we had set aside a granary to store this ice, all of the layers of blocks covered and smothered in sawdust. By mid summer the blocks would have melted down to about half size, but it was still good cold ice and in the icebox it kept our cream fresh, our butter cold and held our meat easily for a few days. We used the same sawdust over and over year after year. No other farmer in the country seemed to care about the summer heat, in the wintertime.

Some of the farmers joined in what was called a "beef pool." Each farmer would contribute a good steer and each Saturday there would be a butchering from which each farmer would get his share. Theoretically in the course of a season each would have had an equivalent of a whole steer. It didn't actually work out that way.

In the winter, meat could be kept frozen for long periods but there was always the danger of a Chinook wind coming out of the southwest which could melt all the snow and bring temperatures above freezing for two or three days, taking all the snow away in streams of water. So the staple meat diet in winter was canned beef. Actually it was the most delicious beef I have ever tasted.

In the fall we would kill a steer of our own and my mother would can virtually the whole steer in quart sealers to be used in the coming year. The men who worked at our place thought it was delicious and they partook ravenously. My mother had the reputation of putting on the best meal in the country. With the storing of ice we also had the luxury of ice cream. We had a gallon freezer and my mother made the most delicious ice cream I have tasted yet. As I got older into my teens I had the job of turning the freezer which could get very tough when the gallon of contents became the general texture of ice cream.

My mother had dreamed of a nice house on the farm. As a small boy I can remember her well, working over plans late into the evening and probably over the course of a few years. There was a major argument in our house after the bumper crop of 1916 when we had enough money to build either a house or a decent barn. My dad opted for the barn because he said now with the two farms our whole livelihood was based on the horses. They had to be kept in very good shape or they would play out before the season was through, working in the hot sun under heavy load day after day, morning til dusk. My mother dreamed of the house and almost ached for the house; it was her one big reward, her life's ambition. It was never to be.

Things were moving along toward her ambitions in 1928 and 1929, but the crash of 1929 and the resulting plunge of the wheat price - next to nothing - put the house plans into limbo. She still clung to one hope; that she and my father could visit her hometown in Germany. That was never to happen either.

My mother seemed to know no fear. If the cattle broke down the fence and got into our grain crop while my father was away, she would get on a horse, bridling and riding, although she had never ridden a horse before. Sometimes she fell off.

It was on my mother's urging in 1917 that we bought the second farm of three quarter sections, homesteaded by old Osteimer. I don't know the price but I know that my father was against it. He said that we had enough land with the three quarters. We would have to get extra machinery and extra horses. There would be extra work. But my mother was persistent. She said if we were ever going to get anywhere we would have to have more than our present holdings. Her point was made probably at the cost of her house a few years later down the road.

My mother, of course, was from the first responsible for my education. And even in the darkest days of the 1930 depression when the land blew away in black clouds and the droughts reduced the crops to a very scanty harvest and when the price of wheat had fallen from $2.00 a bushel down to 25 cents in 1932, she scraped every corner and groove to see that my education was not interrupted. With that objective she would not compromise.

A bright new light came into her life in the prosperous days of 1927 in the shape of a brand new Maytag washing machine with a gasoline engine. That ended the hand work and many hours of toil. It was equipped also with a power wringer. Previously all washed clothes had to be put through a wringer turned by hand which was really hard work. Electric power and the magic of electric lights would not come until the rural electrification gridwork arrived nearly 20 years later.

With the coming of fall and winter the housework lightened, but even throughout the long winter I seldom saw my mother idle. She was heavily occupied in the autumn with the canning of our food for the coming year. After that she seldom left her sewing machine.

When the snow flew and the outside work was done my dad became my mother's helper. He nearly always did the dishes and often cooked the meals. His hardest job was to get my mother to leave the sewing machine and come to eat. She was completely absorbed in repairing all of our clothes, using big patches where a garment could be saved. We bought few new socks because she always kept them darned. When that was done she could resort to the luxury at last of making a dress or two for herself. I can remember as a very young boy the paper patterns laying around the house and talk of crepe de chine, which I thought was a funny word, satin, lace and silk.

Looking back it's no wonder to me that I got the damnedest licking of my life for losing my overcoat when I was about twelve years old. I had been sent in the buggy with my horse, Old Joe, to get some supplies in the town of Lomond ten miles to the east. I guess I put my coat down hanging over the buggy seat or perhaps over the back. Anyway, when I got home the coat wasn't there. My mother had got a real bargain on this secondhand coat. It was a terribly tough year and she didn't know how I was going to get another coat, and here I had lost it through sheer carelessness. I never saw her so upset and never did she lick me more severely. Not once, but at least three times. She gave me a licking and sent me to bed without supper and then while she and dad were having supper she got herself worked up talking about it again, and she came in and licked me again. An hour later she got worked up again and came in and licked me again. Finally on her next trip to the bedroom I was saved by my dad. "Now here," in a very strong voice, "this has been about enough."

I never heard about the coat again, although I'm sure that she continued to be bothered by the thoughts of what a grievous and unnecessary loss this had been.

A licking by my mother was not altogether unusual. There was one other occasion that I never forgot. It was my job each night to get the kindling in; the stove could not be started in the morning without kindling. It must have been about 1917 because I was getting the kindling from scrap lumber around the new barn. On this night I was comfortably in my bed (my dad was away) when the door opened and in comes mother with a switch. "Where's the kindling?"

"I forgot."

"Get out there right now!"

I leaped from my bed and began to run but she kept up with me and switched me every step of the way to the barn. I never forgot the kindling again. And I am convinced that only corporal punishment can have such lasting affect. It certainly taught me responsibility.

I was a boy of seven years old in 1919 and a few of us in school were out in the boys' outhouse saying bad things about the teacher, a certain Mr. Youres. I can't remember all the things that were said and I don't remember if I had any particular name for Mr. Youres, but a pal of mine, Ross McIntyre, said that Mr. Youres was a shit-ass. This had been at the morning recess and at the noon hour my pal and I had a school boy's disagreement and we were quite angry. When school opened my friend marched up to Mr. Youres and said, "Vernon Myers called you a shit-ass."

Mr. Youres got beet red and he called me to the front and he said, "Did you say that word?" And I said, "No sir, I did not." He said, "Well, Ross McIntyre says you said that word and I believe him. You don't seem to have much defense." And I told him, "Well I didn't say it and that's the truth. I didn't say it." Mr. Youres said, "You come in and apologize to me in front of all the school tomorrow morning at nine or you will receive a whipping. That's all."

Now Mr. Youres had a very cruel strap. In those days the tires were thin and small and the inside rubber rims of these tires were about an inch and a quarter wide. They came up in a v-shape. Mr. Youres had a strap made out of the rim of one of these tires which was about sixteen inches long. You held out your hand open palm and he would take one hand after the other and deliver his blow with this treaded piece of rubber. I had never had a strapping from Youres but I had seen another kid that had, and I was pretty scared of that.

I went home and told my mother my problem. I said, "Ross McIntyre told Mr. Youres that I had called him a shit-ass and I said I never called him that. Ross McIntyre was the one who called Mr. Youres a shit-ass."

I never received more severe questioning from my mother. She said, "Are you absolutely sure that you didn't call Mr. Youres a shit-ass?" And I said, "I'm sure." She said, "On your honor you tell me the truth; you tell me the truth!" I said, "I never said it."

My mother said, "Well then don't you apologize to Mr. Youres."

I said: "But if I don't apologize I am going to get a licking tomorrow morning." She said, "If you apologize you're going to get a licking when you come home."

I didn't have a very good night. I was only a small boy but here I was caught between two powers just as decades later I would someday be caught between two governments. I felt; I am going to get a licking anyway and I might as well be right as be wrong. I didn't say it, I shouldn't apologize and if I do I'm going to get a licking. So I decided I would not apologize.

I went to school the next morning in great trepidation. My courage was at low ebb and when the bell rang and we all sat down. Mr. Youres asked me if I was ready to apologize. With some bravado I replied: "I didn't say it and I'm not going to apologize."

It was a very severe strapping and the palms of my hands swelled up red. But I had a certain inner satisfaction that I had not betrayed the truth, I had lived up to what was **RIGHT**. But I have to admit I cried. It hurt so much!

It was one of the lessons that sank in. Throughout my life I never missed a bill that I owed, and I never paid a bill that somebody claimed if I didn't owe it. I never apologized unless an apology was due

When Revenue Canada charged me with having cheated the Canadian government out of $800,000 I was back in grade school. I wasn't guilty.

* * * *

I got into one mess in school that had nothing to do with my mother, and I never told her about it. Every morning at the bell all of us kids, about thirty from grades one to nine, had to stand up and sing "Oh, Canada, our home, our native land," accompanied on the piano by our teacher, Mrs. Mannen. We boys agreed to form a pact against singing of *Oh, Canada*. If we all stuck together, we reasoned, there wouldn't be anything Mrs. Mannen could do about it. She wouldn't lick all of us. The key was to stick together.

I remember being quite enthusiastic. As Mrs. Mannen began to play I locked my jaws. It seemed like all the class were singing like birds. After a few bars I saw Mrs. Mannen look around and focus on one of my friends to the right and a little behind me. She was glaring. A second later I noticed my friend had commenced to sing. Mrs. Mannen pivoted about four threatening glances. In my position I couldn't see all my friends, but I did see two or three others start to sing. It was a sinking feeling but I wasn't going to let my pals down, the others behind me and out of my view. About half way through the song Mrs. Mannen stopped playing.

"Vernon, you're not singing. What's the matter?"

"I'm not going to sing," I said. She said, "You're going to sing! Now sing." She resumed with the piano and the class started singing. I saw now that my stalwart friends had caved in. But there might be one or two still holding out and I determined I would not be one to break the trust. I did not sing.

Mrs. Mannen stopped the piano. "Vernon, you can come up here and sing a solo to the class!"

I was speechless. I couldn't imagine a more terrible punishment. "Come up here!"

Who could resist it? I went forward. Mrs. Mannen started to play, but I did not sing.

She stopped abruptly, got out her strap. She strapped me in front of the class.

The others had abandoned me. I was taking the rap. If I consistently refused to sing, she would consistently continue to whip me. Mrs. Mannen was no panty-waist.

Trying to hold on, but half sobbing I sang haltingly. I felt betrayed, even bitter, if a small child can be bitter. It was probably my worst single experience in school and it maybe taught me one of my best lessons.

When much later in life OPEC, the organization of petroleum exporting countries, was organized I had little faith that that organization would endure. Sooner or later one of them would start to sing. With one singing (exceeding the quota) others would start to sing. When the quota was busted OPEC would be busted and the price of oil would be busted.

OPEC did last for a time, but eventually I turned out to be right. They broke off one by one. The price of oil plummeted

For my own part I vowed never to count on anyone else to see me through. I never joined forces with others. I remained completely on my own. Sink or swim. Sometimes I very nearly sank. But I didn't.

* * * *

I never held any resentment against my mother because I automatically knew how deeply she cared about me. I can see her yet standing in the yard, the wind blowing her apron, waving her dish towel as I took off for school on my horse down the road.

"Be careful. I dreamt about water last night and that's a bad sign. Sonny, you be careful!"

There were times of relaxation and enjoyment. In the fall and winter there were dances at the school house where the whole community would meet and sometimes there were community suppers where the parents would visit and all us kids would play. The women would be dressed up in their new crepe de chine or silk dresses, and on Sundays we often went to Sunday school and church where we had a social time with all the neighbors. All in all, though, the pioneer life was drudgery. The amazing thing is that it never seemed to break pioneer spirits. The modern world can hardly comprehend it. And even I, having lived through it, can hardly understand it. These were self-sufficient and fearless people.

Soon after harvest my mother applied herself to the annual shopping via the mail order houses of Robert Simpson and the T. Eaton Company. For most of a week when she was immersed in those catalogs filling out several pages of order blanks, the job of cooking and housework fell to my father. He didn't mind. He'd much rather do that than apply himself to the paper work.

In those catalogs there were listings and pictures of every-thing imaginable from children's, men's and women's clothes to groceries, household wares, hardware. The mail order sheets consisted of everything from coffee to toothpicks, tea, spices, sugar, salt and pepper, baking powder and soda, scribblers and pencils for school, wrenches, saddles and bridles, and almost any item one might name. The size of the order was dependent on the kind of a crop we had and that was the reason it was never made out until after harvest when we knew we had the money to pay for it. All purchases in those days were strictly cash, including the freight cost. If it was a good crop there would be some luxuries in the way of candies for Christmas, birthday candles, a nice new sweater, or dress. The list had to be complete. There would not be another shopping trip until the following year, only minor items from the small stores in Vulcan.

My mother added the long columns, as a part of her bookkeeping. While my father had a grade five education in Oklahoma, my mother had no English education. She had a grade eight education in Germany and she put that to good use in learning the English language. She taught herself to read and write English, and though her accent never completely left her, her book work was rather good, her writing legible and clear in meaning.

Of course the income tax nightmare had not yet descended upon these poor common people, who if they lived long enough would later find themselves completely swamped in a mass of figures they did not understand. For the most part they were left to live unmolested until the years immediately following the war. After the mid-twenties their living pleasure was immeasurably improved with that miracle which came to be commonly known as radio.

Probably the most illustrative event pertaining to my mother was the time she drove up to confront the premier of Alberta, the Honorable Ernest Manning.

This was much later, probably the mid or latter 1950s. My first wife, Amy, was in the mental asylum in Penocka about two hundred miles from home. She had been there for a number of years following a tragic nervous breakdown. My divorce was many years behind, but my mother continued to have great sympathy for Amy and about once a year she would drive up to the asylum to visit Amy. At this time she became almost fanatically convinced that there was nothing wrong with Amy, and righteously indignant that she should be held in Penocka against her will. The premier of Alberta was one of the biggest politicians in Canada. He had by then already served a dozen years in his post. When all else had failed, my mother decided to go to see the premier to get Amy out. Although nearly seventy she made the three hundred-mile drive to Edmonton all on her own.

When she got to the parliament buildings she found Manning totally inaccessible. But my mother was not giving up. Manning was a preacher. Every Sunday he preached over the Alberta Network from his large Baptist church in Edmonton. Unable to make contact any other way, my mother stalked the premier at the church steps and when Mr. Manning emerged she collared him. He had to stand and listen to her story about Amy's detention. "How can you live with yourself when you're keeping this woman a prisoner?" When Manning tried to excuse himself out of the situation, to his embarrassment, my mother made her pronouncement in no quiet voice. "This woman is no crazier than I am or you are. You should let her go."

Although our family looked upon the trip with some amusement we couldn't help but be impressed with the dauntless spirit that had propelled my mother through her lifetime.

She was feisty from the beginning. She never lost her fierce individuality. Her spirit of independence persevered to the end. She didn't see how the government had any right to force us to divulge every cent we spent and every cent we made. "What business is it of his," she would demand. "He didn't make it, he didn't do anything." She always personalized the government. She never came to understand that government was deteriorating toward a mindless bureaucracy operating, for the most part, without common sense.

My dad, when he died in 1946, had left all the land in my mother's name. She wanted each of us three kids to have one quarter section and she gave us those quarters without ever transferring the titles. But we farmed the land or had it rented out and took proceeds. After a few years Canadian Revenue came pouncing down on my mother. They tried to compel her to assign the quarters legally to us kids or else pay the income tax. She refused to assign. She claimed there was no law forcing her to assign and she claimed since she did not have the income there was no law requiring her to pay the taxes. That stymied them for a while, but they came on in a second rush. They said that she had given us those quarters - whether legally assigned or not - and she would be required to pay a gift tax on each quarter. My mother's response was that she had given us nothing but an opportunity. She had given us the **right** to use those quarters to our advantage. If we had let them grow up to weeds there would have been no income. There was no real gift. In tax court she won.

My mother looked with great disfavor on the social security payments. She did not believe people should receive money for nothing. She heaped great verbal abuse on the government, "he." She said, "I don't want nothing from him and let him ask nothing from me." The social security checks kept coming. After my mother passed away we found them all neatly together in an elastic band in her desk drawer. She hadn't cashed one of them.

She was a pioneer woman par excellence. For perseverance, industry and dauntless will, I couldn't hold a candle to her. And I don't know anyone else that can.

Although my mother has been dead these twenty-five years, this picture still persists: I'm on horseback riding out to school. She's standing in the yard, her apron blowing in the wind, waving a dishtowel, "I dreamt about water last night. Now, sonny, you be careful!"

My old home. Later expansion consisted of the addition on the right. The 12' X 12' original shack is on the left - now on a foundation.

My new home of the last nine years near Spokane, Washington.

Remains of the old tank wagon, capacity of 120 bushels hard red wheat - main transport vehicle for scores of thousands of bushels between 1912 and 1928.

My dad about 1935 beside our 1928 Dodge truck, successor to the tank wagon.

At age of about 45 (1933), my mother had weathered the storms pretty well.

A motor trip about 1928: My dad, one-year-old Richard, six-year-old sister Ruth, myself at age sixteen. Star car.

PERMANENT EXECUTIVE CLASS '32

MAYME MATTHEWS
Vice-President

VERNON MYERS
Class President

MARY COUTTS
Sec.-Treas.

Happily sandwiched between old flame Mayme Matilda and later friend Mary Coutts; but it's been a long time since the last meeting of the Executive.

Clark Hall on the right, men's residence on the left, roof of low ceilinged chapel between. Miss Morgan's window is shown on the upper right center. Big enough to get through.

Chapter Eight

RELIGION

As I look back on my life, trying to bring to the surface the significant beliefs and deep-seated motives, the first to come to mind is a conventional one. When I think about it I soon realize that the real belief goes back much further, and that the surface belief is not the real belief at all. I think back to an important event in my life when I was sixteen years old. I had come home from college to learn, a few days later, that my best friend on the first Sunday of his vacation, had been hit in the head by a baseball, and killed instantly. This set me to thinking deeply for the first time about life and death. I couldn't believe it was the Lord's will that this fine young man should be struck down on the threshold of his prime.

And if it wasn't the Lord's will, apparently there were some things that happened without the Lord having anything to do with it. This put a question under the old concept of God as I had learned it over the years.

I soon became aware that my idea of God did not emanate from what I had been taught in Sunday school at all. It was coming from a lot further back; from passively absorbed impressions that challenged all of my Sunday school teachings and all of the sermons I ever heard.

Early on in my boyhood, a Russian family had moved in a mile north of us. Mr. Lipsock was a preacher at the sect's weekly Sunday religious ceremonies and, as I see it now, somewhat of a fanatic. He used to come up in the evenings during the week and argue with my parents about religion, especially with my mother. My father seldom joined in, but he often listened. I recall that one night Mr. Lipsock was emphasizing how a baby that remained unbaptized would be burned in hellfire. As this argument progressed, watching my father, I saw that he had began to pay active attention. Of a sudden he interrupted Lipsock.

"Do you mean to tell me that if I have a little innocent child here and that if I have shirked my duty in not having him baptized that God is going to burn this little child in hellfire?"

Mr. Lipsock told my dad that, yes, if the child had not been given over to God it would most certainly be burned with the rest of the unbelievers in the eternal hellfire.

My father spoke quite severely. I could hear something new in his voice: "Well, it don't look to me like a loving God could burn an innocent little baby because its parents just didn't bother to have him baptized. I wouldn't want to have anything to do with that kind of a God."

With that my father got up, left the room and went to bed.

Right there, in my young mind, without anyone being aware of it, the benevolence of God came into question, a cornerstone of religious belief. The question lay dormant these many years until I lost my friend.

My father would frequently go to bed, leaving my mother to argue with Mr. Lipsock. But I remember one later occasion when he responded.

Mr. Lipsock had praised Abraham for his great obedience to God and as he put it "his love of God" because Abraham was ready to sacrifice his son Isaac just because God commanded him do to it.

I recalled at that point a picture in my Sunday school paper which showed Abraham standing over a naked Isaac on a slab of stone, a large knife in Abraham's upraised hand.

My father, who was eating an apple as he usually did just before retirement, stopped eating quite suddenly. "Do you say that God commanded Abraham to kill his own boy just to prove to God that he would do whatever God told him?"

"He had to show his love of God," Lipsock replied.

"Did you say, love of God? Who will love that kind of a God? And what man is going to kill his boy just because somebody told him to - even if it is God?"

Lipsock replied bluntly, "You must obey God!"

Once again my father left the room, and he left the apple on the table. I had a good feeling because I knew never never would my dad kill me no matter how many times God told him to do it. And I guess in my young mind I couldn't help but feel safer with my dad than with God. In a choice, it was a hands' down contest so far as I was concerned.

I realize as late as today that two seemingly innocuously brief conversations, reaching forward through the years, have constructed a basic gridwork which is at the center of my religious philosophy. But it took a while for this to happen.

Really, why would God kill Dunlap or at least condone such a stupid accident? They said that God watched over all his creatures, even the birds. And if it wasn't God's will, why didn't He stop it? When this happened where was He? A universal God truly should not be sleeping on the job. Of course preachers would reply that perhaps this was all a part of God's plan; that we can never know what God's overall plan may be. I say that this way, right or wrong, God always gets the credit, but manages to get out of taking the blame for anything.

I thought about a lot of other children that had died in our area, children of all ages, from infants to adolescents, the young adults, but mostly children because children were the victims of so many diseases, and medical assistance was so rare that their headstones were the largest group in the cemetery.

In those years I encountered serious questions but I did not reach any crystallized conclusions.

As far as Dunlap was concerned I just couldn't come to terms with it, I could not conclude that religion was only a bunch of theory, maybe lies; neither could I believe that God would strike Dunlap dead. I decided to leave it for the time being just as a mystery. The following poem was my expression of that.

THE MYSTERIOUS SWORD OF DEATH

It takes the young and leaves the old,
Where warm hearts beat it leaves them cold,

Where cold old fingers ache to die,
The sword of death flits lightly by
To strike the young man standing nigh.
The Mysterious Sword of Death!

When life is sweet and filled with joy,
The sword of death will take the boy;
While weary lives that writhe in pain
It views, and then, with high disdain
It lifts its blade afar again.
The Mysterious Sword of Death!

When future's gleaming large and grand
And in the palm of fortune's hand
And everything is bright and gay,
The sword of death will make its way,
Transforming all to lifeless clay.
The Mysterious Sword of Death!

We know not when the sword is due;
Perhaps it's hovering over you
And poses o'er you while you play;
Or while you wind your homeward way,
It aims to strike at close of day.
The Mysterious Sword of Death!

We know not why it strikes or how
But the sword is striking even now;
And even now some life departs
And leaves behind those bleeding hearts
To learn the sting that it imparts.
The Mysterious Sword of Death!

During the last two or three years of my studies in geology, astronomy and evolution my mind was increasingly beset with doubt about matching dogmatic religious teachings with the principles and the obvious messages of science. How could Jesus physically make one hundred fishes out of one? Was it actually possible that anyone could turn water into wine, imparting by magic the alcoholic spirits which are a part of wine?

At home in the summertime I would spend hours in the long cool evenings telling my dad about how the earth had been formed through the course of millions and millions of years and that if all of time could be represented by a day on the clock, human life would have only been here for the last half minute or so; and I told him how coal had really been trees that had been compressed and subjected to tremendous weight and heat to become coal and how all of the mountains had arisen one or more times and had been eroded down by rivers and laid down in ocean beds and later became sedimentary rocks which were found later on to contain oil, the brew of millions of organisms in the sea. The brew had risen within the curvatures of the porous rock to form reservoirs.

To a man raised on the Cherokee Strip of Oklahoma who had never been beyond grade five, and who had never read anything at all of this, these ideas were supremely fascinating. My father believed what I said was true and he questioned me often closely about the evolutionary process, and I was sure that through these years he himself was wrestling with the new facts that were challenging his old beliefs, taught to him by mostly unenlightened people in his childhood.

I know he wanted to believe in God. But I never did find out whether he really did. I know my father would never try to convince me of something that he didn't know himself to be true. And I'm sure that he probably didn't know the truth about atheism and he would therefore be very careful not to let me believe that he was a disbeliever. But as much as he fought the idea of the cruelty of a loving heavenly father, he dearly wanted to believe that he would see his father and his mother again. As my college years passed we still continued to talk sometimes about the sciences, but we did not talk again about the sciences as they related to religion.

I had gone to Sunday school regularly and at a Baptist boys' camp, very early on, I was the first boy on his feet to answer the plea of the preacher and come forward and "give my life to God" as it was put. The preacher later told my folks how proud he was of me to be the first one, and how many of the others had then followed. Throughout my life I have never shrank from what I believe to be true, and from saying it, even if no one else agreed - this was probably my first demonstration of that characteristic. But sometimes in my profound beliefs I have been wrong; more often, thankfully, I have been right.

But I had still to come to my own personal accommodation with religious beliefs.

It was very natural that these influences would permeate the realm of sex which was and always has been fundamentally intermingled with religion, finally fusing like two atoms to make a new molecule.

Chapter Nine

SEX

Sex and religion are so hopelessly intertwined that they often merge. One finds that in speaking of sex he is often also unavoidably speaking of sin. Borders become hazy. Sex and sin are often by inference synonymous. Yet, even a small amount of thought will generally reveal that our very existence is sin because it arose unavoidably out of sex. We are goners to start with.

In order to get around this bothersome question, the church had to isolate the original sin, and then forgive it. So all the rest of sex is sin but conception is not. Still, the inference remains that there should not be any enjoyment out of it because that will bring it right back into the category of sin.

Still, except for the enjoyment of sex, none of the species of the animal kingdom would inhabit the world today. Sexual pleasure is universal.

Do they believe that a horse breeds a mare out of duty or that the bull jumps the cow so that he can see new calves in the field?

Clearly, in the interest of our survival, sex rates right up with hunger in the preservation of our species. Without hunger we would starve to death. Without sex we would live only through one generation. We would nearly all disappear in a hundred years.

The inborn urge to satisfy the sexual appetite is truly on a par with the necessity to satisfy hunger. It is a necessity of on-going animal life, an inherent inseparable part.

The more liberal churches will allow as how it is okay for married couples to enjoy sex, but only under the authority of their permit by the preacher or the priest.

Priests must defy nature - their God-given nature - or quite illogically face the prospect of eternal hellfire. It's okay to eat though, and even enjoy the food.

It came to me early on in my adolescent years that we were living in a huge matrix of hypocrisy, despicable, dishonest to its core; indeed, in an intelligent society, deplorable.

I learned that in the earliest societies and in the primitive societies today sex has held an honorable and celebrated role. Tribes have fertility dances. In India the phallic symbol is a symbol of worship. Since eons past, the boy's emergence into manhood (the ability to reproduce) has been a celebrated ritual. In Africa I witnessed sexually symbolic celebrations in their unrestrained dancing and the beating of the drums. God is the only deity that admonishes His people to "go forth and multiply" and then hits them with the sex rap when they do.

Of course the results of sex are of major social consequence, and obviously, for the collective welfare it cannot be practiced indiscriminately; there has to be a lid on it. But there has to be a lid on hunger too. The visible and disgraceful avoirdupois, resulting from an appetite gone mad, may be more immoral than illegitimate pregnancy. Both are unwelcome. Both are foolish and both are unprincipled. But the attempt to squelch this second most fundamental drive in our nature is not an intelligent answer.

Sex education for our young children is not a good answer either, because it tends to deal with sex separately from the rest of life.

In my own life I had some misery with the problem. It was for me the most flawed portion of my education.

* * * *

My earliest remembrance goes back to about five years of age. My parents had bought another farm bringing our holdings up to about 1,000 acres. My mother's brother Carl and his wife and family were having a hard struggle in Denver, Colorado. To farm 1,000 acres was a little beyond the human capacity of my father, and my parents got the idea they could perform a great favor for Uncle Carl and at the same time run the two farms without hardship. Consequently, in 1917 my Uncle Carl and Aunt May and two girls, Marie one year older than myself, and Louise my age, and a couple of younger brothers came to Vulcan and moved into the house of our second farm. My father had built a barn for my uncle and the house had been fixed up. It had more room than our own house. I don't remember the arrival but I do remember that I often played with the girls being about my age and full of wonderment about the farm.

I remember being with the girls one day in our chicken house. I recall unabashedly bringing forth my penis and marching around the chicken house urinating, much to the delight of the two girls, when all of a sudden the chicken house door opened and I found myself staring into the face of my mother. Shock of shocks! The world stood still. I had never known such shame. My mother took me into the house and lectured me very severely with the admonishment never, never, never to do such a thing again. I weepingly and gladly made this eternal promise if she would please, please not tell my father. She made the deal. Whether she kept it I don't know, but my father never showed any sign that he had heard of my misbehavior. But it surely slowed me down, and I don't have any other such memories until a year or two later when I recall that in a small tent up at Uncle Carl's place the girls and I played doctor. I believe they were the instigators just as Eve was the instigator of Adam's troubles, but in spite of my solemn promise to my mother I lacked the resolve against the temptation.

Once I told a dirty joke to my parents, but I didn't know what I was telling. It seemed stupid to me, in fact, and as far as "dirty joke" is concerned I never remember that expression until somewhere in the early 30s when I was in the university.

In this case one day after I had been playing up at Uncle Carl's my Aunt May called us in for cookies and she said, "When you get home I want you to tell this to your parents. Do you think you can remember what I'm going to say?" I thought I could.

She said, "You ask your mother and dad if they know what are the three principal parts of a stove. They will say no. When they say no you tell them: The principal parts of a stove are lifter, leg, and poker. Can you remember that?"

I nodded, and faithfully I went home and repeated the obviously silly words to my parents. I can't remember their reaction because I had no idea what it was about.

The only other incident that I recall from my childhood is a visit from a friend a mile down the road a couple of years younger than I, now since deceased, who once again down to the chicken house exposed himself and wanted to play. The remembered terror of the episode with my cousins sent me shuddering from the idea. When my friend left I told my mother about it and she gave me high praise for my purity. She told me that boys who played that way or who played with themselves would come to a very awful end. They could go blind, or they could lose their minds. The results were horrible.

I suppose these ideas would affect me in later life although I do not understand how. My mother was the top of the mid-Victorian age.

My father, on the other hand, was a very down to earth man. A spade was a spade and you didn't call it a club. And a bull was a bull and you didn't call him anything else.

I recall one day my father rang up the neighbor to ask him if his bull was at home. My mother went into a dither waving her dishtowel. "Not bull!" she exclaimed. She whispered, "Gentleman cow - gentleman cow." My father went on:

"I got a cow up here that's in heat and I want to bring her over." My mother, whispering tensely, "Not that, daddy; not that. You say 'in season'."

My father ended the conversation, "I guess I'll bring her over this afternoon."

If my father said some woman was pregnant, my mother would say, "Not pregnant, don't say that. Say 'expecting'."

I don't know if the old timers used birth control, but my parents were married four years before I was born, my sister was born five years later, and my brother was born still ten years later. A number of people had large families but a greater number had small families. On the other hand they surely had lots of time on their hands in the long winters where there was nothing to do but read a book. In any case I had no further adventures and no further understanding until I reached adolescence in my fourteenth year at Brandon College.

There I heard a lot of sexual talk and it excited me erotically. I couldn't figure it out but I knew it was wrong. And then I recall one day performing the unforgiveable sin, hell fire and damnation!

I had accidentally brushed the corner of the desk and the pleasant feeling that resulted caused me to lean on it. This brought one action on another to the uncontrollable and finally cataclysmic end. To my amazement sperm shot fifteen feet across the room and seemed like it would not stop. After countless emissions the end came and I sank down, realizing I had now committed the unforgiveable sin. I could never do this again.

I relate that only because there are in-built hungers and desires of human beings that cannot be denied any more than hunger itself can be denied. One way or another these urgings will bring themselves to the surface and be recognized. I think it's important that this be mentioned because it brought to me one of my most distressing periods.

After the "Sin" I began to have regular nocturnal emissions. These were highly charged erotic dreams related to the few pictures of women I had seen in magazines or in the picture shows with low cut dresses and high skirts. The first night I had such a dream I awoke with remorse and terror. I had unconsciously committed the crime which brought this on; I had sewn the wind and so now I had to reap the whirlwind.

The next night when I went to bed I prayed to God that this would never happen to me again. But that night it happened three times. When I got up my pajamas were soaked. I fell into a state of dejection. I couldn't talk about it to anyone. I thought this was the punishment for my act a few days before and I could just hope that it would go away before it drove me out of my mind.

I prayed again. Again the Lord didn't listen. From then on this happened two or three times a night every night. If I had ever pleaded and prayed in my life I prayed those nights. But God didn't listen. It came to have an important influence on my concept of the loving Father and religion generally. Surely if there was ever anyone in remorse, ever any repentant person, ever a person in dire need, ever a boy who wanted to be good, that boy was I - and God wouldn't listen.

I don't know how I got through that spring; I know I was glad to reach home in early May and go to work on the farm. There I worked from early morning 'til late at night without relief, and as my life began to round out with contacts among the neighbors and some pride in what I was doing, my obsession began to disappear and so did the results of the obsession.

My mother was away when I returned and she had never allowed me to drive one team of two horses. My father was driving eight horses on a double disc in the field and I asked him to let me try. He took me out and gave me the lines and instructed me on what to do and during that day he gave me a lesson of such competence that I was able to pick up the lines on this eight horse team every morning of the summer thereafter. When my mother got home from Denver she nearly had a fit. She cried, "That boy has never driven any horses before and there you let him go with eight horses. He could be killed!"

My dad said, "He didn't drive any horses before because you wouldn't let him because you thought he would be killed. Now he's doing the job. Quit babying him and let him be."

Often my mother could win her arguments but not the ones that really mattered. From then on as long as I was on the farm in the summers I drove eight to ten horses from early morning 'til six o'clock at night through the summer season. Instead of allowing my thoughts to wonder to eroticism I began making up poetry, as I have explained. One poem I made up was called "Fantastic Dream." As I remember, I did it on the plow during the day, putting it down to writing by kerosene lamplight at night. But people who have seen it and read it aloud seemed to have been fascinated with it. Some find a deep allegorical meaning. It was all a part of my effort to become a writer which I shall deal with later.

I make mention of it here because it indicates to me that the adolescent needs to be fully occupied both in mind and body if he is to escape the dangerous eroticism that wells up uncontrollably from his unconscious mind. I believe the poem is a manifestation of an internal storm, an urging that would not be suppressed but luckily for me was deflected. I think it may have helped rescue me from dangerous brooding and a resulting discontent which perhaps in these modern times drive the adolescent in the direction of drugs and resulting hallucinations.

Chapter Ten

GETTING MODERN
THE FORD CAR

The process of getting modern may seem fast in retrospect, but to those living people on the prairie it was tediously and painfully slow. Then two amazing developments came one upon the heels of the other, the advent of telephone communication and the Ford car.

It's hard for me to comprehend even now that until I was seven years old there was no way to get a message from one farmer to another or from home to town or to a doctor except by walking, on horseback, or by horse-driven vehicle. Even though the distance to town had been shortened from 40 miles to Stavely to 20 miles to Vulcan it still took a day for the trip. With the introduction of the telephone one could call a neighbor to find out if he knew who might be going to town and then call that person and ask him to call at King's Drug Store. It was possible instantly to call Mr. King and ask him to prepare a package to be handed to the neighbor.

The effect of the telephone was to bring the people closer together. Neighbors cooperated, one would bring back the mail for four or five people if asked and bring back certain supplies. The long tedious journeys to get the simplest message across were over. The telephone greased communications and the Ford car greased transportation amazingly.

We got our first Ford car in 1917, a year before the rural telephone system was developed, and on the heels of the bumper crop of 1916. You might wonder how we clod-hopper farmers ever managed to get our driver's licenses. Are you kidding? Who ever thought of a driver's license? You didn't need a driver's license to drive six horses into town, why should you need a license for one horseless carriage? There was no road expense because the roads amounted only to wagon trails. In dry weather transportation was fairly fast. Whereas you might average seven miles an hour on a saddlehorse you could speed along in the Tin Lizzy at 25 to 30 miles an hour.

Nor did you need a license plate. I was with my parents when we went into Mr. Jennyjohn's garage to pick up the Lizzy. It was a shiny black double seater with a top on it and eisen glass curtains to keep out the rain and dust. Mr. Jennyjohn got us into the car and got behind the wheel and showed my parents how to make it go. He explained how you pushed on the clutch to make it start out in low and how when it got up enough speed you just quickly lifted your foot off the clutch and it would whip into high. There was a middle pedal for reverse. And there was a right-hand pedal for the brake. I don't remember the trip home but we must've made it all right for I do remember that after supper my father went out to drive the car into the brand new garage that we had prepared for it.

I can see it very clearly. He carefully advanced the gas and spark to the proper setting and then got out and grabbed the crank, turning it energetically. "Twist her tail," was the common expression. Suddenly the bright black little new car began to shiver and shake and he got in and put his foot on that clutch.

The hired man and I were standing to the side of the garage when the car, like a frightened steed, leaped forward and bashed straight through the garage. The studding cracked and splintered and the boards flew. My father was hollering "Whoa! Whoa! Whoa!" Until the day he died he never did completely rid himself of the habit of hollering "Whoa!" when he wanted a vehicle to stop quickly. Lizzy paid no attention.

I'll never forget Sam going around to the north side of the garage doubled over with laughter he couldn't contain. My father managed to stop the car about 40 feet past the busted end. He sat in the seat of the Tin Lizzy dumbfounded. After a while Sam was able to make his appearance, still yielding to wild bursts of laughter as he bent forward, slapping his knees.

I remember my mother driving the car out of the yard and me running along after, trying to catch her. I could have caught her in a horse and buggy but there was no way I was going to catch this new carriage with an engine in it. She dusted down the road and soon was out of sight. My father assured me she would be back, and she was.

My mother was known as the daredevil driver of Prospect Slope. That was the name of our school district. People told stories of how she went around corners on two wheels. I'll say she really got the speed out of that machine. A much later nickname for her was Sir Malcolm Campbell.

It changed our lives completely. We could go visiting on a Sunday afternoon if we had the time. We could go to church and Sunday school. My mother could visit the neighbors. She could make a 20 mile trip into town and back and buy what she wanted. A great new world of freedom was opened to us all living out this primitive life on the windswept plains.

I don't remember when they started calling for license plates or driver's licenses but I do know that in grade nine in 1926 I drove the car back and forth to school and never thought about such amenities.

Those were pretty good years. We had outlived the Tin Lizzy and bought a new Star car, and in 1925 we took a trip a thousand miles to Denver, Colorado where my mother had many relatives.

What a trip! We had a storage box for groceries and utensils built into the right fender the length of the car and we had an umbrella tent folded and tied on behind and a Coleman gasoline stove, and I don't know what all else.

At nights we pitched the tent and on the gasoline stove my mother cooked supper, including super baking powder biscuits, pancakes in the morning. My sister was about eight years old by then and she went along without ever causing any trouble that I can recall.

We closed in on Denver, Colorado at the rate of about 45 miles an hour. Even at that some big smart guys with sport cars passed us like we were standing still. This was the day of the McLaughlin Buick - the car of cars. The Star car company was really a company formed by Durant and it made the Flint, a car meant to compete with the McLaughlin Buick built by two merged retailers, the McLaughlin Carriage Company of London, Ontario which had always made horse drawn buggies, and the auto company started by Buick. Durant turned out also a middle car called the Durant. All of the Durant line would go up in smoke in the crash of 1929, but many different makes of cars were appearing on the scene in 1925 and in 1926, including Auburn, Studebaker and others.

The way you bought a car in those days was to get out and test it on Heath Hill or Horn's Hill. If a car could make those hills in high it was a good car and you probably bought it. The Heath Hill was halfway between my home and Vulcan. It was deceiving because it was about three miles long and the nearer you got to the top the steeper it became. No matter what speed you started out at you lost it before you got to the top and you usually had to push the clutch into low on the Ford car. But with the Star car we could make that hill on high. We could also make the twisting Horn Hill on high. Today these hills are not even noticeable in any make of new car.

The Star cars operated at high speed revolutions per minute. As a result they didn't last too long. But they sure had the pep. So much so that in 1926 we traded in our Star car for a new one which was still superior. One night on our Denver trip we pitched our tent near a garage which held two cars. One was a spanking new McLaughlin Buick, the king of all cars. I spent a great deal of time peering into the window admiring this car and I determined that when I grew up I would someday own an automobile just like it.

We passed through Yellowstone Park and I wondered that my mother didn't have heart failure around those curves. We got behind one driver who was going about ten miles an hour and my mother insisted that my dad should stay behind him. She said, "You can see that this man knows what he's doing. He's used to this road." So about an hour later when we got to the bottom, our leader stopped and pulled over. He and his wife stepped out and two paler people I had never seen, deathly white, shaking and scared to death. My dad said, "Well, now you see just because a man goes slow don't mean he knows what he's doing."

I carved my name in a tree on Yellowstone Park with the idea that on my honeymoon I would come back there and read the name. Unfortunately, when it came to my honeymoon we were in the depth of the depression and I didn't have the money to go to the downtown park, let alone Yellowstone Park. I guess my name is still in that tree if it didn't get burned up in the great Yellowstone fire of 1988.

We came back from Denver through the mountain road, through Salt Lake City and saw the Mormon Tabernacle and the Great Salt Lake and the Statue of Brigham Young in the Central Square. And my father told me about Brigham Young and all the numerous wives he had, but he praised the Mormons for their road work. The road out of Salt Lake was the only stretch of paved road on our whole trip. That was for about 60 miles. Other than that we always felt ourselves lucky if we were on gravel roads. We dreaded the dirt roads which sometimes we had to take for short distances. If it rained you were in deep trouble.

We arrived back via Shelby, Montana on the eve of one of the biggest events in Montana history, one of Jack Dempsey's famous world championship fights. In this case I believe he took on the South American giant Firpo, knocking him silly in short order. We didn't have time to stay over for the fight because the harvest was ready and my dad was already getting into the state of great urgency that consumed him annually for the duration of the event. It was the only time he ever got excited, but there would be no let up now until the grain was in the bin and I guess we made the fastest mileage of our whole trip on the last one hundred and fifty miles from Shelby to our farm. For once my mother made no objections to our excessive speed, now fully 45 miles an hour because within the next six weeks I had to be prepared and ready for the totally new phase of my life, my college career.

Chapter Eleven

EVEN A RADIO

When we got our first car we certainly had no reason to expect that this miracle would be followed by another even bigger one in less than ten years. The present generation can no more comprehend a time when transportation depended on horses, and communication depended on word of mouth than they can comprehend the Stone Age.

Why, no radio? What would you do at night; night after night; year after year? No newspaper? No telephone? No comics? No kidding? News of the world war a week after it had started?

Living, working and surviving, long nights when the sun set early on the world and rose late.

Loneliness? What about nights? Above all, no television? Never to watch New York or living people in Los Angeles, never to see a hockey game, football, baseball? Stone Age? Where is the difference?

I believe more of significance has happened during my single lifetime than in the 500 years preceding it. What's more, the changes are occurring faster year by year.

It was just as impossible for us to visualize the future as it is for the current generation to visualize the past. I well remember the implausibility with which radio was greeted. I first heard the word when a neighbor of ours rode into our yard on horseback to bring us the mail. I see it yet, so clearly. A wet afternoon, a horse standing in an inch or two of mud and puddles around our yard, my dad on the kitchen porch accepting the mail and then Art Fitzpatrick with a meaningless question.

"Well, Aim, are you going to get yourself a radio this fall?"

"A radio," my dad said, "what's that?"

"Well it's a kind of a box that you set up on your table and you turn knobs on it and you can get music from hundreds of miles away. You can get music from Hawaii and the news every night from Calgary." Art said this with a quizzical grin. My dad said, "Aw, go away with you. I don't know where Hawaii is but I know it's around the other side of the world."

Art Fitzpatrick said, "It don't matter how far it is, Aim. You just turn these dials and inside this box are these tubes or bulbs of colored light and then you get the talk or the music from wherever it is."

"You gonna get one?" my dad challenged.

"Well, no, but there's a lot of talk about them and I hear Ben Munson is getting one."

My dad said, "How about the wires? How are you going to get music from Hawaii? Some damn long wires?"

"You don't have wires," Art Fitzpatrick said. "It's just in the air."

"What the hell are you talking about?"

"Well, it's just in the air. I don't know how it works. But I know there's no wires."

My dad said, "If it's in the air here, you mean to tell me it's in the air over at Stavely too?"

"It's in the air," Art Fitzpatrick replied. "It's in the air all over the world."

My dad said, "You're crazy!"

That must have been about 1924. I was about eleven or twelve, and that fall or the next fall old Ben Munson got a radio.

Ben Munson was a maverick homesteader, a plunger, an up-to-date homesteader, always on the cutting edge. He had the first big car with a strange name. He was the first person to buy solid rubber tires so he wouldn't get flats. He had a small bachelor shack but big enough to keep a housekeeper or sometimes a married couple.

One time he fell in love with a 16 year old girl and was sporting her around the country in his new car. I remember them calling in at our place. I remember how disgusted my mother was. Then I heard afterwards that the girl's parents were up in arms. And Ben Munson had threatened to kill himself if he didn't get the girl. He never got the girl and he did later make an unsuccessful attempt on his life by slashing his wrists. Meanwhile, he was into anything new, and I was the first kid in the whole neighborhood to be invited over to Mr. Munson's place to hear his radio and spend the night. An honor for me.

I remember well that winter evening; bitter cold, and about 20 below zero. After supper I saddled up my pony and set out on the five mile ride to Munson's place. Mr. Munson and I put my pony in the barn. I followed Mr. Munson into the house and I saw this brand new machine on a stand in the kitchen. It was three or four feet long, about fourteen inches high, and twelve to fourteen inches deep. There were buttons all along the confounded thing. Ben Munson sat down in his chair for the evening's entertainment; I sat beside him facing the radio.

We each had a pair of earphones and he started in with the dials. In all my life before or since I never heard such squawking and crackling. Once in a while we could hear a fleeting voice, a bar of music. "I think that's Hawaii!" Munson exclaimed. We heard a couple of voices for a few seconds and we persevered until midnight. Suddenly Mr. Munson hit the silencer button. Abruptly the squawking, the screeching and roaring stopped. "It's not a good night for reception," Munson announced.

About three years later we had a radio. It was a Westinghouse. It was a nice looking machine and was powered by a car battery. We used to listen to Denver and Salt Lake City, many other stations, and of course to Calgary which was only one hundred miles away. My dad listened enthusiastically to the Texaco news and to Amos and Andy. He would imitate Andy talking about the Fresh Air Taxi Cab Company, and Amos the driver. I can remember some of Amos' romances and the efforts of the KingFish to fix it up. What a transformation of the world for my dad.

My mother was impressed by the soap operas. I think the leading one in those times was "Big Sister." Another was "Ma Perkins." The radio changed life completely on the prairies. I guess it did everywhere else too, only the change was more dramatic in the outlying rural areas because of the long dearth in communication. You couldn't go across the street to speak a few words with your neighbor or drop in for a loaf of bread at the grocery store. You stayed there, listened to the wind, looked at the sky and waited for your husband to come home.

It was at least twenty-five years later before I heard the mention of television. I heard there was a man in Italy by the name of Marconi who was fooling around with it and that they had it on an experimental basis in New York City broadcasting over a distance of a few blocks. I didn't think there would ever be such thing as television in our country. Imagine! Not only hearing what people were saying 2,000 miles away but actually seeing them opening their mouths and saying the words.

By 1954 I was the owner of a television set, one of the first in our part of the country at Mindapore, Alberta, about ten miles from Calgary and one hundred miles from the old farm. My father had passed away on my 34th birthday, June 15, 1946. He never got to see television.

But radio had changed our lives.

Chapter Twelve

COLLEGE

One day in June 1926 I had to say good-bye to our single room schoolhouse.

My next step was cold turkey into a new world. There was a high school in Vulcan but as a boarder I would be unsupervised. The question was where in the world to send me. The student minister of our country church, Norman Todd, who in fact serviced two or three churches each Sunday, was going to study at Brandon, a Baptist College about a thousand miles from home.

Todd suggested to my parents that they send me with him to Brandon. The supervision was strict he said and it was a wonderful place for me to take my education right on through university. Todd offered to take me under his wing.

We spent some time getting me ready. We had a new wardrobe trunk with drawers in it and hooks to hang my coats on. I also had to have a napkin ring with my initials on it. I had never used a table napkin.

My teacher, Mrs. Mannen, told me that I would have to watch my manners and I was real scared about that. I knew from the brochure there were some dozens of tables arranged so that a senior class member sat at the head and a third year member at the foot and two members of other classes on either side with a pitcher of ice water and glasses on the one corner. I saw a picture of it. At suppertime there was the blasting of a gong and the racing of feet down the stairs, four flights of them from my room, three steps at a time, piling into the dining room in the basement. I found my assigned place standing next to the water pitcher and glasses next to the foot of the six person table. We all stood as the dean said grace. This was followed by a loud noise as everyone at once moved his chair to sit down.

As the dean said "Amen" I whirled, knocking the water pitcher and all the glasses shattering to the floor. Everyone in the dining room looked at me. I thought my education was ended right there. The dean gave me a smile; it saved my life.

Two waiters came in now with broom and mop and cleaned up the mess. With a shaky hand I poured water from the new pitcher into the new glasses and passed them around to the other members of our table.

College was a **totally** new world. The grounds were surrounded by a fence at least ten feet high. I thought the fence was put there to keep us inside. Someday I would learn what such a fence would look like.

At first I was like a fish out of water. Everything was absolutely brand new. When supper was through I had to fold up my serviette and stuff it neatly into my personalized silver serviette ring marked "CVM" which my mother had beforehand bought for me. We all walked out together.

At home I'd been so shy that I even dreaded the trip alone to the tiny town of Lomond to get the mail where I hoped I wouldn't meet people on the board sidewalk because I didn't know whether to look up at them or to look away or to say hello or to keep my mouth shut. I always got out of town as fast as I could. No wonder that to me the city of Brandon with its twenty-five thousand people was a world metropolis. This surely must be the big time.

I didn't know anything about street crossings and when I walked downtown on Rosser Avenue I watched the cars with great concern. I didn't wait for a corner, and there were no marked pedestrian lines then in any case. I would stand in the center of the block and wait for traffic both ways to go by. When I could see an open spot I'd sprint for all I was worth across to the other side of the street.

I learned a little later that the traffic would be going one way on one side of the street and the other way on the other side and I realized that if I watched the traffic on the first side when it was free I could cross to the center without being hit and then over the other half if I watched that traffic carefully. This sure wasn't like the farm.

I had seen only a few picture shows in my life and now at Brandon I was free every Saturday afternoon to walk downtown to see the show at a price of fifteen cents. The world boxing champion, Gene Tunney, was playing in a continuing series. At the end of each program it seemed a boulder would be falling down the mountain just in time to crush him. Each ending looked like he was a goner; each new opening proved it to have been a narrow escape. I couldn't think of missing an installment.

After each show I took another dime and bought either a pastry, containing whipped cream, or an Eskimo pie. The Eskimo pie was brand new; a piece of ice cream coated with frozen chocolate and a stick in the center to handle it. I was really living it up!

A new system had been installed in the high school; (I was taking grade ten) by the principal Mr. Porter and it was called the Dalton Plan. Under this plan the teacher of each subject made out a monthly assignment, split into days, and students could do them in the order of their own choice and as many as they wished at one time or as few. The only rule was that all of the assignments had to be done by the end of the month. The plan was aimed at establishing responsibility, foresight, and individualism.

Most of the kids didn't care for it but I thought it was great. On the first night I took out my month's assignment in algebra and worked on it without pause from suppertime until the eleven o'clock gong signaled lights out. I had completed my entire month's assignment in algebra. I was pleasantly surprised the next morning at my teacher's proud announcement of this achievement to the class. It must have appeared to Mr. Porter that his pet new project "the Dalton Plan" was working. My work was correct too; I got 95 percent on the assignment. I got a boost of self confidence that made for a strong jump start.

Coming from the lonesome plains, even though we had a telephone and a car, this was a life I could never have dreamed of. A picture show every week and an Eskimo pie!

I had a roommate that I got along well with, who was a few years older than I, but we never developed any real friendship. I was so independent I didn't need friends. Everyone back on the farm had predicted that I would be very homesick. From the first on to the end of my Bachelor of Arts degree I was never homesick.

Strangely, much later in my life, I could be overcome with a homesickness that was crushing, debilitating, devastating. At Brandon I had my freedom. I was living, I realized later, the best years of my life.

My transformation from a frightened farm boy into a self confident kid was fast. I came home that Christmas of 1926 surprisingly changed. My folks were happy and they never tired of asking me questions about my life, a kind of a life that had never touched theirs and never would.

I spent hours over the breakfast table on Sunday mornings relating incidents from college life and many of the picture shows I had seen. I had almost a photographic memory for the picture shows. I believe my parents were entertained more than if they had been watching the show themselves. When at the end of the year I won a medal for the grade ten class they were very proud and pleased that they had sent me to Brandon College.

Of course there were times that were less than exhilarating. I was the youngest kid in the institution; most students were university age, ranging into their twenties and mid-twenties. I became a sort of college mascot. Sometimes out of nowhere would come the shout; "Let's bounce Myers!" Four to six guys would get on two sides opposite each other and join hands. I would be placed on this bed of hands which would go "one, two, three," and on the third count the locked arms threw me into the air. As this was repeated time after time I might sometimes be thrown up more than four feet to land back on the bumpy hands. This was all great fun to them.

The following year, 1927-28, I finished grade eleven thereby graduating from the academy in preparation to begin first year university the next fall, but without particular distinction. The novelty of the "metropolis," had worn off.

I was a seasoned resident of the school by this time. I was dealing with the sexual awakening as I have already described. I waited anxiously for the day when I could get home and get on the farm and get to work. From May to October I worked with a vengeance returning to another new phase of life in my first year of Arts.

In the academy I'd an entirely wrong impression of the seriousness of university work. Whereas in the academy we went to school all day, in the university we had certain scheduled classes throughout the week which hardly took up half the time. In the classes also we were never asked to show any evidence of our learning or our progress. Instead we were expected to take notes of what the lecturer was saying. I didn't take the notes very seriously. I considered university to be a piece of cake.

I daydreamed through many of the lectures, particularly if I was not interested in the subject matter, which was most of the time. Also I was madly in love. I couldn't concentrate. But my class attendance was good because this gave me a chance to see my golden haired beauty several times a day. I even started going to church Sunday nights and I always aimed for a seat in the balcony that would be somewhere near her.

I never minded asking other girls for a date but it took me the longest time to get up my courage to ask Mayme Matilda; I always especially referred to her with both her first and middle names because I thought they sounded so beautiful together. Since we were in the same class we did attend the same class meetings and I was overjoyed when I was elected president of the freshman year, and she was elected vice-president. This allowed for an association which I wanted with all my being but which I was nevertheless afraid to pursue for fear of rejection. I was so bogged down in an unexpressed love that my studies frankly went to hell.

The first year term exams were coming up right after Christmas and we had preliminary examinations before Christmas. I found out that the difference between academy and university was taking responsibility. The preliminary tests were a disaster. We got the results shortly before the Christmas holiday and I had what they called a "BL," meaning below the line, in four out of six or seven subjects. Unless I pulled up my socks I could get sent home after Christmas. I'd have to work all holiday or I was a goner.

I think then I gave my parents probably the biggest disappointment they would ever have in me. I wrote home and told them I would not be able to come home for Christmas because I had to study for my first term exams, early in January.

A few other students stayed during the holiday, including a couple of my friends, which was somewhat of a blessing to me. I hit the books like never before but my love-sickness was undiminished. I walked around downtown Brandon all Christmas Eve in the hope that I might get a glimpse of Mayme Matilda entering or leaving a store, or walking the street. No such luck. I went to bed feeling foolish and terribly depressed. I just didn't have the nerve to phone her.

Then to my amazement three days before Christmas she phoned the boys' residence and asked me if I would come and have Christmas dinner with the family. Terrible, debilitating, devastating luck; one of my professors, the day before, had invited me with a group from the dormitory for Christmas dinner and I had accepted. I knew I couldn't break that acceptance. It had been drilled into me all of my life that my word once given had to be fulfilled. The one chance that I would have given my heart for had been, by means of some unlucky star, smashed.

There was no better cook in Brandon than professor Lager's wife and gastronomically the dinner was a delight. But all the time my mind was on that other dinner. I could have rather eaten cold potatoes and bread with Mayme Matilda. I didn't see her throughout the whole holiday.

From the standpoint of the January exams, however, my position was much improved. I didn't know whether I had improved it enough; where I had to depend on notes taken from professors I didn't have much to go on. But where there was a textbook I set my memory to work at top efficiency.

They had a rule that a "BL" (between 40 and 50 percent) could be offset by a corresponding first (between 80 and 100 percent). I was taking a Bible course which was relatively easy and a biology course which was all contained in one big textbook, I got BL's in trigonometry, physics and chemistry; firsts in English and Bible, and I wrote a biology paper such as my professor said he'd never seen the equal of. My work was 98 percent. Overall, I had scraped by; I would not be sent home.

Beginning the second term I had a reformed attitude about

my classes although I was no less wild about my unrequited love. My most satisfactory contact with her was what they called "the Lit." Each class of the university was required to put on a literary evening during each term. This had to be original, strictly the work of the class. Since I was the president of first year I had a big responsibility with that and I even had to have meetings with the executive which consisted of Mayme Matilda and another very attractive blonde girl, Mary Coutts. I wrote a number of songs adapted from popular tunes and I translated what became a tremendous hit. I made a German translation (I was now studying German) of a popular song of the day; something like: "What do I do when my baby cries, do I shout, fret, and fuss? No! I lift up my finger and I say tweet tweet, now now, come come!" In German the result was uproarious.

The rather corpulent German professor, Mr. Lager, practically laughed himself into the aisles. I thought he would roll down the alley between the benches. It was the highlight of that year, though, in all, the year had been a painful one.

Back home about the end of May, I hit the hard work right away, shoveling and taking to market the last of the previous year's crop, and then into the fields for the summer-fallow, arising at five o'clock every morning and working in the field the full ten hour day. Just as the hard physical work of the previous summer had eased and cured the psychic distress of that college year, so once again the work rescued me from the love obsession, although it never did completely disappear.

My second university year was uneventful, my scholastic performance undistinguished, although this time I had no close scrape with failure in any of my subjects. I got to taking out other girls and I had to watch with some pain as other guys "stole my red-hearted sweetheart from me."

Then came my third year.

Now, seventeen, and very strong, I had developed a self confidence that surprised me and stayed with me for a long long time throughout many adversities. But for all of that I never got over the feeling of inadequacy because of my failure to openly press forward to what I emotionally wanted so much. I felt a certain cowardice.

The initial wave of the crash of 1929 came in August when the bottom fell out of the wheat market. It marked the beginning of a ten year period more devastating to my parents than the worst of the deprivations of the earliest homestead days. I shall defer telling of those events now because my college life rolled on as if there had been no change in the outside world. Although Lindbergh's solo crossing of the Atlantic had caused great excitement in our campus in 1927, the historic market crash passed almost without notice.

As long as parents could continue to cough up the tuition and the board, there was no break in the continuity in my new world. Each year was an extension of the last, the love affairs, the exams. Only in my third year, in the fall of 1930, did I learn that faculty members had agreed to take a deferment of half their pay until the college could raise the money. And in the year beginning in the fall of 1931 conditions got worse. The faculty members took even less. Fund raising was a disaster area. We heard of this but we were supremely unimpressed. College life went on as usual.

I was a few months past eighteen when I returned to commence my third year in the fall of 1930. There had been a tremendous change in me since the first day I entered the college in short pants in 1926. I had reached my full growth, just a little under 5'8", and although a great many were bigger than I and taller than I, very few seniors were of a mind to cross swords with me even in a good natured rough and tumble fight.

After my first year I'd had about enough of my life as "the kid." I started to work on my physical inferiority and with a vengeance. Norman Todd, who was still my roommate, had a pair of wire stretchers that he occasionally used and gave me permission to use whenever I liked. I don't think he expected me to wear them out. I had a full routine of exercise with them. Over my head, across the chest, from foot to the height of upraised hand. I used them after class, morning, noon and night.

The strong man of the college, known as Stuart Purdue, had a fifty pound dumbbell that he used to play with. I got his permission to go in his room and use it when I liked.

Hardly anyone was aware of what I was doing and I never

spoke of it. But one day it became quickly apparent when one of the college athletes playfully began to push me around. It happened in the college chapel which had rows of twenty foot benches running from back to front well over one hundred feet on either side of an aisle. When the rough and tumble began we were at the front of the chapel. Instantly one of the great pictures came down from the wall. Onlookers scattered. The benches began to tumble like dominoes. About a dozen of the fellow students of the dormitory stood by in amazement at this exhibition of physical ferocity, completely unsuspected up to now. Their disbelief was even more apparent when about a minute later the fight ended with Ralph Adams laid out on his back over a bench, at my mercy now and motionless in a powerful and punishing headlock.

The performance was repeated again soon when a Freshman smart aleck from Vancouver, quite a lot bigger than I, thought to make an impression. He ended up on the floor in nothing flat. He said later on it was the most amazing experience he had had at Brandon.

The word soon got around and now even among the twenty and twenty-four year olds there were no longer suggestions of "let's bounce Myers."

I felt good about that; it was another reinforcement of my confidence. Unfortunately, the confidence was not transferable to my relationship with the girls. I was to remain all my life reticent to make any advances to the members of the opposite sex who impressed me the most.

I suppose this cowardice must have sprung from my mother's teachings because from my very early adolescence I became very mindful of her stern admonition. "Don't you ever let me learn of you having a girl in trouble. Daddy and I are sacrificing everything to put you through school."

She never spelled out what she meant by "in trouble" but by this time I had a pretty accurate idea. I suppose that because I feared powerful temptation would loosen forces I couldn't control, I remained petrified of starting a fire I couldn't stop. I must have proved to be a dull companion to some of the girls of less stringent standards I went out with.

But by the beginning of my fourth year which began in the

fall of 1931 I had managed an almost complete transformation of the timid boy I was when I started. I was now confident in my work, confident in my strength, confident in most of my relationships. And I was experiencing a dangerous growth of confidence in my association with the girls.

I went through two or three mild courtships in the last of my second year and the early part of my third year, but I had been held back to a certain extent by a strong attachment I had made for a neighbor girl back on the farm, the daughter of some friends of the family that were renting our other farm. She was a sweet country girl and I had reason to believe that she was really in love with me.

In the consequence of the moral principles as they had been taught to me, I felt that I was being less than fair and less than honest if I abandoned the faithful girl at home for the classy girls of the college. But by the beginning of my fourth year I was taking measure of the real world. I wouldn't graduate for at least another year, I had no job opportunities in mind, thoughts of marriage were out of the question. In the light of the implausibility of the practical situation, I began to see where I would be as unfair to my girl back home by leading her to hope for a state of marriage. This attitude made it a little easier for me and I wasn't long in taking advantage of it.

Brandon College and Clark Hall, the girls' dormitory, were separated by a one story building of classrooms. It was possible to climb out the window of Brandon College, cross the roof of the adjacent building, and climb up into one of the rooms in Clark Hall. They always had this room occupied by a faculty member. In 1931-32 Miss Morgan, the singing teacher, had been assigned the room. But she always went away on weekends. Don White, a dormitory friend of mine and I became quite venturesome. In spite of the obvious dangers, we managed for our two girls, who were also friends, to go into Miss Morgan's room about the time of lights out Saturday nights. At that time we would steal silently across the roof and climb half a story up the side of Clark Hall into Miss Morgan's room. The window was waiting and open for us. We probably got more kick out of the hell we were raising than from our dates in Miss Morgan's room, although I have to confess that what was at that time known as "hot necking" did take place quite regularly.

We were taking a terrible chance, the chance of expulsion just as we were about to finish; the girls were taking an even bigger chance. The rules in Clark Hall were very strict.

The closest I ever got to real trouble came on the occasion of the Brandon College basketball team travelling to Winnipeg by train, a distance of a couple of hundred miles. It was possible for a student who had the fare to go along with the team to see the game. Don White and I scraped up the money and, not coincidentally, his girlfriend and mine also scraped up the money with our help. Once in Winnipeg we separated from the rest of the college people and they never saw us again until the Sunday night train home. This gave us almost forty-eight hours. Quite brazenly we went into the Marlboro Hotel and each of us couples separately registered under an assumed married name. To this day the nerve of it makes me shudder. I'm sure the clerk knew we were kids.

I shall not describe the events of the evening or the night. I shall simply say I forget. But I very well recall the next morning when Don White and his girlfriend entered the room. How well I see him in a spell of laughter, "If only Dr. Evans could see his president of the Student Council now."

It was a chilling thought. I had a flashing vision of headlines in the college paper. "President of Student Council takes co-ed into Winnipeg hotel. Registers as married couple." Awesome!

The realization of the consequences of what we had done, should it become known, crystallized enough in the next twenty-four hours so that we made certain that the girls entered the train for the trip home separately from us. We came back at the other end of the car, drifting back to socialize with the team and any other students. Somewhat ominously, no one ventured: "Where have you been; we didn't see you at the game?" The lack of conversation seemed to me to be an indication of suspicions and I knew we better get ready to take some heat and to be damn convincing when we got home. If we failed, expulsion was almost certain. My girl was the daughter of a very important Baptist and a financial supporter of the college.

Only now was I struck with the magnitude of the consequences of this daredevil scheme.

Monday morning it was classes as usual, but later on I heard that the Dean of Women, Mrs. Wright, had called a meeting of the girls' Student Council of Clark Hall to discuss the possible situation of our weekend escapade. I knew the story had to be stopped in its tracks. Right there.

The best defense, I figured, was not to try to defend ourselves against accusations, and get into the position of telling a bunch of lies and having to back one lie up with the next and not knowing exactly what the girls might say under similar questioning. So I screwed up my courage and marched over to Clark Hall and asked to see the lady dean.

I was admitted into the office to see Mrs. Wright, a very very plump lady, looking very very severe.

I said, "I hear, Mrs. Wright, that you have made an accusation to your girls' council that I may have spent some time with Helen in Winnipeg last weekend." I said, "I hope this isn't right because I'm sure that you realize even more than I do, how serious a charge this is. Frankly I'm shocked by it." When Mrs. Wright continued to glare at me unblinkingly, I continued.

"All I can say, Mrs. Wright, is that whoever makes this claim, whether it's student or faculty, better have solid evidence. I'm in a position to **know** what didn't happen, and the rest of the people are not. This story is pure guesswork. And it's vicious. I hate to think of the mess there's going to be if this kind of gossip gets around, and gets around to Helen's father. And I think that you will find that Helen and I, when it's all over, will come out better than anybody else. This is all I have to say, but I thought I better say it to you now."

Mrs. Wright blinked; grudgingly gave me the faintest hint of a half smile. She nodded, "Okay, thank you."

I left with the feeling, mission accomplished. And I hadn't lied.

It was accomplished. I never heard any more about it and neither did Helen and neither did the other two. My strength was the fact I knew we had not been seen by anybody. No one could say we had been together. The girls might have been together; my friend and I might have been together without ever having crossed paths. No one could have anything more than a suspicion.

It was a close shave, especially when I was hit with the full impact of what this would have done to my parents, their life's hope cruelly dashed on the cusp of realization.

Thus was the Winnipeg episode put promptly to rest and permanently sealed away. As far as I know the secret has not been exhumed these past 57 years. I always felt the authorities remained suspicious but I knew that without something to back them up they would remain fearful of a scandal that could hurt the college financially and lead them personally in deep hot water.

Now was my last chance to make a name for myself, to validate the hardships my parents had endured in order to give me the chance they'd never had. The college offered a gold medal for the special geology course to the student with the highest marks, above a certain stiff minimum. I determined I would win that medal.

I knew a fellow student by the name of Paul Bugg was expected to win. He was the serious kind of a student, conforming to and supportive of all that tends to impress a faculty. So I knew that unless my marks were well ahead of Bugg's, something would be stretched to fulfill the faculty expectations. My prior performance had remained undistinguished.

Once I'd set my sights, I never relaxed. A large part of the geology course depended strictly on memory. Professor Evans, who was also the geology prof, furnished each of us special geology students with a whole set of his lectures in historic geology. That was one of the courses that I zeroed in on. When the exams came, both the mid-terms and the finals, I gave Evans a paper that was practically a carbon copy of his notes in answer to each of his questions. I knew he'd have to give me 100 percent on that course; there wasn't a single doubt. I applied similar diligence to all of the geology courses. I never learned what the specific marks were but I learned who the medal winner was, and with some pride. I learned also that certain members of the faculty had disfavored giving me the medal but that the great divergence in marks between Bugg and me gave them no choice. There was a lot of satisfaction in that.

All in all I ended a distinguished year. Apart from the scholastic achievement I was class valedictorian, class president, president of the Student Council for the boys' residence. Also I had composed the class song from the tune of, according to my memory, *The Marines' Hymn (from The Halls of Montezuma)* - and the class yell.

From the fair Assiniboine, to the east and to the west
From the land of Manitoba, to the ocean's foamy crest
In all sections of our country, from the centre to the sea
May the honoured name of Brandon,
Stand for truest liberty.
> *CHORUS:*
> *To the gold and purple symbol*
> *Of our final college year*
> *May our hearts beat ever loyal*
> *O, our Alma Mater dear.*

We, her faithful sons and daughters, must extend our
> *parting hand.*
And we say adieu with sorrow, in one brave unbroken band
Thou hast bound us Alma Mater with a tie we'll ne'er regret.
May the honoured name of Brandon, be the last we'll 'ere forget.

Once again we'll sing her praises, with a voice that's loud
> *and strong*
Once again we pay our homage to the spot we loved so long.
So adieu our Alma Mater, we have turned the final bend;
But the memory of Brandon will remain until the end.

CLASS YELL
Rickety, Rackety; Rickety Zoo,
Nineteen Hundred and Thirty -two
'32!

My valedictory address was published on the front page of the Western Baptist magazine. It was my first published work and I was very proud to read my words in print.

But I think my parents were the most pleased of all. They had produced the first university graduate in all the history of all of the Myers family and all of the history of all of my mother's family, the Feys, and in all of thousands of square miles in Southern Alberta up to that time. They had given me the tools to make an outstanding future for myself if I had the good sense to apply the necessary ambition and wisdom. But I soon learned a necessary ingredient was a **chance**.

Right up to the end of the term, as we waited around a week for the graduation ceremonies, I was hoping for and expecting a job with the Canadian Geological Survey.

Meanwhile, in a final meeting of the class I was elected permanent class president; the permanent vice president was Mayme Matilda and the permanent secretary was Mary Coutts, coinciding with the executive of our freshman year. The night of the graduation ceremonies we were arranged in line alphabetically for the graduation dinner and later to the ceremony to receive our sheepskins. There being no alphabetical name intervening between Matthews and Myers I had the final satisfaction of ending up beside the girl whom I had always thought of as my girl, but who never was.

The job I had looked for did not come. The year was 1932 and we were advised that the government was hiring no university students; the survey project had been cancelled for the summer.

When I was in first year Arts the Canadian Geological Survey was taking a few top students from second year who were beginning a course of special geology. When I was in second year they were taking no second year students but a few from third year. As the depression worsened, when I was in third year, they were taking no third year but some from the graduating classes. It was only natural when I was in fourth year they were not taking any at all. They were taking nothing but graduate students.

Here I was with a university education back on the farm, eating the dust and shoveling the wheat. It looked like I really had become what my mother had always warned me against, "an educated fool."

That condition would last a while; quite a while!

Chapter Thirteen

DEPRESSION

M y parents' happiness over my graduation was not due to last long. No job. No job anywhere. It seemed that my stars were mistimed. I was always just a step behind. My real ambition had been journalism but they didn't teach journalism in Brandon. My second ambition was to be a lawyer but they didn't teach law in Brandon. I chose geology because I found the history of the earth to be of tremendous interest and the revelations engulfed me with a new insight into the human race and a perspective of time. It was all a brand new idea and a very exciting one.

The Canadian Geological Survey was busy in those days in an effort to complete a geological study of all of this vast land of Northern Canada. For four years I followed the carrot but never got a taste.

When I was in my fourth and graduating year they took only post-graduate students. I was always just a step behind and it seemed as there was no way I could ever catch up. It was decided, however, that since I had no job I'd better take one year of post-graduate work. Then for sure I'd get on the government survey the next year. Well, the next year they didn't take anybody. The survey department shut down. I knew they wouldn't run out of land to survey. I hadn't thought of them running out of money.

In 1929 the market had crashed and the price of wheat after gyrating violently began its long term descent that would take it from a high of $2.50 a bushel down to a low of 25 cents in 1934. Besides that we had run into the Dust Bowl era that forced the "Okies" out of central Oklahoma, on west, onward to California, but in Western Canada there was no place for us to go. The dry hot winds wilted the crops and what was worse stirred up the dust on the land to where it practically at times obliterated vision.

Up until then land had been farmed in quarter section blocks, that is a half mile square, sometimes bigger. This gave the continuous winds a chance to stir up great volumes of dust to sweep on just as the wind on a wide expanse of water will whip up tremendous waves. I recall in one terrible storm that I had to go to the neighbor's house to get some yeast to make bread. My mother had run out of yeast. It was a rare occurrence for her to run out of anything essential, because from the very beginning the long trip to Stavely had taught the homesteaders to look ahead. But on this day we were out of bread, and the dust was so bad you could not see from the house to the barn.

My dad saddled up my pony and brought it to the house; my mother fixed cloths around my face to stop the direct dust out of my mouth and nose. I kicked my pony into a gallop and never stopped until I had arrived at the Chapman place about two miles away. I came home with the yeast; we had bread, but the land sure wasn't raising any bread; it was just blowing away.

The crops that had ventured above the surface were now slashed mercilessly by the wind and silt to a pitiful sight. The sand piled up along the fence lines where the Russian thistles blew and made a barricade. All fence lines running north and south were obliterated by the bridge of dust which covered them. It didn't take more than a year or two for the farmers both in the United States and in Canada to smarten up by cutting the size of their fields from quarter section acre blocks to twenty acre strips; twenty acres of grain, twenty acres of summer fallow, twenty acres of grain.

But through the early 30s there was plenty of wind, little rain, and a plague of grasshoppers. By this time we had a truck and I recall making several trips to the Municipal Grasshopper Poison Center where I would pick up a truckload of wet treated sawdust, free of charge. That was about the only thing I ever remember getting free.

The poison was instant death to the grasshopper, but when we got the poison home we had to drive around the fields with the horse and buggy, one person driving and one person in back using two hands to broadcast from the one hundred pound sacks of the poison sawdust as far and wide on both sides as he could. If the field could be caught before the infestation had got more than a quarter of the way in, the grasshoppers could be stopped by this poisoning method.

Pestilence and drought seemed to come together, one year we had the invasion of the "army worms." I don't know their biological name - these were green worms about an inch long. They were so proliferous that they blackened the ground and the ground was green. Locomotives' wheels skidded on the tracks. The worms crawled up the side of houses and I know in the case of our own house the east side (the invasion side) was almost solid green. Your car would skid on pavement corners because of the smashed worms. They would get in any nook and cranny and then fall and then spread around in the house.

The worms knew no limitations. They crawled up bedposters into beds. They crawled up tables and counters. They kept housewives sweeping most of the time unless they lived in very tight houses. They climbed up their legs too.

Some people ingeniously invented the tomato can trap. They would take an empty tomato can, fill it about a quarter full of kerosene and then set the bedposters in the tomato cans, four to a bed. The worms would crawl up the can and tumble into the kerosene. That guaranteed a full night's sleep without slapping squishy army worms spreading across the body.

I thought my mother would go out of her mind. We spread thick axle grease around the door jams and windows to immobilize the worms.

They invaded the garden like an advancing army. That's where they got their name. They stripped every leaf to the stem. To save the potatoes we dug ditches along the rows with a one foot pit every six feet. The worms would travel down the ditches like a stream and tumble into the pits - filled with lye. We saved the potatoes.

The worms were a one time phenomenon. No one knew where the worms came from or where they went. Suddenly they were just there. Never to this day, again.

Not enough green seed was grown to keep the cattle and they were slaughtered by the thousands across the country. The price of pork was so low that farmers fell to killing their hogs and burying them in ditches.

I can remember taking a crate of eggs to town; that would be 12 dozen, a dozen to each layer, in a box with thin cardboard dividers. I recall distinctly once getting 10 cents a dozen for one crate of eggs from the Chinese cafe, then buying a breakfast of two eggs, a piece of toast, a couple of pieces of bacon, and coffee for 30 cents, three dozen eggs for two.

We of course always had our food. We always had our milk cows; our beef, our pork; our milk, our cream; we raised enough wheat to take it to town and have it ground into flour to make bread. But cash was a commodity of the utmost scarcity.

My parents had been doubly hit by the depression; crop failures as well as the market crash. My mother was the more venturesome of the two and she got into the market of wheat futures. This was the craze all over the country before the 1929 crash. Everybody was gambling on something and the idea was that if you bought wheat futures you could take your **own** wheat to the elevator and sell it and avoid paying storage on it and then since wheat was usually low in the fall and higher in the spring, sell in the spring. The theory was good on paper and it might have worked earlier, or later, but it wasn't worth a damn in the disastrous market of 1929 and 1930.

Until then we'd had good crops; we were farming nearly 1,000 acres; the prices were good and we had money in the bank.

I recall that my mother was in Denver visiting relatives when the bottom went out of the wheat market and her losses amounted to $3,000. This was big big money in those days. I urged my father to sell all of the wheat contracts, to forget the market, and to take the money we had and put it away and use the rest to buy a fine new car. We planned to get a brand new green Hudson sedan and we would drive down to Denver to bring back my mother, my sister, and by then my infant brother.

My father followed my urgings and I was very excited about this great trip, happy to be away from the gambling pits, when one day about three days before our planned departure and two days before the planned delivery of the car my father came home from town and he announced: "Son, we're not going." I was thunderstruck. I couldn't believe it. I hardly dared to venture "Why?"

My dad had never had any experience with marketing or with stock markets and I don't know how he arrived at the drastic and dramatic decision he made that day. He simply said; "Your mother has lost $3,000 in the wheat market. I believe wheat is going to come back. I'm going to buy back her futures and we've got to stay here and ride it out and make this money back."

I was devastated but I knew there was no use setting up any objections. If my father once made up his mind you were not likely to get him to change it.

To my amazement after my father bought back the wheat futures the next day or two wheat began to go up. I don't remember the time interval but I don't think it could have been more than three weeks until wheat had come back to where the sale of the futures would recover my mother's losses. He'd told me that when wheat came back to where we were even he was going to sell out, and he did.

However, wheat continued to advance on the market, and the selling looked like a mistake. That didn't bother my father, he'd had an objective; that objective was to get back the money my mother had lost. He said fine. That was all there was to it.

But when my mother arrived home from Denver and found that the futures that had been bought had now been sold and the price of wheat was far higher and still rising she was upset. She announced her decision to buy the futures back and ride the up-market.

Unfortunately, the up-market had finished its move. It went down. It began its fatal tumble that would never really end until wheat got down to 25 cents a bushel in about 1934 or 1935.

There was a time interval here, a rather short one, and in that interval we had bought a new 1929 Buick car. What an amazement! What a luxury! What a marvel of technology of the modern age; a windshield wiper, a self starter, even lights in the interior. And bright headlights that could go either dim or bright. I remember my sister and I standing in the kitchen window looking to the road north for my parents' return on the day that they brought the car from Calgary and when I saw the very bright lights I knew that was the car. And sure enough it was. A wonderful moment in our lives.

But any joy we had out of the car was short-lived, as the wheat market continued to tumble.

I recall that my mother had bought about 5,000 bushels of wheat and that when the margin ran out Tull and Arden Ltd. of Calgary called our home and wanted more margin. This had already happened a couple of times. And my parents decided to put in enough margin this time to hold it for a while. So they sent Tull Arden $5,000, above the margin requirement, the remainder of their cash savings. That ought to satisfy it. That ought to stop it. And actually it temporarily did. But there was another fly in the ointment.

We had made extensive inquiries in town about the solidity of Tull and Arden brokerage firm because by that time firms were going broke across the country, and we had been assured by our banker that this was one of the most solid companies in the business. So I will not forget the morning my mother came out of the house, her apron blowing in the wind to announce that the radio had just stated that Tull and Arden had gone bankrupt. Unless they paid up that meant that the $5,000 above margin - really banked money - had gone down the drain with the rest.

Of course there was the usual talk of making good. There was the usual upbeat talk. Mr. Tull and Mr. Arden would personally make good all cash losses. There was the plea, as usual, for patience. But none of it ever came true. Tull and Arden were busted and whether the partners had the money to make up the losses or not, I do not know, but never again did I hear the name either of Mr. Tull or Mr. Arden, and never did my parents see one green dollar out of the $5,000 they had sent to support their contracts in addition to the $3,000 lost in the market.

You might think we were badly off; we were among the best off in the country. We had never mortgaged our farm. I had heard my mother vow many a time since my earliest years that they would never mortgage the farm. We hadn't borrowed on anything. We had no money, but we also had no debt.

I recall my dad saying, "Hell will freeze before they can squeeze us out of here." That was a comforting thought and it was a true one, and it was illustrative of the solidarity of my father. I knew no one would ever budge my father.

96

That didn't provide extra dollars to send the son a thousand miles away to college. Or if he did go to college it meant sacrifices undescribable. But those sacrifices were made. I went back to complete my third college year at Brandon. Nothing would deter my mother's determination that I should graduate from college.

I do recall that at one stage we sold a carload or two of wheat when wheat was about 35 cents a bushel. I recall we had held 1,000 bushels hoping for a better price in the spring. It didn't come. We sold at 25 cents a bushel. Our carload of wheat had a storage bill of 25 cents a bushel; we had to sell that wheat to pay for the storage on it. It was indeed all gone with the wind that had piled up the dust knee high along the fences.

We had by 1930 the grain truck and we had the car and the machinery and the horses and we had grown enough oats and greenfeed to keep the horses going the following season and we had saved back previously seed wheat from earlier crops to tide us over. Not many other farmers had done this. There was no use looking to the government for help. In fact no one even thought about that.

But I can recall my 1931 return trip to Brandon for my fourth year, when my mother was getting my clothes ready for the coming college season. I had two suits, one which I wore every day at Brandon and one for better occasions. It cost one dollar to get a suit cleaned.

She told me to get some tractor gasoline and had me pour a washtub about half full. It was purple gas because the government charged no tax on tractor gasoline and they colored it purple to stop farmers from using it in their cars.

My mother dumped my suits in this purple gas, brought out the washboard and washed my suits in the gasoline, then hung them up on the line to dry. She left them for about two days to get all the gasoline smell out of them, then pressed them and never had they looked better when they had come back from a cleaner. But I still see my mother's poor hands, red and sore, from their work with the gasoline. There was no doubt I was going back to college.

Luckily college didn't start until near the end of the farming season when all the grain had been moved into the granaries and much of it already hauled to market. My father didn't need any help through the winter season but in the spring and summer until I returned in May he was able to get a hired man - they now had 1,000 acres - for board and room and $10 a month. When I came home in May I took over the eight and ten horse teams required for the farm operation. I used eight horses on the eight foot disc which would do about twenty acres a day and I used ten horses on the three bottom plow which would do about ten acres a day.

I got up before five each morning, got on my pony, rode a couple of miles to where the horses were pastured and drove them back to the barn. They would all go automatically into their own stalls and I would feed each of them a gallon of oats and an oats hay bundle, two good bundles down the loft hole above every double stall.

Then I put on the collars and the hames and hame straps, belly band, and traces and leave the horses to eat while I went into breakfast. When I finished breakfast I got the horses out again, often with the help of my father, led them two teams at a time to the water trough, bridled each horse, made the connections of the several lines of each team, there was a lead team and a wheel team, and so there were two sets of lines, one set for the right hand horses and one for the left hand horses. It was a religion to be standing up on either the plow or the disc at seven o'clock sharp and saying "Gettyup." I worked till twelve when I would break for noon, unbridle the horses, water them, feed them again, have dinner, come out and hook them up again and work until six when I would come in as black as any of the blacks in Africa, and the wash water in the basin was nearly mud. I'd have to wash my face at least twice.

Along about nine o'clock in the morning each day I'd see my friend drive up to their new tractor. He would get on that thing, quit at noon, rest a couple of hours in the heat of the day, come out and get on the tractor again for a few more hours - maybe in the cool of the evening - and at the end of the day he had done three times as much as I. I'd start out a quarter section and, when I was about a third finished, he had his quarter finished and was moving on to the next.

It was sure hard to take and I told my dad we'd better get a tractor. And he said we'd have to wait and see how these new tractors worked out. They worked out all right. Inside of three or four years most of the people were getting tractors, including my dad. We tearfully parted with twenty good work horses to get it. By that time, I was away from the farm and I never had the joy of doing as much land in a day as my friend, Fred, on the next farm.

In the fall we had to haul wheat to town with the horses. We had to go ten miles and that would take about four hours with a heavy load and, between the two or us, we might haul about 200 bushels. We'd get into town by noon, unload at the elevator, put our horses in the livery stable, feed them and go to the Chinese restaurant for dinner. At one o'clock we'd be on our way home. We'd get home about four o'clock. But we wouldn't go to the house; we would back up to the granary and with a scoop shovel we would shovel on our loads for the next day. After about an hour of sweating in the granary at the hardest work I've ever known, we would pull our loads to the house, unhitch the horses, put them in the barn, feed them, go in and have supper, go to bed early so we could get up at five o'clock the next morning and do the same thing all over again.

I will not forget when our neighbor got a fancy Reo truck. It was harvest season then and he was hauling from the threshing machine. So was I. After about four miles out, or nearly two hours, he would pass me in a cloud of dust. And when I'd gone another couple of miles, he would pass me coming back. When I'd gone another couple of miles, he would pass me again going into town, and by the time I got into town, he would pass me again coming back. This went on all morning and all afternoon. When I got home, I'd hauled about 80 bushels to town with two horses and he had made seven trips and hauled about 600 bushels. I told my dad we should get a truck, and he said we would wait and see how these new trucks worked out.

They worked out all right and in another year or two my dad had a truck, too. Tremendous numbers of hours were saved as the combine replaced the binder, the stookers, the threshing machine and the wagons, and as all loading of grain became automated over the scores of millions of acres in the breadbasket of the United States and Canada. So if millions of hours were saved, people by the hundreds of thousands were no longer needed. And this changed agriculture, but more importantly it changed the culture of the nation. The farms became quickly bigger. The small guys sold out. The young people went to the cities to get jobs. Today you hardly ever see a farm of less than a section and most farms are several sections. The job killers have scourged the land.

Now if you drive around in the country where I lived, you will see the ghost of an era gone - gaping old houses, doors hanging, windows knocked out, roofs leaning, old barns still faintly red and caving in. The laughter of children running in the schoolyard, or the family beings that inhabited that country have passed into history. The huge machines work around the old houses, hardly noticing them.

The descendant children now go to city schools. They get the chance at better education but I doubt if they learn more. When we came home we had work to do, and the city kids miss that; they have nothing to do. In short, the nature and texture of our whole society has changed.

There are no country rubes anymore, they are the city smart guys, the motorcycle gangs. To be sure, there are millions of good students, but there are also millions of very poor students and their values are different. They have shaken the dirt from their shoes and they no longer realize they live off the dirt which produces their daily bread.

I actually finished school in the summer of 1934. I had gone on to a year's graduate work in geology in the fall of 1932 and when this brought no job I took a year of the School of Education at the University of Alberta. This gave me a qualified teacher's certificate to teach all high school grades, nine to twelve inclusive. Then came the job of getting a school. The education had seriously crimped all of the resources of my family and I knew that this had to be the final course that would pay off. I began at once to try for a school beginning the fall season of 1934.

Through that summer I sent dozens of applications, I drove around the country talking to members of school boards wherever there was going to be a vacancy and putting forth my best foot.

My best foot wasn't too convincing. I remember one farmer on his hay swather stopping his horses to talk to me as I approached him across the stubble. I explained to him what I was after and gave him the reasons why I thought I would be a very good teacher.

I was a university graduate which many teachers were not. I had been the gold medalist in my class. I had been given the honor of delivering the valedictory address for my class. I had been the president of the boys in residence in Brandon College. (This was opposed to the presidency of the whole student body which in an election I had lost.) I showed the school board man many eloquent praises I had received from teachers in Edmonton who had used me for practice teaching classes. After I was finished the farmer raised the visor of his cap about an inch, spat tobacco juice straight into the swather, and said: "Hell, son, we got kids in grade twelve that look older than you do." With this final assessment he said "Gettyup" and that was the end of that interview.

I had many others similar to it, if not quite as specific and quite as harsh. Most of the board members would start with the question of what experience I had. Of course I had to say none. Their reply would be "Well, we need someone with experience, and you know there are lots of teachers out of work with experience."

Sometimes my father would go with me when I went to see these board members over a radius of maybe 100 to 140 miles, but always the answer was the same, "We want someone with experience." And my dad would come out sometimes with the practical question, "How the hell you gonna get experience if nobody will hire you to give you any experience?" We never got a good answer to that one, and finally at the end of the summer I got my one and only offer of a school.

The Bentley District would employ me to teach grades nine to twelve inclusive, all classes, some thirty pupils, and they would pay me $500 a year and supply a little shack at the schoolhouse to live in. I told them, "Thank you, but no thank you."

Quite a number of our graduates of the School of Education in 1934 did get school teaching jobs. I don't know how they did but I was admittedly very young to be teaching kids that were nearly my age, and worse than that I looked a lot younger than I was. It took a few rough tumbles in life thereafter to give me a good set of wrinkles which now are quite up-to-date.

Anyway I started a commission job of selling washing machines through fall, winter and into the next spring. I made between $40 and $50 a month, about the same as the Bentley School Board had offered me, selling washers door to door where about a third of the houses were occupied by people who were unemployed. The first question we used to ask was, "Where does your husband work, Mrs. so and so?" As soon as the lady said he was out of work we moved on to the next house.

When we found someone who was working the next question was, "What kind of a washer do you have?" If it was of recent vintage we moved on to the next house. When we found a lady where there was employment and who had no washer, or a poor one, that was our prospect. But even such people could not be easily persuaded to spend their money. They were barely making it and when our initial payments on the washing machine took five dollars a month that was a major item to a lot of the prospects. There was a gimmick, and I have never been quite sure if I was fully honest in the use of it.

The Beatty Washing Machine Company put out cheap porcelain tub washers at $59.95 with payments of five dollars a month. The next step up was the $99 washer, better built and still with payments of just five dollars a month. The third step was the copper tub which was a washer of lifetime duration at a cost of about $124, but the payments were still just five dollars a month. But the commission was $25.00 instead of $5.95 on the cheap machine.

I got the idea that if copper were to become scarce and if the company were to withdraw copper tubs from the market there would be a considerably greater demand for copper tubs. I used to bring my assistant manager along on some of the best prospects and I would tell the prospects in front of the manager that I thought it was only right to inform the prospects about the copper tub. There was a chance, only a chance, but still a chance that copper tubs would not be available next year. As a result the company was not pushing the copper tub in order to conserve what models they had left.

We would point out to the prospect that he could buy the

copper tub for the same amount of cash down and the same monthly payments as he could buy the cheap machine. Mind you we already had the contract signed on the cheap machine before we moved into this stage of the sale. I pointed out to the prospect that "all I have to do is change the model number here on the sales contract; we will not ask you for any more and we will deliver the copper tub next week; you just keep on paying the same amount only for a longer time."

It was surprising how often this worked. I didn't regret selling those people the copper tub because that machine is probably still working this fifty years hence. There was just a little bit of trickery, however, involved in the sales proposition, just a little white lie, and I have never liked that. When I quit the washing machine company it was partly because of the sales presentation that I had to use to make a decent commission, partly because the money was hardly a living anyway.

I had very poor winter boots, couldn't afford new ones and I was determined not to ask my family for help. It was only a commission job and you could get other commission jobs during the depression.

Another thing was that I had obtained a guaranteed salary with a collection agency. The pay was about $70 a month. I wasn't sure how tough I could be with collections from poor people who didn't have the money to pay and I didn't look forward to that job. At about the same time I was offered a job in the packing plant at 30 cents an hour as a shipping clerk. I had married the daughter of one of the founders of an Edmonton packing house. And the hourly wage here would fetch me about $65 a month on a job that I could do. That's what I thought. And while people with great minds and grade ten educations could do fine on the desk in taking down orders and getting them quickly delivered to the shipping department, and keeping the records on them, I found I couldn't. I was always making mistakes. The word went out that "Art's son-in-law can't cut the mustard." So I was moved from shipping clerk to shipping boy.

I was glad for the move. The wages were the same and I didn't have to deal with the confounded business of figures and detail, and a jungle of errors. I went to the shipping room from 7:00 A.M.

to 12 noon and from 1:00 P.M. to 5:00 P.M. I would line up with the other shipping boys - I say boys intentionally because usually they were under 20 years of age - and the shipping clerk would bark out the orders to us, "five pounds of hog liver, ten pounds of tripe, twenty pounds of wieners, three full hams; - -" All of these items had to be brought back to the shipping clerk, put on the scale, the weight registered, and the butcher shop that was doing the buying, marked on the white paper which I used to wrap up the order. I carried hundred pound orders of tripe from the lowest floor to the highest floor, and all in all it was not a very impressive job either to my employer or to me.

However, I thought I saw a chance for improvement. I got books from the library on the packing industry and on the chemical controls of the packing industry. I'd had enough ground work in chemistry to figure out a program for the testing of the vital statistics such as free fatty acids and percentage of phosphorous in bone meal, and I don't know what all. I was able to persuade the superintendent of the plant, a man by the name of Jack Pheasey, an Englishman, and a progressive one, that they ought to have a chemical laboratory to keep control. With the help of some professors at the university I set up and ordered all the necessary equipment for the lab and started in a month or two later as the chemist.

The job was better and it carried more prestige, but it didn't carry any more money.

Chapter Fourteen

GETTING TO BE A WRITER

The writing profession is probably less understood than most. Thousands of people would like to be writers. Dozens of people are heard to say; "My life would make a book - when I get time, I'm going to sit down and write it."

While they would readily admit that a skater must spend years on skates before he becomes a professional in his class, a tennis player the same, a musician the same, it never occurs to them that the same holds true for a writer. They think a writer just sits down and writes a story or a book and if it's a good story he sends it to a publisher; and that's all there's to it.

A published author rises to his position on the back of three prerequisites. The first is an inborn talent; the second is facility with the language which can only be learned by doing the scales as the piano player learns his scales, and the third is the willingness to stay with it in the face of unending rejections. The true writer writes because he can't help it - not someday when he gets the time - and he continues to write whether he is published or not because he can't help it.

I think the writing talent shows up early. If it is a strong talent it persists, if it is a weak talent it withers and the would-be writer abandons his ambition.

In my own case, looking back, I can detect the natural bent at a very early age. The creative writer isn't necessarily driven by an instinct to pick up a pen and start putting words on paper. He is driven by a compulsion for self expression. In my own case, I believe that the beginning of this drive expressed itself when at the age of about three years I was gratified to stand up on the counter in Mr. Fitz's Londale store and sing to the customers. No one had to force me or coax me, I just happened to be a kid that enjoyed doing it. I suppose I also enjoyed the applause, and I certainly enjoyed the reward of a chocolate bar. I think you might say that a writer is driven by a deep-seated and often obscured desire. The writer is driven to show off his innermost thoughts and feelings while he is at the same time restrained by his nature from doing so openly, in the real world.

A great many of the best writers and the best performers are very shy. Under the protective armor of the covers of a book or a production of the theater or the movies he can bring this exhibitionism to the fore while he himself stays in the shadows.

People who say that if I had the time I would write a book, never write one. The true writer will make time for the book if he has to give up time for all manner of other purposes. He is propelled, whereas the man who says "if I had time", is not propelled. If he did sit down to write the book he wouldn't know how to start. In the first place he wouldn't have the skill with the language which he already takes for granted. The easier it is to read, the easier it is to write, so the reader thinks.

The truth is actually the opposite, just as the case with the singer. In every public activity the best of the professionals make it look easy. I have even noticed this in the equestrian sport of stadium jumping. Put a top rider on a top horse and he will come around the course and every jump will look simple as pie. Put an amateur on the same horse and on the first or second jump you will probably see the wreck of your life. It wasn't easy at all for the professional. He arrived at his stature through guiding horses over hundreds and maybe thousands of jumps and learning the fine points about riding before he ever took a jump.

A practiced editor or writer can tell the work of an amateur at a glance. Give him a short paragraph to read and he'll give you the answer. It may sound unlikely; it's true.

When I was in grade five or six I recall my first opportunity to write. Our school teacher in our country school asked the class each to write a composition and each to pick his own subject. I had just finished reading "Tarzan of the Apes" and I was so mightily impressed that I practically lived Tarzan. I got out my school scribbler and started right in. I wrote like fury until the end of the class when Mrs. Mannen picked up the papers. Other kids had sat there writing a few lines, or chewing their pencils trying to think of something to put down. Mrs. Mannen was impressed with my story which was my own idea of what Tarzan did after he came out of the book.

The next time I had such an assignment was in my first year university, and the English teacher told us to write a composition and she said it could be as long as 1,000 words.

I put up my hand and asked the stupid question: "How short can it be?"

She said severely, "Mr. Myers, you can write 1,000 words."

I went to my room and started to think of what would be exciting. Once I had read "Twenty Thousand Leagues Under the Sea," and I wasn't able to stop reading. Now I thought a Trip To Mars would be an exciting story. I wrote the title at the top of the page and started to write the composition. That night I wrote it all in one session and somewhat well over 1,000 words. I revised it a little and turned it in the next day. My English teacher was much impressed.

Mrs. Whitmore was known for her strong likes and dislikes. If she thought you were good she would go overboard in her marks and if she thought you were bad she would go overboard too, in the opposite direction.

When the essays were handed back I proudly received mine with a "Very good!" and a mark of "<u>A plus plus plus</u>." I thought, "Oh boy, is this a piece of cake!"

After Christmas she gave us another assignment to write a composition of our own choice. At home during the Christmas vacation I had been talking to my dad about the early days in Oklahoma and he told me about a lynching he had witnessed. It made a very strong impression on me and I thought it was a very good, if gory, story, so when we got back I decided to write about the lynching.

The age of realism had not yet arrived. I unfortunately strove to expound and depict the harsh realities of the story. I had such quotations as, "Bring that damn nigger over here and let me get this rope around his neck."

107

I described the death of the lynched man, the kicking and the twitching and a bystander who shouted, "Let the son-of-a-bitch kick." Well, this was a Baptist college and Mrs. Ella Whitmore was a devout Baptist, a very proper one, and I should have known that even the word "damn" would be enough to paralyze her, and enough to paralyze my future in English Literature. My story came back with a "<u>C minus minus minus</u>."

Never again in all my four years of university did I get more than a C or a C minus in a composition. It was not yet my day.

My God, for that story it's a wonder I didn't get expelled!

During my two post-graduate years I did very little writing but I remained fascinated with the fiction of the masters. I read Thomas Hardy's *Far From The Madding Crowd* whose author is today renowned as the father of the modern English novel. I read nearly all of his books, *Tess of the d'Urbervilles*, Arthur Conan Doyle's *Hound of the Baskervilles* and many others. I dreamed stories, and I wrote poetry, nearly all of which has been since lost. As soon as I went to work in 1934 my interest in prose composition returned. I wrote a few stories which came back with a sound rejection every time. Then, through the *Writer's Digest*, I got hold of a book by Thomas H. Uzell, a teacher of the art of writing and at one time the editor of a leading magazines. But Uzell laid it on the line and I listened:

Uzell told his readers and his pupils that the first thing you have to do is learn your scales, as a piano student learns his. You have to write. You have to write, and write, and write and write. You have to develop a professional facility with the English language. You have to eliminate clumsy expressions, redundancies, many of your adjectives. And you will find that as time goes on that the best thing you can do with a story you have written is to deliberately cut off the beginning and cut off the end. And in looking at some of my stories I realized that this was true. You don't use a meandering beginning. You get down to business right away. You develop what is called "the narrative hook." And at the end you don't overdo the conclusion or preach about it. You simply end it.

Well, there was a lot more than that. But the biggest thing I got out of it was the necessity to write, write, write. Uzell said that when you have written a million words you will probably be proficient with the use of the language. So I thought "okay, if I have to write a million words, I'll write a million words, and then maybe I'll be able to get a story published."

So the first thing I did was to buy a second-hand typewriter and an instruction book from the business school. I tackled the typewriter, going through all of the exercises as instructed and going over them again until I had developed an ability to type about 45 or 50 words a minute in good form. "Okay," I said, "here I go on a million words."

I started to write short stories. I wrote mysteries. I wrote detective stories. I wrote science fiction. I wrote true confessions. I wrote what I thought were sophisticated stories for the slick magazines like *Cosmopolitan* and *Ladies Home Journal*. I wrote *The Blue Lace Curtain*, and *Compartment 76* and dozens and dozens whose titles I don't remember. I wrote a novel *The Woman Came Back*. It was about a woman who had left her husband and she had been absent seven years and presumed dead. He had married again and was living on the farm when the woman came back. It wasn't a bad story, but it wasn't good enough to get published. I simply could not find anyone who was ready to publish my stories, although here and there I did get some encouragement.

The truth was that the middle and late 30s was as tough for writers as for everyone else. The competition for magazine space was furious. Everyone who was out of work, who thought he might like to write, was sending in stories. Also the magazines were cutting back and even the professional writers were getting rejection slips. They had to change their style and change fast because the style of the published story was changing to fit the times. Their big houses and their Cadillacs were going down the drain. You were competing with them to get space in a magazine. I never succeeded.

The disappointment was sometimes bitter. The scores of rejection slips, with the knowledge that I was on my way to having written a million words, didn't give me much satisfaction. I just kept on.

Of course I was working as I have related before, in the sales of washing machines and, later in the sales of life insurance. And when that ended I began finally a new chapter in my life.

* * * *

I had been married about 1934 to the daughter of the founder of a meat packing house. My father-in-law was a very strong Baptist, an important businessman, and one of the big contributors to the Baptist College of Brandon. It was through this inside pull that I got the job at 25 cents an hour as a shipping clerk in the packing house. I had a wife and a baby daughter to keep and the pickings were pretty slim. I can remember a lot of hamburger. I remember that I would try to make my haircuts go five weeks instead of four, even though a haircut I believe was only 25 or 30 cents, and though I had a terribly heavy head of hair. I remember making a 10 cents package of tobacco last for a week to make roll-your-own cigarettes.

After 1939, as the war progressed, I listened religiously to the news commentators and I pictured myself as a commentator. At least once a week I would write my news column and recite it to some of my friends. They were duly impressed, and that was fun, and it was writing practice, but other than that it didn't do any good.

My in-laws were not very impressed with me. They were even less impressed when I quit them and went to selling insurance on commission. I had a friend who was selling for the Metropolitan Life, and working under a guaranteed salary and some commissions, he was able to make about $120 a month. I put my application in there and I must have waited nearly a year for the job. Every month I would call the manager, Mr. Peavoy, and he would keep encouraging me to come back.

Meanwhile, I wrote. I still wrote.

I had a very good close friend during this period and we sustained each other. I used him as a testing board on some of my writing. His name was Barney Jones. No matter what the editor said, Barney always thought my stuff was good. Meanwhile, he was barely sustaining himself on a few odd jobs. Then out of the blue came a big opportunity.

He had been promised a job in the north by a budding air transportation company headed by a man who called himself "The First World Flying Ace." There was great excitement in our house when Jones told me about this opportunity. The catch was that the job was in the far north and he had to have a sleeping bag and few other essentials to take the job. He didn't have a cent. I had $25 in the bank and that was about what was needed to get him on the way. I was very glad to have reserve capital to put up for Barney. In a couple of days he was airborne at pretty good wages, a lot more than I was making. When Barney got back a year or so later he got married after a whirlwind courtship with a new girl in about two weeks. The flying company had started up a transportation center in Edmonton and had a growing business with the north. Barney had the job of moving some of the aircraft around in and out of hangars. One night he came to our house as pale as death. He said, "Myers, I'm going to get fired."

"For God sake, why?"

"While I was towing an airplane out of the hangar this morning, I got too close to the building and ripped a wing off."

This looked to me like a disaster. When jobs were so scarce, losing a good one was almost like losing your life. I suggested to Jones that if he wasn't fired yet maybe he wouldn't be fired. He said that the boss had been away but that he would have to go in and see him in the morning.

Imagine the celebration when I learned the result of the meeting. Jones appeared before his employer's desk; he stood there frozen, facing the inevitable.

The famous flyer said to him; "Jones, you cost me some money yesterday by knocking that wing off the Beechcraft. I guess you think you're going to get fired. Maybe you should be fired. But I'm not going to fire you, Jones. If I get a new man in your place he may do the same damn fool thing someday but I know you'll never do it again. Go on out and get to work."

That may have been part of the secret for Barney's company's success in building a large and prosperous air transportation company when Edmonton was being called for the first time THE GATEWAY TO THE NORTH.

Just before Jones returned from the north I had been successful in my application to the Metropolitan Life Insurance Company and I was doing a little better too. It surely wasn't what I wanted. We had to balance our books every Friday night on the debit and credit system and it nearly drove me crazy. But I was a good salesman and Mr. Peavoy gave me what he called a District Office account. This was an account where insured people pay their premiums directly in at the office and didn't have an agent collecting from them. So my time was 100 percent free for selling. In my first year I qualified for the Star Salesman club and got a free trip to Qualicum Beach on Vancouver Island for a convention where we would be addressed by Mr. Lincoln, president of the company, a direct descendent of a relative of Abraham Lincoln.

While I was gratified with my success, I despised the work. I hated selling. I hated selling washing machines and I hated selling insurance, and I hated being a shipping boy at a packing plant as I had been. I was about five years beyond graduation. I had applied for the job of reporter to every newspaper in Western Canada I could reach by mail and I had applied in person many many times to the newspapers in Alberta. The editor of the Edmonton Journal, which was a member of the eastern chain of Southam newspapers, asked of course about my experience, knowing very well that I had none. When I admitted that he said, "Well then, how can you expect to get in here? There are experienced newspaper men in Canada who are out of work. Besides that, if we do have a cub reporter's job, we have some very good delivery boys who are lined up for the first opportunity." When I told him I had a University degree and I had practiced a lot of writing he asked me if I had ever had anything published, and of course I had to say no. He said, "Well, you're out of college about six years now; my advice to you would be to stay with the job you've got or try for something else."

It was always the same; "What's your experience?" I understood the utter dejection I saw on the face of so many men who were without jobs and receiving bare subsistence allowance for themselves and their families. I realized that I was lucky to have what I had but that did not make me happy about it. And I realized that the further I moved beyond graduation the less likely I was to qualify for a job of cub reporter - which I would have to be - before getting to be a full fledged reporter. And even if I should get employment as a cub reporter the wages were about equivalent to what they had been at the packing house. And now I was married with a family. My future as a writer looked very black indeed. Nevertheless I kept on. I kept on because I wanted to.

Sometime, I felt to myself, I'll surely hit. I've written my million words and maybe some to boot. And I am a good writer. There's just no way for me to show it and I don't know how to try to show it except more short stories.

So sometimes I would just write for fun.

Going through some of my very old stuff of half a century ago I recently came upon a poem that I wrote during this period. I wrote it just for the hell of it, and I'm going to reproduce it just for the hell of it.

I recall sitting down one evening and thought I should write about a dream - a fantastic dream. I wrote out the title. The first line:

"I had a vision yester'en" and then the second line,

"Unparalleled, before unseen".

At that moment I had no idea what the next line would be, but it came to

"I dread to think what it could mean,

"For when I looked the moon was green."

And then quickly the line,

"Two horns it had and one between,

"Divulged a light; 'twas such a beam

That living stars did rise and scream

In deadly terror of the beam."

I would not strongly disagree with a reader's conclusion that this is a pile of nonsense but then so was a lot of Edgar Allen Poe's poetry, I believe, nonsense. Of course, Poe was thought to have been on drugs. I have no such excuse.

As far as I can remember I wrote it all in a couple of nights, with tremendous satisfaction, and I read it now with some satisfaction. The imagery gives me pleasure and I think it truly is, if nothing else, at least fantastic. So here it is; I hope there is some enjoyment in it.

"FANTASTIC DREAM"

I had a vision yester'en,
Unparalleled, before unseen;
I dread to think what it could mean
For when I looked the moon was green;
Two horns it had and one between
Divulged a light; 'twas such a beam
That living starts did rise and scream
In deadly terror of the beam;
I dread to think what it could mean.

The sky a battleground became;
The starry vault was all aflame
Where fought the moon with might and main
As one possessed, as one insane,
And single handed 'against the train,
Endless multitudinous train,
Of stars the sky could scarce contain,
Whose war gods plied their swords in vain
And struck and charged and charged again,
Yet seemed no single inch to gain
Upon the moon who still did reign
Supreme, serene upon the plain,
King of kings amidst the slain,
Yea what can we of men complain
When even stars have gone insane!

Such visions I had never seen;
I dread to think what they could mean.

"Save us now, oh God," I cried.
"Let not protection be denied
For night is come and Hell is loose
and even stars become obtuse."

The mystery, then, so long concealed
In flaming letters was revealed;
A phantom painted them on high
Stretching far across the sky.

"The battleground," it said, "is life;
The moon is poor humanity
Which since its birth hath borne the strife
Of war and hate and jealousy.

The horn is love upon the right,
The greatest weapon in the sky.

And truth it is the leftmost horn,
Which long and loud doth boom,
And whatsoever enemy of sore distressed Humanity
Shall lend his ear the voice to hear
Shall swiftly meet his doom.

The middle horn that gleams so bright
Sheddeth wisdom's searching light,
And all the stars, the friends of Mars,
Do rise and scream in mortal fright
And wave their hands and take to flight,
Instantly upon the sight
Of death approaching with that light."

But some have gleaming armour borne
To shield them from the deadly ray
Of universal love, the horn,
The greatest saviour of the day.

What was the armour? Man's distress,
'Twas narrow minded prejudice.
And Mars hath all of it supplied.
Hath universal love defied,

Now he strutteth in his pride,
How laughingly doth he deride
The moon whose useless beams swing wide,
Back and forth on every side
And hath not yet one foe espied,
Who cannot 'neath his armour hide.

The voice of truth were better still,
For none can hear and no one will;
In helmets are the heads concealed,
With ignorance all ears are sealed
No vital part is left revealed.
To all the light of wisdom's field
Selfishness becomes the shield.

Then of a sudden Mars arose,
Reigning right and left his blows;
Like hail from heaven down they came
And then the moon began to wane.

Right and left his sword he swings,
He raises high and down he brings
It down upon the horn of light
Which shines no longer on the right;
Then down upon the horn between
And cleaves it off so slick and clean
That nevermore will it be seen
Upon the waning moon so green.

Humanity is now deprived
By war of wisdom's light;
Howe'er before he had contrived
To win, he now must fight.

He shakes his lowered head in rage
And bellows forth in pain;
One sturdy horn may still engage
The foe yet once again.

Like a crackling pistol shot
He leaps from off the cloud;
Possessed with action once forgot
With all his strength endowed.

With all his might he pounced on Mars
And gored him to the earth.
"All this will be the end of wars
Of peace the blessed birth."
But peace that night was never born
For there were none to rear her,
She needed parents to be borne
And none were fit to bear her.

He fought with war to end all war
And believed that wars were through
Deprived of wisdom's guiding ray
'Twas all that he could do.

Then from the bloody battleground,
He slowly limped away,
Bleeding forth from every wound,
Exhausted from the fray.

Upon a feathery cloud of down
He laid himself to sleep.
In confidence that Mars was done
He slumbered long and deep.

The horn of love grew not again
But fear sprang up instead;
It caused the moon such aching pain
It split his aching head.

Oh woeful sight! Oh woe betide!
The moon is sore distressed
And Mars is turning on his side
Reviving with the rest.

The moon is slumbering on in pain,
Oblivious to fear;
But Mars is growing strong again;
Hark; hear the Henchmen cheer!

The moon believed him safely dead
From war that ended wars,
But Mars is raising high his head
From cloud to cloud he soars.
He chooses one of crimson red
He takes his stand and roars
And all the stars in mortal dread
Do tremble when he roars.

He raises high his warrior hand
And it sufficeth to demand
Silence from the henchman band,
Who seem to know and understand
He still is king within the land.
Each move is now minutely scanned
As he assumes supreme command,
And takes his place upon the stand,
Lord of ocean, sky and land!

"Ever since the birth of man,
Since Immortality began,
I have scourged his every plan,
Through his territories ran,
And still I scourge where scourge I can,
And I shall be the death of man.

I have armed you well my friends,
Armed you well to suit my ends.
How well your prejudice commends,
How well your ignorance recommends,
Your selfishness how well defends
What I have done to please my ends."

When next I looked the moon was blue
The body green, the face was blue,
And half the face was clove in two,
Where warrior Mars had cut him through.
From cloven head his sword he drew,
Again he cut and hacked him too,
I saw the slice'd face turned blue
And then I knew the moon was through.

Oh horrible sight— the blood was blue!

Such horrors I had never seen;
I dread to think what they could mean.

And snakes I saw up in the sky;
And even snakes began to fly,
One wing in front and one behind,
On sagging middles out of line
Rode the mermaids from the Rhine.

With flowing hair and graceful ease,
And clothing none above the knees,
They seemed to float upon the breeze,
And nothing more my heart could please
Than what they sang upon the breeze.
Straight towards the moon they flew,
And as they flew the reptiles grew;
Their flapping wings could well be seen
To near the moon so blue and green.

Upon a cloud they landed there
To watch the sport, the joy to share;
And many a warrior passed the lair
And closed his eyes upon the snare,
Lest the temptresses so fair
Should break his will and lead him there;
To his comrades called "Beware"!

And woe to him who turns his glance
Upon these maids from north of France;
The reptiles writhed around and round
About their bodies on the ground.
They harm the maids no mite at all,
But when they round the warrior crawl
They crush the bones and gnaw the meat,
And then the cursed serpents bleat
And fly away for more to eat.

Such horrors I had never seen;
I dread to think what they could mean.

A rainbow stretched from earth to sky
And stars got on that they might fly
To where the battle raged on high,
But I was lost; Oh where was I?

Soon the rainbow car was heard,
In noisy silence like a bird,
To lift its cargo heavenward;
But I was lost; Oh where was I?

Then my fate did I recall,
Of all humanity the fall
And I a part, with one and all
Had perished with them in the brawl.

I found my soul and took to flight
Disgusted with the gruesome sight,
Through the winding bowers came
To the graveyard by the lane;
Twixt the graves I scarcely stirred
Lest the dead should be disturbed,
Thinking, "These departed slumber,
They will waken if I blunder."

Each stealthy step I took with care,
An ominous tension charged the air;
No single corpse must be aware
That I was walking midst them there.

Extreme precision too precise
But proved itself a poor device;
Upon some monumental mark
I stumbled headlong in the dark.

I saw the grave at once unfold;
The corpse arose, and, Lo Behold!
Ten thousand dead men slowly rise
And turn on me with cold dead eyes.

God Almighty! Virgin Queen!
Come protect what I have been.

Their cold dead eyes on me they bound;
Their clammy hands they raised
Nor spoke nor made a single sound
But steadily they gazed.

I could not move nor turn nor stir.
What dreadful stupefaction?
Their faces all became a blur
And I a petrifaction.

They crowded round in circle form
To hem me in it seemed;
I first grew cold then grew warm
And then a woman screamed.

Like shot from gun I left the ground;
I leapt into the air;
I cleared the circle with a bound
And not an inch to spare.

I ran as ne'er before I ran;
My flying feet the breeze did fan;
Pursuing corpses in the van
Were thirsting for the blood of man;
I stumbled headlong; rose again
And ran; with all my might I ran!

I came unto a blood-filled stream;
The purplish blood was flecked with green;
Upon the bank a crowne'd queen,
Was drinking from the putrid stream.

And snakes were writhing in and out
Her naked bosom all about
For she had charmed them there no doubt
And loved to have them frisk about;
Then spying me she rose and shouted
"Hallelujah!"

Such sights before I'd never seen;
I dread to think what they could mean.

Her eyes she cast upon my eyes
And held me spellbound with her glance
And I succumbed. In dumb surprise
Fell victim, captive in the trance.

Her raving beauty cast the spell;
Bewitching charms to which I fell,
Indescribable to tell,
Irresistible as well,
Her voice so sweet, so clear a bell
No man alive could now repel
That wily temptress sent from Hell.

Resistance proved no use to me
And I abandoned it with glee.

I walked upon the bloody road,
Across the bloody river trode,
Nor sank an inch within the slime,
Until I touched her graceful line,
And touched her figure's full design
Upon the bank this witch of mine!

I stroked her golden locks so fine
In all their lustrous gleam and shine,
Hanging round her form divine,
Which intermingled then with mine;
Intoxicated by the wine
Of her emotional design
My whole resistance did decline
To less and less and then in time
Sore victimized did I resign.

Oh woe is me! for then she rose,
Assuming now a hideous pose.

The golden tresses snakes became
Growing from her head the same,
Writhing, wriggling, squirming chain
Straining forth with might and main.

An evil masculine glint she wore
Within her eyes so soft before;
Her pearly teeth were there no more
But tusks replaced them four on four.

She laughed a laugh to stir the dead,
A laugh that rattled through my head
And made me shake in mortal dread,
Which would not let me move or tread,
Her victim now whate'er she did.

The bloody river flowed anew,
Through caverns down to hell it flew,
Dark dismal caverns passing through
The likes of which no mortal knew;
She raised me high and then she threw
Me far upon the murky slough.

A swifter stream you could not find,
A moment left her far behind
I heard her laughter on the wind,
Faint thin and rattling ill defined,
High praise to heaven's grace so kind
Which brought to me the peace of mind
Of any fate with her behind.

I floated on the foamy tide,
Upon the bubbles did I ride,
Through the caverns all we ran
And darkened lands unknown to man,
And o'er a great and vast expanse
Of bloody waters in my trance,
Until we came unto the end,
End of earth and round the bend,
Straight o'er the cliff I forthwith fell
Down, down, down, straight down to Hell!

The lightning flashed its light on me
And blinded me, I could not see;
The thunder filled my heart with fear,
It deafened me, I could not hear.

Rain and sleet and snow came down
And froze my body all around,
Faster! Faster! Hurtling down.

Through the universe I fell
Bottomless, abyssal well;

I could not breathe, my heart was still,
Until the devil rang his bell,
Then all was clear, my sight as well;
The sights I saw I cannot tell,
For I was heading straight for Hell.

I could see and I could hear,
I could breathe; the end was near,
I heard the devils rise and cheer,
Anticipation feedeth fear.

But yet I must prepare to land;
Terrific shocks must I withstand,
If I could cheat the devil's band
And all his secrets understand.
He issued forth a stern demand
That all the furnaces be fanned,
Waved aloft his magic wand,
And just as I came down to land
He stopped me there by his command
In mid air, resting on his hand.

With evil eyes and smacking lips
And serpents dangling from his hips
He holds me in his fingertips;
With ugly claws my throat he grips,
With grimy fangs he nips and nips
And from my jugular vein he sips
And licks his vicious smacking lips;
Whirling round he falls and trips,
And bangs my head upon the strips
Of iron on the furnace.

When I awoke upon the floor
Three bumps upon my head I bore;
I did not have to look for more
For all my body'd seen the war;

And I was marked with blood and gore
From head to foot all bruised and sore.

I rose and to my bed I went;
The sheets in tiny shreds were rent;
The frame was battered, smashed and bent,
From the wildest night I ever spent.

The sun was riding noonday high;
No single star was in the sky;
How thankful then to know was I
'Twas all a dream and all a lie.

For stranger things I've never seen;
I dread to think what they could mean.

BOOK TWO

CAREER

Chapter Fifteen

WORDS FOR DOLLARS

War broke out in August 1939. My wife had left me and I was down on the farm helping my dad with the harvest. Amy had taken our daughter Bettie May and moved back into her mother's house. Her dad had died.

I was left to abandon the small home we had put together. It had always been fully understood by us kids that if any of us ever needed a home we would always find the door open there on the farm. At this low ebb in my life I was grateful. I was physically in good shape, 27 years old, and I knew the hard harvest work would be good for me. But when my mother drove out through the stubble field in the car to tell us England had just declared war, we became instantly a part of a shocked world.

Of course there was no question of my going to war. I had long ago resolved never to offer my life for a foreign cause. I couldn't see where Canada had any business to get involved in a war, thousands of miles from home, declared quite independently of us. I was lucky never to be drafted. Although it lasted five years I was always just a step ahead of it, the same as in the job market I had always been a step behind. As time passed the draft age got higher and higher. It rose to include single men up to 30 years old. But I was married. Then it rose to include married men without a family, but I had a family. But at the time the war ended I would have been next on the list, even at 32 in 1944.

By this time we were well up on the news with radio reports throughout the day and the summaries at night. I remember a wild and dramatic day when the Germans blew up the *Hood*, England's pride and joy, her newest battleship on its maiden voyage, and then the very next day when the English blew up the

Bismarck, the pride and joy of the German navy. I well remember Dunkirk; one or two of my acquaintances were in it. But on the whole, the war never really affected my private life. I was still stumbling, still searching for something to do.

It was altogether a very dismal period of my life. My parents, I knew, must be bitterly disappointed, although they never said anything about my failure. They had sacrificed so much, hoped so hard. They had in fact endured poverty, given several years of their life so that I could rise above the drudgery which had been their lot. Now seven years after graduation I still didn't have a job to amount to anything. My marriage now a failure, I was back on the farm without a cent to my name. Actually, I was worse off than the other kids of my age who had never taken a day of school past grade eight.

My parents were aware of my efforts at writing. Even at the farm I banged away on my typewriter with more short stories that never sold. Who could continue to pin their hopes on this grandiose but unlikely career? No realist certainly. My father, I'm afraid, was a disappointed realist, although he gave me his support to the end. My mother, I think, suffered my every rejection slip more than I did. I had to do something to try to pull myself together.

When I had been at the packing plant I had done quite a bit of reading about hogs. In fact I entertained my friend Barney one night with a story I had written about a guy who invented some medicine that would make hogs the size of elephants. These giant hogs would sell for a very high price but they became dangerous to handle and had to be sold very young. I don't remember what happened in the story but I do remember that on the farm I followed up on the pig raising idea, on a mass production basis.

I had read all the literature, including special scientific feeding programs. I had it all down to the cost of feed per pound to put on one pound of pork. I had devised a program which would grow to a point where I would turn out hogs like Henry Ford turned out automobiles. It would be all streamlined and it would be very much like the huge hog establishments of the present day. My only competition, I reasoned, would be the general farmer who really knew nothing about nutrition. I surely ought to be able to produce pigs at a good profit and I could see unlimited growth to where, when fully established, we would be turning out thousands every year. Actually it was a real good idea as has been proven since, but it did not work out that way in my case in 1939.

My father added to my meager savings to help get me started with a basic 50 feeder hogs, or so, in the late fall of 1939. I had designed small hog huts which would house pigs in units of half a dozen or so, all lined up in a row with a small run for each section of pigs. They were doing real well until I caught a terrible cold in January 1940, so bad that I had to go to bed with it. My father was looking after feeding the pigs.

From scientific study I had concluded that it would be necessary at all times to protect against worms which was a very special hazard in the hog raising business. The key to keeping pigs worm free was a potent drug called phenothiazine. You mixed this with their ground feed in a very tiny amount. I think it was about five tablespoons full to several bushels of ground grain. First of all you would mix it with a couple of shovels-full and then you would take that amount and you would mix it with an amount of several times its size, until you had two piles on the floor. Then you would mix the two piles together by piling the unmixed pile on the main pile and letting it run down on the side. It wasn't complicated but you had to do it right.

My father willingly took over my work for me, but one day he ran into a complication; he had accidentally spilled about a third of a can of phenothiazine while he was mixing. He picked up some of it but the most of it was still on the floor. He knew that it was expensive stuff, and my father just could not bring himself to waste all that good phenothiazine. So he mixed it in with the piles of feed in the usual way.

As I grew better my hogs grew sicker. We couldn't figure out what it was. Then he told me about the phenothiazine he had mixed in to prevent wasting it, but with his very unsure assurance, "I don't think that could have had anything to do with it - do you?"

Right then I knew. These pigs were going to get a lot sicker.

It was January and 40 below zero day on day. We discarded the whole pile of feed he had been using and put in new feed without any phenothiazine, but the damage had been done. Every day the hogs looked worse. Their backs got slick and greasy, they came out of their pens on stilted legs so stiff and sore they could hardly walk. A more sorrowful bunch of pigs I never saw. The end was near.

Soon we had to start shooting pigs. We dragged the frozen carcasses out in the snow with a horse, leaving my carefully constructed hog houses sadly vacant. This was a disaster I didn't need. A failure on top of a failure, on top of a failure. I felt that for my parents this was the mockery of a purpose. A Bachelor of Arts, a gold medalist, back on the farm feeding pigs. And now even the pigs were dead.

Disheartened, I got in touch with the Metropolitan Life Insurance Company and was immediately accepted for a District Office job in Victoria, about a thousand miles west of my home. I took the job. What else was there to do?

My wife and I, after several months of separation, both began to have second thoughts, so with our three year old daughter, Bettie May, she came out to join me. I was making enough money to keep us comfortably, but right off the bat we ran into a snag which in her mind proved her parents' contention that I wasn't much good.

I had arranged for a nice house - nicer than anything we had ever approached in Edmonton - and we were to move in the day she arrived. But when I went around to the house to make the final arrangements a few days before her arrival the woman wouldn't come to the door. Repeated visits brought no answer although I could tell there were people in the house. I began to suspect that she wanted to go back on her deal and I was sure enough right. I saw a lawyer but he said it would be very difficult to dislodge the woman even though I carried a receipt and an agreement for the rental of the house. Meanwhile my wife and daughter were arriving the next day. I got what emergency accommodation I could find and rather ashamedly moved my wife in there. It wasn't the greatest reunion.

She said her parents had always told her that I couldn't make a decent home for her and now this was my second chance and

I had flubbed it again. I felt terrible. But what could I do? I got real busy the next day and within two or three days I had found another place close to the ocean that was every bit as suitable as the first place, and so within a week after her arrival we did move into decent housing.

But we were off on the wrong foot. In the background her powerful parents could always give the necessary shove to make us lose our balance.

Victoria, British Columbia has an ideal climate and even in February winter I could take my daughter walking along the sand of the ocean beaches. I didn't like it though because I could never get out in the country. Once on a Saturday afternoon, longing for the country, I tried it. I drove about 70 miles but I never came to any country. The island seemed to be semi-settled all over.

I worked in Victoria for a couple of years much to the consternation of the manager there. He liked my selling results but he found me unwieldy in the manner of all kinds of regulations he was prone to impose. I guess I just wasn't made for regimentation. Old MacDonald announced to all the sales force one day: "If we want to win the war we ought to get Hitler to take Myers into the German army. He would demoralize them in six weeks."

I hated regulations for regulations' sake. I hated red tape. I felt if you got the job done that was the big answer right there and none of the red tape made a damn bit of difference. Sergeant personalities, however, never see it that way. You don't deal with army types like that, as I was later to find out. But with MacDonald I pretty well had my way; I had a very good record which he was in no hurry to lose. Finally, when I left, it was of my own choosing. Back in Edmonton some new avenues were opening up.

As I mentioned briefly in an earlier chapter, the Japanese had landed on the tip islands of Alaska at Kiska. Japanese ships had been seen along the west coast. Pearl Harbor had given the U.S. a mighty scare and they were afraid of an overland push by the Japanese through Alaska down through Canada. It didn't take long until they began work on a 2,000 mile highway from Edmonton, Alberta north to Skagway, Alaska to be known as the Alaska Highway. It was a mighty undertaking, but the Americans felt that they would have to supply their forces in the north and there was no alternative to a road. They were apprehensive about sending supplies along the coast by sea because of probable interference by Japanese submarines.

So they started to build these powerful bases in the north, among them strong air defense facilities. But there was a real problem about that. No oil was known to exist in Alaska in those days.

Oil was known at Norman Wells on the MacKenzie River in the Arctic Circle in Canada. That oil was a thousand miles east of the new Fairbanks base. The only way to get it there was by pipeline. This daunting project was undertaken. It was an unbelievable objective under the circumstances. There was not a thing between Edmonton and what was to be called Camp CANOL (Canadian Oil), a thousand miles to the north. Not a road, not a trail, not an outpost except one or two along the MacKenzie River. This most formidable project in the history of construction was undertaken in the fall of 1942. It was hush hush and top secret with the Americans. It never made the newspapers. People didn't know what was going on. But the Americans were establishing a fundamental home base in Edmonton.

From here all men and materials would be brought to this central staging point and from here it was the job of the project managers to get them out north into the Arctic Circle and to make sure that before they got there there was warm and comfortable housing to receive them. Despite the fact that this housing was mass produced in the form of half moon circular buildings, sent in sections, the freight involved for the housing alone was awesome, never mind the pipe that would have to be brought up to go a thousand miles; never mind the explorers who would be needed to find a passage across the MacKenzie Mountains which had never been crossed before; never mind the bulldozers, the thousands of Caterpillars for this purpose and that; never mind the cabooses that would need to be used as tractor trains to haul material and personnel into this outpost at the north end of the world; never mind the trucks; never mind - - never mind - -.

Before airplanes could be of great use, flying fields had to be made, and before flying fields could be made, someone had to be there to construct them, and someone must have previously built the housing of those constructors. The plan was for freight to be taken by barge down the MacKenzie River toward its mouth in the fall of 1942. But winter came early; the MacKenzie froze. Plans now hastily changed. All freight henceforth would have to be moved overland out of Edmonton, unloaded and then loaded again and transported and taken across the northern ice in the winter. The CANOL project was the joint effort of three large U.S. contractors, the Bechtel Company, the Callahan Construction Company and the Price Pipeline Company. They were headquartered in a newly constructed California redwood building near the center of Edmonton. Their need for personnel was great and it was urgent.

Gwen Jones, who was married to my friend Barney, had got a job with the man named Spivey who was assistant to the general project manager J. P. Shirley, Jr. and Gwen got me an interview with Spivey. He hired me almost right away.

In 1942, I was 30 years old, ten years past graduation and I still didn't have a future. I had by that time written a million words all right, but I still didn't have a word published. The only positive thing I can say about my writing career is that I hadn't given up yet - I don't know why.

The CANOL job didn't give me an opportunity to write, but it did give me the opportunity to be useful in a new situation and I advanced pretty fast. I was soon made responsible for expediting personnel from various points all over the United States into Camp CANOL at the Arctic Circle. They couldn't be just any personnel. The requisitions would come down, send a hundred cooks, two hundred carpenters, thirty welders, five accountants, twenty time keepers, and so on and so on. I don't know how many men we took in and out to Camp CANOL. I know eventually there were a thousand men stationed there, but these were only the remnants of those who had been sent up; most of them went back to the United States after a short time. They sure didn't like it in the north. But we kept them coming, the project advanced.

We at Edmonton comprised the headquarters for only half the force. The line was attacked from both ends, Fairbanks at the west end to go five hundred miles east and Camp CANOL at the east end to go five hundred miles west, awaiting the triumphant day when the two forces would join.

There was no comparison between the two jobs that had to be done. The western-based outfit had by that time the Alaska Highway to back them up for supplies. The eastern-based outfit had nothing but an untamed river that froze solid in its banks half the year and great expanses of ice and snow. But objectives were set and objectives were met - somehow. I'll never know exactly how because Caterpillars could vanish in the permafrost. It was soft and mushy, a semi-frozen coverage the year around. There were mighty storms on the lakes and the rivers. It was killing cold, one of the severest winters ever seen in Canada. In Peace River, not far north of Edmonton they left trucks running 24 hours a day because if they ever let them stop they couldn't start them again.

Anyway, I worked diligently at my job and got substantial praise for my efforts. At Christmastime after working ten months, I was given a bonus that would today amount to about $5,000, $500 at that time.

But there was a fly in the ointment up there. The U.S. Army Corps of Engineers were the watchdogs on the project. It was a cost-plus project. The contractor got 10 percent above everything he spent. So he had to get clearance from the Army on every expenditure if he wanted to get paid for it. And masses of paper were moving back and forth between the contractor and the U.S. Army Corps all the time.

I saw a lot of things that I thought should be brushed aside as trivial, considering the importance of the project and the necessity of getting it finished on time. It wasn't my job to pass judgement on that, but I just had a dislike for the Engineers.

By the spring of 1944 conditions had changed enormously. The Japanese were no longer a threat in the north but the pipeline had been built just the same. It was a rather flimsy affair lying, for the most part, on the ground surface because conditions wouldn't allow it to be buried.

Just after the new year 1944 the engineers, having passed the critical stages, got to looking for other things to do and new regulations to make - at least in my view. As I said in chapter one, they put through a memorandum stating that none of the employees were to be allowed coffee breaks hereafter. They complained that too much time was being wasted on the mid-morning coffee break at ten o'clock when all the employees would swarm out to the big coffee shop across the street.

Seeing where it came from, I didn't like that a little bit. I worked many hours far into the night if I needed to to get my work done and I would come early to get my work done. And I thought to myself this is pretty damned high-handed of the Army Engineers when they don't even know what the hell is going on. Besides that, it's even more high-handed to think that they can keep us locked in. You see they didn't have the power to hire or fire, so they couldn't threaten you with the loss of your job if you didn't do what they wanted. It was trouble tailor-made for me.

The morning after the memorandum I went down to the revolving doors. A guard stepped up in front of me (there were always guards) and said, "You can't go out!"

I said, "Who the hell says I can't go out?"

He replied, "It's the regulation!"

I said, "You tell your bosses maybe they can keep me out of this building but they sure can't keep me in."

The guard threw himself in front of me, red faced to the neck. I just pushed him aside and went on out.

When I came back he put himself in front of me again and said, "You can't come in!"

I said, "Who the hell says I can't come in? I have a job here. I'm reporting for duty." Once again I pushed him aside and walked in.

I went through this performance two or three days with the guards losing some of their bravado and belligerence. After all, what were they going to do?

I soon found out what they were going to do. Their bosses went to J. P. Shirley Jr. and reported the incident to him. Shirley called me into his office and he said, "What the hell is this with you about the guards at the door and coffee break?"

I said, "Well, I do my work no matter what it takes. I think that I ought to be entitled to a break for a cup of coffee."

Shirley said, "Regardless of what you think you are causing me a hell of a lot of trouble - and I want you to stop it!"

So of course with orders from J. P. Shirley Jr. I stopped; I'd had my last cup of coffee with the time paid for by the U.S. Army Corps of Engineers.

I kept on working.

As spring came Bechtel, Price, Callahan began to move men out of the north as fast as at one time they had moved them in. J. P. Shirley, Jr. picked me to go to Camp CANOL and expedite the men out. After all I was experienced in it and it made sense. But, of course, while the U.S. government was supplying airplanes, there was nevertheless a paper charge for every flight in and out of CANOL. When J. P. Shirley Jr. applied for approval of my flight plan the engineers vetoed it. Shirley demanded to know why. Back came the answer. "This man is a nonconformist, and therefore detrimental to the organization."

This sort of made Shirley mad and he sent them an ultimatum; either order him to fire me or grant the travel authority. Well, the Corps of Engineers didn't want to overstep their mark. They could get into a lot of trouble. It was not their job to hire or fire employees of the contractor. It was only their job to approve or disapprove expenses. The result - they did nothing.

The result of that was that I sat at my desk drawing pay for doing nothing.

The result of that was that I got to thinking why don't I make use of my time? I've been on this project since the early days. I know it backwards and forwards. I have pictures of much of the operations. The story has never been told in the newspapers. The press censorship is off it now; why don't I write it up?

And that's exactly what I did. I spent my office hours digging through the literature, writing the history of the project from the start to the finish.

I made arrangements with the printing company in Edmonton to do the book. When I got the prices I found out I could only afford about sixty pages so I had to cut it down to that. I took every cent of money I had in the bank and all I could out of my life insurance policies, and every cent I could scrape anywhere, and turned it over to the printer and told them to produce 1,000 copies. The title of the small book was in a very large script on a yellow background, *Oil to Alaska.*

As the men came swarming out of the north they picked

136

these books up like hotcakes. It was something to take home to show their families to give them some idea of the job they'd been working on. I sold some 5,000 books priced at $1.00 each in a very short time.

I was making about 80 cents a copy. Bill Grafe, the president of the Callahan Construction Company, bought 1,000 books from me himself. The books were on sale at the newsstands in Edmonton and they sold remarkably well; also at certain CANOL hiring centers in the States. It was the first noticeable money I'd made in my 32 years, after twelve years of single minded persistence from my graduation date.

But somehow I was denied that glorious feeling of being an author. After all, no one had accepted my book to publish it. I'd done it all myself. I had the prize, but without benefit of the judge. So where did I stand now with newspapers?

I went once again to see the editor of the Edmonton Journal. When I showed him my book and told of its sales he seemed, if anything, more negative than previously. Almost resentful, I thought, that a rank outsider could snatch and capitalize a hot subject from right under the noses of the local professional writing establishment. I don't suppose he himself had ever made five thousand dollars in less than three months.

About July I went down to the farm again which was about a hundred miles south of Calgary to help my father once more with the harvest. What a proud reception I got at home. Here between two covers was the proof of my success. I felt I had begun to vindicate myself. My mother wanted to buy several books to mail to our relatives, never realizing that she had bought and paid for the whole proposition several times over with her years of drudgery for me.

On my way back I stopped in at the *Calgary Herald* to talk about a job. I didn't really go in there with much hope; I'd been turned down so many times before. And there were only two worthwhile papers in Alberta and not more than about fourteen city papers across Canada. Chances were very scarce. But I felt now a certain confidence. If worst came to worst I would do something else and publish it myself; readers had been enthusiastic.

Not intending to use *Oil to Alaska* as a lever, I brought one along nevertheless - just in case.

The editor's name was Allen Bill. The first thing he asked me was what kind of training I'd had and I said I was a graduate in geology. I noticed right away that got his attention.

"You know with this new Princess field down here out east, Western Canada could be one of the greatest oil fields on the continent." He said, "The prospects here are tremendous." He let that sink in. I let it sink in too. I didn't know the first damn thing of what was going on in the oil industry; I'd never even heard of "Princess", but I had sense enough not to open my mouth, and thus reveal my ignorance.

Allen Bill resumed; "We need somebody here that understands oil and that understands oil exploration, the whys of it - you know. And we have tried two or three geologists. But geologists can't write." He stopped and seemed to study me. "Can you write?"

In reply I brought out my copy of *Oil to Alaska* . I knew right there that if Allen Bill liked my writing I had the job. He was really keyed up about the oil industry and having a qualified observer to write about it. I watched him open the book about three or four pages in and I watched him read a paragraph or two. Quickly, he opened the book further in at random and read a paragraph or two, then again, very quickly he closed the book and handed it to me. "Come in and see me at ten tomorrow."

I was sure I had the job. And I was right.

When I went into Allen Bill's office he said, "We have decided to hire you. You will start as '*Calgary Herald* Oil Editor' and your stories will carry your by-line. We can't pay what you were getting paid up north, but we'll pay you $250 a month to start."

Hired as a writer, I never thought I would hear words like that! I never thought I would be hired by a newspaper. And most of all I never thought that my first stories would carry my name and call me an editor. I got out of there pretty fast so as not to betray my astonishment, my disbelief. But I'll tell you one thing, I wasn't late for the start of work on the appointed day.

As I got to thinking over it afterwards I saw how the whole thing had eventually come out in the wash. I had determined to be a writer. I had accepted the advice that if you want to be a writer you'd better write. Write a million words. I had done my scales. I was indeed already a professional. It had only taken a few paragraphs to prove that to Allen Bill, and on the strength of that he was prepared to bestow on me not only the job but the title of editor and my byline on every story, immediately. Here at last was the glorious day when my four years of college geology would start to pay off unexpectedly after a long drought, 1932-1944.

I also saw that if I hadn't been a *nonconformist*, as branded by the army bureaucrats, I would have received travel authority to go to Camp CANOL, I would have expedited personnel out, I would have come back, I would have been without a job, there would never have been in my career "*Oil to Alaska*", and consequently my lifetime career to this day might never have materialized.

Newspapers could have continued to use the old excuse; if I hadn't made it in twelve years after graduation why was I putting myself up now to compete with twenty-year-old kids?

With me there were three prerequisites: utter determination, a lucky break, and a character trait.

I didn't realize that in later life this very quality of challenging the bureaucrats would end me up fighting city hall both north and south of the 49th parallel, and simultaneously.

Chapter Sixteen

WRITER TO EDITOR

One of my proudest moments came when I picked up a copy of the *Calgary Herald* as it rolled off the presses carrying my first story, carrying the proud line **"by C.V. Myers, Calgary Herald Oil Editor."** From then on every day the MYERS name was circulated across Southern Alberta and became known, as my mother had predicted, far and wide. It had been a favorite saying of my mother; "He who laughs last, laughs longest." My parents were laughing last and surely it was the greatest laugh of their laborious lives, the laugh that forever put the end to their disappointments. There was still more to come.

There was another laugh too. Editor Allen Bill, by appointing me editor, a man with no previous experience in newspaper work, ahead of all others, had opened himself to a storm of criticism. If I failed or blundered he was subject to the resentment of his own staff and also probably by headquarters in eastern Canada. I'm sure he waited for my first story that day and in the many days following with some tension.

But he could have saved himself the stress. From the very first it was plain to members of the oil industry, geologists, managers, service industry people, that I knew what I was talking about. And they were pleased to have someone presenting the activities of the industry clearly and with insight. Soon new events made my column even more important.

My first story had appeared in the *Herald* in the fall of '46. On February 10, 1947 the well that would put Canada on the oil map of the world blew into production. It was the harbinger of hundreds of wells in an oil search that would cover millions of square miles eventually from the border to Yukon and the Arctic Circle. I immediately sensed the tremendous potential of this well. And I wrote it for both industry and public consumption.

It was a landmark to be remembered and when all of this had happened, forty years later, on the anniversary, the *Calgary Herald* ran a feature recounting that day in oil history. It said,

"C. V. Myers (Herald Oil Editor at the time) wrote:

"The well made its debut in somewhat spectacular fashion, snorting and puffing with great bursts of gas and watery oil. They put a flame to the pipe and the flame rose 30 feet in the air as the well belched oil and black smoke.

". . . . it blew a dense black ring in a perfect circle, a ring 30 feet in diameter, 50 feet in the air as the monster puffed and heaved, struggling for life."

If Allen Bill had been inclined to wonder about his choice, that doubt was wiped away February 13, 1947. I interviewed geologists and managers from several of the oil companies to get an idea of its significance, to get more detail about the kind of reservoir we were dealing with and the prospects as a whole. I had several page one features in the next few months; all of the oil industry and a great deal of the business community followed my every story. I had done my writing scales, which together with my background in geology, made a powerful combination.

A newcomer is rarely accepted by the rank and file, especially if he is good. And many were my detractors. **"A new broom sweeps clean"; "Just give him enough rope and he'll hang himself"; "This guy won't last."** But my competition couldn't match me and I sold some of my stories to other publications and occasionally sold them to oil companies who were promoting their own oil interests but wanted descriptive material about the area. In all that time I never boosted an oil company or never praised or sided with a promoter for gain, although there were many opportunities for me to get stock in various companies if I would go along and tell the public how good their proposition was. It wasn't too long before all the promoters knew that along these lines Myers was unapproachable. I missed making a lot of money that way, but my reputation for integrity was worth all of those losses.

Quite a few exciting things happened in those early days. The war was over in 1946 and newspapermen were allowed to visit Great Bear Lake, the source of the uranium which had supplied the plutonium for the bombs of Hiroshima and Nagasaki. I was among the reporters chosen to go into the mines in the far, far north at Great Bear Lake and later to go to Norman Wells, the site of the oil production for the CANOL pipeline.

This oil operation had been handled exclusively by Imperial Oil, the biggest oil firm operating in Canada. When I went to see Walker Taylor, the manager, he was mum, seemingly under the impression that the war was still on and this was still a classified project. I got all the information I could and when I got back I wrote a story that blew them apart. It said "IMPERIAL OIL DROPS IRON CURTAIN AROUND NORMAN WELLS."

I never was the darling of Imperial Oil after that, or any of the majors. Later on they would come to court me; to ask me to stop writing stories in support of a pipeline to Montreal and thereby serving eastern Canada, which was now buying its oil from the Middle East production of the major oil companies, at a cost to them of only about ten cents a barrel. The eastern Canadian market was to them a valuable plum. If it was replaced by oil from western Canada the plum would disappear.

Even though they invited me down to Toronto to see the bigwigs who took pains to explain to me why I should not pursue this line, I nevertheless kept on plugging the trans-Canada oil pipeline. Eventually the idea matured and was in place before the Arabs called their first oil boycott.

I never had a word of criticism from the editor and I don't believe there was any open criticism from the oil company headquarters in the east. If there had been those complaints would have looked bad in print.

My competitors were rather afraid to launch out in their writing. And I saw then that the difference in having an education and not having one was mostly a matter of confidence. When I wrote a story about oil I would know what was predictable and what was not predictable. I could make statements with confidence, not so much because of what I knew, but because of what I knew was unknown. My competition, on the other hand, was always subject to the fear that knowledge unknown to them could make their statements look silly. Their greatest drawback was that they did not have the background knowledge to judge what was foolish and what was not.

My oil writing attracted the radio station of CFAC, owned by the *Calgary Herald*, and I was asked by the manager, Fred Shaw, if I would like to do a 15 minute program on agriculture every week. He had a sponsor for such a program, and because of my farm background he thought I might be able to handle it. He asked me to prepare a sample 15 minute broadcast. I did this and within a few days he gave me the signal to start in. I would get $25 a week from the sponsor for this broadcast, which at that time seemed an awful lot of money for 15 minutes.

My radio program too attracted a very large audience. It came on at six o'clock in the evening when farmers were home for supper. It was the only agricultural comment of its kind.

Now my parents could laugh twice. It was not totally unknown that some neighbors snickered at the Myers sending that damned kid to college - all for nothing. He couldn't even hold a job. The boys on the farm were working with their fathers or had been given a piece of land and settled down; they were married and going ahead. The Myers' kid had to sell washing machines in the snow. What sense did that education make?

But now the boy failure was a dark horse that had come up suddenly from behind and passed everyone. What farm boy had ever even known an editor, much less an editor of the most talked about subject in the whole country - oil?

My father glowed with pride when neighbors would stop him on the street and ask him about my success or refer to some story I had written in the *Calgary Herald*. "Where does he get all the stuff, how does he get to know so much?" One time my mother, travelling home on the train from Denver, Colorado, saw a man reading *"Oil to Alaska"*. Her visit with that man and his enthusiasm over the book was in itself enough to satisfy her for all of her sacrifices.

Every Friday night when the clock stood at six my parents' ears were glued to the radio, that wonderful invention now no more than ten years old, and they would gratifyingly hear the voice of their own son. No doubt about it, the hard, hard battle had been fought and won!

On a 1945 press junket, following wartime declassification of far north Great Bear Lake mine, which supplied uranium for the first nuclear bombs.

Calgary Herald oil editor, 1945.

Chapter Seventeen

REVERSAL

My downfall came from some of my inherent characteristics, the same ones that caused me to challenge the U.S. Army Engineers and the door guards. From the beginning truth, with me, has been very real, as solid as a mountain of granite, immovable, unshakable. A spade has always been a spade and never once have I seen it in the form of a club, a diamond or a heart. Black is black; no one can ever make me believe it is white, although I see every day plenty of examples where our leaders, both financially and politically persist in trying to make us believe that black is white.

My first trouble came from the newspaper, or rather the editor of the newspaper. How that happened is rather an involved story. Telling it, though, is unavoidable.

The trouble really started when my wife refused to follow me to Calgary. Her family was very much against her leaving Edmonton, opposed to placing her future and the future of our daughter in the hands of an n'er-do-well that kept jumping from job to job. I tried to impress upon her the importance of this writing job. I explained that it was really the object of my entire life and to me it was the chance of my lifetime. At last I could do what I wanted to do and still make enough money to support us reasonably well, that I was confident my future lay here, if there was any future for me at all. I have to say I was sorry for my wife, pulled as she was, between me on the one hand and her very powerful family on the other. I guess she thought my record wasn't strong enough to trust me and she continued in Edmonton at the job she now had of teaching music. She was a very good musician, her job was certain, and she would have to leave that if she came down to be with me in Calgary.

I give the impression of being a loner but I am basically not a very good loner. I was bent on going my own way; at the same time I very much needed companionship, and especially moral support. While in my early college years I had been an invincible loner, now in my late twenties I suffered veritable attacks of loneliness. As Dean Martin sings, "Everybody needs somebody sometime;" this was my time. I was in a totally new environment, starting a totally new job. After the beating I had taken getting there I was internally shaky now. I had an inner need for loving support.

I believe the things that happen to us are the results of the driving forces inside us, of what we want, of what we reject, of what we despise, of what we admire. Whatever position you may be in, I believe the cause in most cases is inherent within you.

At a newspaper party soon after I started with the *Herald* one night I met a girl who struck me like a thunderbolt. I knew she was married, but I made a date with her. What made it dangerous was the fact that she was married to a nighttime sports editor of the *Calgary Herald*. In fact that was the major problem of her life. Many times she had urged her husband to try to get a daytime job so they could have some life together. He promised to do so but he never did try. He loved the nighttime job and she was beginning to believe that's where he would stay as long as he lived. She had a child and she worried about his future; she was in fact herself, a lonely lady.

Furthermore, she was a very beautiful lady, a very loving person, intelligent, jovial and witty. I suppose our two problems matched; we were both lonely, both a little uncertain of our futures. I was more confident in mine than she was in hers.

The amazing thing about the relationship was that it never seemed to bother her husband. As long as he could meet with the boys at his scheduled times, and have his night life there he was happy and satisfied. He didn't seem to care what she did in the evenings. At least there was no sign of it.

If a small prairie fire is not curtailed at all, it can grow into a very big prairie fire that becomes finally unmanageable. This was the case. A small fire was building. A cupful of water could have put it out. But nobody bothered.

It started with dinner dates, moving on to picture shows, a drive in the country, or simply an evening at Muriel's apartment. This was the upstairs of her parents' home. It was another dissatisfaction with her life - not to be able to make any move without the knowledge and the censorship of her parents. But the apartment came at a cheap price, and there wasn't much chance that that would be changed either.

Without our being conscious of it, our dating grew more serious. Intensely attracted from the beginning, the more time that passed, the more involved we became. It started to get scary.

I made two strong efforts to persuade my wife Amy to come to Calgary. I saw our whole marriage on the way to disintegration, and I saw the disintegration of another marriage besides, if something wasn't done fast. My trips to Edmonton didn't seem to turn the scales. Finally I arranged to rent a very attractive house in a good residential district and I sent Amy a telegram, next to an ultimatum I fear, urging her to come at once. In return I got a telegram from her family stating that Amy was not moving to Calgary at this time.

Meanwhile, Muriel, basically insecure anyway, as I would later learn, sensed that she was moving into quicksand. She knew that if my marriage worked hers would have to work, or where would she be? She made a last-ditch effort; she phoned Allen Bill, asking him to meet with her to discuss a serious problem. He replied that he was very busy for the next few days and that he would not be free to see her, but he could meet her for dinner and talk her problem over with her.

Of course I knew about the meeting and hoped it would go well. Her idea was to get Allen Bill to change her husband from night shift to day shift. The situation was desperate enough for her to tell all this to the editor. I was prepared for that but not for the shock that I got afterwards.

Allen Bill met her as arranged and after an expensive meal in one of the fine dining places he offered of course to drive her home. On the way home, however, the managing editor pulled over into a sheltered spot to park. I don't know the details of the adventure but Muriel came back pale and troubled. She told me that after explaining her troubles, Mr. Bill had made a serious pass at her and she didn't know how to handle it. She was afraid that her rough rejection might now cause Burt to lose his job. There was no other way he could make a living.

Immediately this created a situation for me with the *Calgary Herald*, and I felt certain there would soon be repercussions. I knew there was a certain amount of talk going on among the staff about my association with Muriel, and I think some of it was pretty bad. I'm sure after that date some of it got back to Allen Bill and here we were; my editor and I were competitors for the attention of the same lady who was already, of course, soundly married.

The rift came about in an oblique way. I had been in the habit of selling my material to other magazines and to oil companies as I have previously related. One day soon after the dinner date Allen Bill called me in and said he had heard that I had charged one of the oil companies, I think it was National Petroleum, for the right to print a *Herald* story of mine.

I said; "Of course I have. And I've been doing that from the very beginning. I believe that when I take my stuff out of the typewriter it is my property except for first publication rights and as you know that is what the *Herald* gets on every story of mine."

Bill got red in the face. I knew right away that this was a trumped up excuse for a showdown.

"Well I want to tell you here and now, the stories you write are the property of the *Calgary Herald* and if anyone wants to publish them all they have to do is come and ask **me**. I won't allow you to charge for these stories, which are our property. Do you understand?!"

I slipped right back into gear; I refuse to be pushed around. I bristled. Allen Bill was flat wrong. I was certain that this had nothing to do with story rights. The fact was he couldn't allow me to stay on in view of what I knew of his advances on the wife of one of his editors.

I told him that if I couldn't sell my works after publication I wouldn't write any more stories for the *Herald*. I was prepared to quit if necessary.

His response was: "If you quit, you quit. If you don't I'm

giving you a month's notice, as of now."

So whether I quit or whether I was fired can be a subject of debate. Whatever, I was suddenly without a job.

I was much better off than before when I didn't have a job because now I had the experience and a name. I was sure I could find work with the oil industry or perhaps with the competing paper the *Albertan* in Calgary. When I told Muriel the news she was more upset than ever. She felt she couldn't desert me at this period and she decided to let the matter with Bill just simply dry up. He phoned her a few times after that without success and I know that he was very glad to see the end of me, even though I was the best oil writer in Western Canada.

Just before the fatal interview with Allen Bill, I had received a letter from Amy that she would be coming to Calgary and that I could go ahead and rent the house if it was still available. It was as much of a shock now that she was coming as it had been before, that she wasn't. I had to tell Muriel about it and I had to tell her that we would have to stop seeing each other. Then it was her turn to be devastated. She had to decide to live with her fate and hope that her flawed marriage, with a minimum of recrimination on both sides, could go on. Burt was very easy going and I thought that that might be possible. I faced a period of intense distress. I knew that by now my marriage to Amy had probably passed the point of no return.

In short the whole situation was a disaster. Now I had to construct some revised plans in order to make a living.

By this time the oil picture was heating up in Canada. Most of the major oil companies had branch offices now in Calgary and exploration and scouting crews out in the field. A great leasing program was in progress all across western Canada. I had a friend who was in the business of putting together huge blocks of oil leases and reselling these leases to the big oil companies. In his business he was looking for thousands of acres from farmers all over Saskatchewan for the sole purpose of turning these leases over to the oil companies at a very handsome profit. He agreed to take me on as one of the members of his team in the leasing program in Saskatchewan.

It was only a temporary job; once again I had to puzzle out

my future.

First of all a couple of independent oil companies took me on to write letters to their shareholders about their holdings and I was paid well for that. Shortly after that I went to see Max Bell who was the publisher of the *Albertan* and a very powerful figure in Canada. He was on the board of many companies, of some banks and of the biggest Canadian industrial company, the Canadian Pacific Railroad Company. He was a big man and he was deep in the oil business. Better, he was also acquainted with my writing. He had been reading it now for two or three years in the *Calgary Herald*. I got the job almost right away and I was back in the groove, same job, same salary, different boss.

Chapter Eighteen

TRANSITION TO TRANQUILITY

"The boy does not become a man as long as his father lives." I read or heard this a long time ago. It left a big impression with me because I believe it to be true. I know that in my case it was true.

My father passed away on my 34th birthday, June 15, 1946.

He had come from the farm to see me in Calgary. He was walking down the main street toward the *Calgary Herald* office when he was seized suddenly by a massive heart attack. He collapsed on the street but was later able to get himself up and walk the remaining two and a half blocks to the *Herald* and up on the elevator to the second floor where I had my office. I had not expected him and I was out on my news beat working on a story for the early afternoon edition. He suffered there for what must have been the biggest part of an hour in intense pain.

As an example of how primitive medicine was in those days only half a century ago, the heart specialist, knowing what had happened, directed me to walk my father over to the clinic for an examination. I could see that he was undergoing excruciating pain and I dreaded every step I had to urge on him, but we made it to the clinic. We had to wait at least forty minutes before the doctor got in to see us. The heart attack was then more than two hours old. The heart doctor told me that if my father could pull through for the first seven days he would probably make it, and so we went to the hospital.

I don't believe the doctor ever thought he would make it seven days, but he did not know the tremendous reserve of power he was dealing with. My father hung on for seventeen incredible days.

When my father left I felt like God had left. Throughout my life my father stood like a mountain between me and the world, between me and nature, even between me and God. I felt the security of a protector, unshakable, invincible. I knew that if my father had been commanded, like Abraham was, by God to sacrifice me, he would stand in front of me and protect me even from the Almighty.

While our loved ones live, we do not concern ourselves with what it will be like when they are gone. And that is good. If we were always to dread their departure, their death, we would miss all the beautiful days and months of the joy of their company during their existence. But when they go, especially in the case of a father, the shock is traumatic.

I don't know how long it took me to get over the emotional earthquake of my father's loss. But I do know that as soon as he was finally put to rest I came to a new realization that henceforth it was me against the world. I was now the protector of my own family and the symbolic leader at least of my heartbroken mother, my sister five years younger than myself and my kid brother fifteen years younger. I was never asked to do anything specific, but was keenly aware of their knowledge that I was there if needed. I was stepping into my father's shoes and I realized that they were mighty big boots.

This feeling did not lessen with the years, it intensified. To this day I see my father as a veritable rock of ages, the rock standing firm in the face of all storms. And to this day sometimes in my worst hours I have no greater wish than once more, for half an hour, talk again with my father. I was lucky in a way that by this 34th birthday my domestic situation, with all its entanglements, had begun to straighten out, although its huge and unsuspected complications remained to be dealt with. My father knew something of my troubles; he knew of Muriel and he had met her. We had talked with great fondness of how, after his recovery, as I had promised, all of us would move to the milder climate of British Columbia and he would sit out in the backyard under an apple tree. I'm sure that he died with this vision still prominent. But it would be a long time before even I alone could get anywhere near an apple tree.

My wife, Amy, having moved to Calgary, quite unknown to me, was in the early stages of a serious mental illness. The constant "Vernon bashing" by her family, the need of our young daughter for her father, matched against the threat of her marriage going over the brink, proved to be a stress too great. I thought her spells of total unreason meant only that she had become impossibly difficult. No day was ever the same as the day before. If one day she pleaded on bended knee and wept copiously with profuse declarations of her love, sobbing entreaties that I return, if that's the way it was one day, then the next day if I came to the house she was likely as not to hit me with a broom and tell me never to enter the door again.

If a couple has difficulty living together when both are in good mental health, then when one or the other is beginning to slip, forget it. There's no way in this world a sane person can live with an insane person and survive. At times I was so distressed that I very seriously considered the awful way out. How was I ever to handle this situation? How was I ever to be able to make life remotely bearable for our nine year old daughter? How was I ever to convince Amy that I was really trying and I needed her help? And on the other side as against all of that, how was I ever to be fair with Muriel who had already lost so much because of a growing loyalty to me and who was now to endure the slings and fortune of outrageous gossip and denigration?

I couldn't see a way. Except one way. And when I considered that way my thought went immediately to my parents and what it would do to them, and I couldn't consider that way either. So in total there was no way.

I thought back to those drama packed days a few years earlier when the Duke of Windsor had given up the throne of England to straighten out his life. I wished that I could do it at such a price. I didn't have anything to trade.

Meanwhile, Muriel was undergoing similar stress of an unending dilemma. Finally I suggested to her we would have to take the bull by the horns ourselves, without thought for anyone else, because no one else mattered as much as we did to our own lives and we would have to either elope and leave the country or simply set up housekeeping together. This seemed like a dreadful solution.

I had been working on my divorce for some time, had it all arranged with the lawyers, when at the last possible moment Amy, as might be expected, had a total change of mind and absolutely refused to consider a divorce. I then, as I had to do on two or three later occasions in my life, brought in my last ammunition and shot the works on the only way out. I told Amy, her family, and her lawyer that if she did not get a divorce now she would never get a divorce from me under heaven or hell, if I lived to be a bachelor forever. This was enough to bring the family to their senses and finally cause them to agree to something which they seem to have wanted from the beginning, but now that it had arrived, they didn't want at all, dissolution of the marriage.

It remained then only necessary for Muriel to get her divorce, and while less troublesome, it seemed to take unending time. I concluded that there was no other solution. I concluded that it was mandatory that we now take our lives in our own hands, and for the sake of our futures, fight it out however we could, leave the country if necessary. In just two or three years I had changed dramatically. A recognized writer now, I was quite confident that if I went to Vancouver, British Columbia I could get a job on one of the newspapers there or in Victoria. I was prepared to use a part of our savings to buy a trailer and to take off for the coast.

In saner moments, however, that seemed to both of us to be rather drastic and we decided first to make a try of it living right there in Calgary. I was able to get - and this was a rare occurrence just after the war - a small upstairs apartment. It was almost an exact replica of the residence of television's "Honeymooners," complete with small gas stove, ice box, and a few shelves. We moved in there prepared to fight the world and that's what we did.

This solution was soon complicated with developments around my radio program on CFAC which was owned by the *Calgary Herald*. It too, now looking back on it, has all the appearance of a script that someone had written out before I was born.

It was about the time when the Canadian government, which is really the government of all of Canada by representation from only two Provinces, Ontario and Quebec, made a move to treat the farmers of Western Canada under a different tax law than those of Eastern Canada. This was a call on my patriotism and on my loyalty to my parents, and to the settlers of Western Canada who had made the country come alive at such a high cost. I had to sound the clarion call and I did.

I started a series of broadcasts which described how the government with the huge overpowering representation from the East Canada was now going to treat the West as a poor cousin, operating under different rules from the favored East. Western farmers under the proposal would be required each year, with their income tax returns, to give a net worth statement. Such a statement would of course include how many chickens there were on hand, how many eggs, how many cows and calves, what ages - even fence posts or building materials. It was an absolute mess. I could not see where my father could ever keep pace with such a conglomeration of bookkeeping. My broadcasts whipped the farmers of the West into anger and I began to suggest that they send letters to their members of Parliament petitioning cessation of Western Canada from the Dominion. This soon got too hot for the separate powers to bear. Firstly, my sponsor Adams, Wood and Wyler, who bought livestock on commission and who bought plenty of it as a result of my broadcast to the farmers, now cancelled their contract with me.

But when it was publicly announced that Adams, Wood and Wyler would no longer carry the Myers program the phone exchange in CFAC lit up for three hours. Within two or three days a representative from the radio station approached me saying that Adams, Wood and Wyler would like to have me back, would I consider it?

I said I would consider it. I did consider it, and by the end of the week I gave them my answer. I would go back, but now at $40 a broadcast instead of $25 a broadcast. The answer was an instant acceptance!

Of course only half the battle was won. The *Calgary Herald* was owned by the *Southam Newspaper Chain*, the most influential publishers in Canada and centered in Toronto. I was told by the radio station that I would have to submit my broadcasts for censorship before I could go on the air. I endured this for one or two weeks and right away I knew that it wouldn't work. I just wasn't going to drop the matter, come what may.

So on the third week I prepared a broadcast which again waded right into the government on behalf of Western Canada farmers, suggesting the cessation of the West from the Federal Dominion. This made headlines in the *Albertan*, but not in the *Calgary Herald*. And in the broadcast I went so far as to relate that this had not made headlines in the *Calgary Herald* because it was the owner of CFAC and itself was owned by Eastern interests. And I said; "If my voice suddenly leaves you, you will know that I have been cut from the air for this remark." There was a click, then silence and then I was told afterwards a general and prolonged illumination on the switchboard.

However, it was too serious a subject for the powers to overlook. I could not be allowed to pursue this trend or Canada would stand in some danger of separation. I was then fired by the radio station itself. That was the end of my broadcasting career.

At one point during this time conditions became so tense that I was prepared to use a gun if necessary to protect myself and the small family unit we were determined to create. Very very late, one night, Muriel awakened me with the urgent whisper: "Wake up! Someone is taking our car."

I sprang to my feet, threw on a bathrobe, grabbing my 32 Colt automatic out of the drawer, on the way out. I knew a lot of stories had whizzed around back and forth around the Calgary Herald and the radio station relating to my mixed up domestic situation and my argument with the paper as well as the radio station. In my bare feet I flew down the steps and out the door, charging my car, and yanked open the door pushing my gun straight into the chest of the man at the wheel, already with the motor running.

He gasped; "Put that thing away. For God's sake!"

To my amazement and to my relief it turned out to be my brother whom I had given permission to use my car. He had his girlfriend with him and it was a cold night and he needed the heater on so he started it up. He told me later there was no doubt by the look on my face that I was prepared to use the gun.

It was during these times of turbulent domestic troubles as well as involvement with the bigger interests that my wife to be,

Muriel, admonished me with quiet wisdom inherent in her statement, "You can't fight City Hall!"

But she never really convinced me of that, nor did anyone else, though she would herself repeat her advice many more times before our marriage finally ended with her death on Christmas 1987.

But in the fight with City Hall at least I had held to a draw. I had accomplished what I had set out to do. The proposal that Western Canadian farmers be required to make out an income tax form differing from eastern Canada farmers was dropped like a hot potato and was never heard of again.

Sometime later on I took off to start my leasing contract, and was headquartered at Regina, Saskatchewan, about 700 miles from home. I believe I made over a thousand dollars a month the few months I was at it, and that was pretty big money back in those days.

The leasing job put some security back under us. Muriel got her divorce and very shortly thereafter we were properly married by a minister of the gospel.

That didn't happen so very easily either.

When, after we had the license and we went in to visit the preacher in the rectory, he first undertook to make sure Muriel knew she was marrying a divorced man, which was not in keeping with religious standards. She agreed that she was well aware of all this and that she was ready to go through with the marriage ceremony. Then the minister asked her about her own situation and found out for the first time that she was also divorced. This about gave the good minister a stroke right there in his chair. He began to fumble as to whether or not he would perform the ceremony.

I said to the minister; "You can do as you like. If you don't perform the ceremony I know where there is a justice of the peace who will do it and I can tell you we will be married with or without you. We would rather be married in the church and be married under your blessing, but if it can't be that way we'll have it the other way, and save an argument."

The minister agreed as to how he would go ahead and do the job himself. He didn't put it in those words, but that was the way it seemed to me, although I assumed that we were going into the situation with the blessing of the Lord behind us.

At least you can say things were beginning to get straightened out.

Chapter Nineteen

THE OIL PATCH
MISSING A MILLION BY A HAIR

I guess the years 1947 to 1952 were about the best years of my life. My domestic life straightened out; my financial security improved, thanks mostly to oil.

As 1947 dawned Muriel and I were still living in the "Ralph Cramdon" apartment, with the icebox and the little gas stove. The most exciting thing domestically was that I learned to bake bread there. There was more activity on the investment front.

The advent of Leduc No. 1 as an exciting oil well in February 1947 set the oil patch literally afire. Lease hounds were criss-crossing north central Alberta so actively they were practically running into one another. Some very promising acreage had been picked up within two or three miles of the Leduc discovery well. The lease hounds who leased this freehold land from the farmers had made companies out of it.

This was the chance for the public to get into the play. The companies were floated with perhaps a million to three million shares for sale to the public at usually about 25 cents a share, the promoters keeping large gobs for themselves. But the public money supplied the wherewithal for the drilling of oil and the cost of the leases. Three such companies were Leduc Consolidated, owned by veteran oil man Mayland, Central Leduc promoted by Neil MacQueen, and Okalta Oils by W. S. Herron, graduates of the Turner Valley days in Alberta and seasoned promoters. Leduc Consolidated looked to be the best promise because it had three quarter sections which were considered to be the best located of all of the independent land and it was managed by a competent but less known man by the name of Phillips.

Soon after Leduc No. 1 came into production, Imperial

Leduc No. 2 also made it into production and Imperial Leduc No. 3 about a mile and a half to the northeast was drilling steadily ahead. The independents were quick to get their drill bits into the ground on the heels of the beginning of Leduc No. 3.

Right here a big surprise was in the making when the oil industry least expected it. The surprise involved the common mistake of taking for granted that the past will be the pattern of the future. In Alberta the "has been" was Turner Valley, a huge gas cap oil field with a very predictable characteristic. That characteristic was that if the oil horizon (strata) came in at a high level the drillers were **certain** either of a wet gas well loaded with petroleum condensate or a good flowing oil well.

From the beginning Imperial Leduc No. 3 began to hit different geological horizons at a higher level than either No. 2 or No. 1. Excitement was at fever pitch. Leduc Consolidated, closest to Imperial No. 3, was not satisfied to commence with one well. It put a rig on all three quarter sections to drill simultaneously. While at the same time Okalta Oils was sinking a well, and Central Leduc was sinking a well in the same general area and to the south.

My daily reports in the *Calgary Herald* always gave the progress of all of these wells and usually gave the elevation of the markers that were being hit by the drill bits. I was offered a chance to buy some of the Leduc Consolidated initial stock at 25 cents a share. This was no gift or any bribe. Lots of people bought it, but after about the third day there was none left and I was happy with my thousand shares.

Almost right away all of these stocks commenced to rise on the market because the initial stock offering had been sold out. Through the next few weeks I saw Leduc Consolidated double to 50 cents and then go to 70 cents; 80 cents, and before too long, without ever a smell of oil, it hit $1.00 a share. I had a tidy profit, but I was not at that point prepared to sell.

Meanwhile, the high markings of Central Leduc were continuing and they began to worry me. The formations were coming in not only somewhat higher than the producing wells but a lot higher. Now in Turner Valley this would have meant that the anticline which is a porous layer of geologic rock slanting upward and sealed off by shale - that this was a sure omen of great success. Two of the Consolidated Leduc wells were drilling and they were coming in also at high levels as were Okalta and Central Leduc. People began to envision ten or fifteen dollars a share for Leduc Consolidated when each of these quarters would be proved out and that meant that the three other wells could be drilled on each of the quarters, a total of twelve oil wells. No words in the *Calgary Herald* were read with a greater sense of euphoria and enthusiasm than the oil column day by day.

My broker told me that when a stock got to be one dollar a share you could put it on margin. That is, you could put up the stock you owned and buy as much again. You would then be on 50 percent margin for 2,000 shares. But if the stock was for instance going to reach ten dollars a share, think of the killing! But don't think of the killing if it should be a dry hole and the stock was worth nothing. No one did think of that.

I had no sooner got my full 2,000 shares of Leduc Consolidated than the market started to move again as the drill bits hit more important geological markers. But I began to get now really scared of Imperial No. 3. I thought that this was coming in altogether too high. I couldn't at once see why this would be harmful, but it just didn't somehow smell right.

I knew that the oil field at Leduc was contained in a corral reef. Back in Devonian geologic times there was a great reef building area in the seas and corals had built beds in some places hundreds to thousands of feet thick. Now these coral reefs were filled with pores and if there was petroleum in the lower echelons of the formations to the southwest it would naturally rise toward the high point in the reef reservoir. You had to think of it like it was a sponge, contained and sealed. Gas would rise to the top where it would be trapped, the oil would follow that, and the water would follow that. And the gas would exert great pressure on the oil, causing it to flow out of any bore hole that penetrated the formation.

My background in geology started to pay off for me at that time because, as I considered the coral reef formation, I knew that we were not looking at the same proposition as we were with the anticline of sedimentary rock at Turner Valley. The corals would build reefs foot on foot on foot on foot, but they would not necessarily be continuous. There might be a huge reef which would, if you could strip the surface away, reveal that after a certain high point the corals had quit building, and after you went over this sort of coral cliff, your bit just dropped off into straight rock. In other words the coral reef could be the replica of a coral hill, 4,000 feet below the surface. If you went over the edge there was no reservoir. There was nothing but salt water to come out of those rocks.

I began to wonder if Imperial No. 3 were not so high that maybe we had passed beyond the end boundaries of this coral reef. And I began to relate that information as to what would happen to all of the independent wells if that were the case.

Consolidated Leduc and the other independent stocks continued to advance without a tremor. I saw the stock go through $1.25 and through $1.50, through $2.00, and my God it was thrilling! People at Leduc Consolidated were just about going crazy. They could see twelve oil wells within a few months - millions and millions of dollars. That kept new buyers coming in that were willing to pay $2.00 for stock the rest of us had paid 25 cents for. And it was obvious that it wasn't over yet.

When one day Imperial Leduc No. 3 hit the critical D-1 zone of the Devonian about 300 feet higher than any other well had. People thought it was great. I waited for the bit to hit the D-2, the zone with the oil, and it soon did, way higher than the other wells but to the amazement of most onlookers there was no oil in the D-2 zone and it was not the regular coral reef rock. As I studied this in preparation for my oil column I began to think the unthinkable. Maybe none of these wells would be any good. I couldn't say for sure yet. Maybe they all would be good - but suddenly I was nervous.

I told my broker, Brian Locke, who was a specialist in the oil stocks, of my suspicions. Brian actually went pale at the thought. He said, "My God, my clients are in this up to their necks! You think it's possible Leduc Consolidated could be a dry hole?"

I said, "I think it's highly possible. In fact I'm beginning to think it's likely."

The Leduc Consolidated stock had risen to over $2.65 a share and all those wells were still hitting all horizons high. Feelings remained high. But we were not far from the day when Imperial Oil would punch its well down another 300 or 400 feet and announce a test of salt water - no oil - no coral reef.

It took more than that to convince the independents and the oil playing public that we could be running into a disaster. People do not like bad news. They will refuse to accredit bad news if at all possible. They will call the purveyor of bad news crazy, irresponsible, a nut. Especially if his idea has never been voiced before.

I said to Brian Locke, "What do you think this stock will be worth if it's a dry hole?"

He said, "Well, it depends on the other two." I said, "But if the first one is a dry hole, I can pretty nearly guarantee you the other two will also be dry holes. What do you think?"

He said, "If they're dry holes it won't be worth a plugged nickel."

I said, "Well you know we live in a very small apartment, Muriel and I. We have no home. Today I could sell my $250 investment for about $5,000. There's a lovely brand spanking new home in Elbow Park with about 1100 square feet selling at $10,000. I could put the $5,000 on the house and we have the home. "

Locke said, "Would you sell all your Leduc stock?"

I said, "Yes, you see I'm betting here. The truth is I'm betting $5,000 cold cash that these are going to be oil wells. If I'm wrong it will turn out I've bet my house and I'll have nothing."

Brian Locke said, "It's hard for me to believe that will happen. But what you say is true - you're betting your house."

I said, "Well, I'm in no position to bet my house that these are oil wells. Sell me out."

He said, "Everything?"

I said, "Everything."

I got some $5,500 for my stock and it did go up a little ways further after that. The next day Muriel and I went down and bought the house. Muriel nearly had a fit because we were taking on a debt of $5,000 which she didn't know how anyone could ever pay off but I urged that we go to the Vancouver Pacific coast for a week vacation. When we got back not only had Imperial No. 3 been declared a dry hole but Leduc Consolidated No. 1 had been declared a dry hole, and all reports had stopped coming from Okalta's well because it was now deep enough to have shown oil. But there wasn't a word from the well site. I remember writing a story with a headline "Herron drops Iron Curtain around Okalta."

The Consolidated stock began to sell off but not as fast as you would think in the first few days. Once it lost momentum it sold off to about $1.50 and then the second Leduc Consolidated well was declared a dry hole. And then the Okalta well, which we knew must be past the oil horizon, still didn't offer any reports and it was being concluded by a few brave souls that it also might be a dry hole.

And the Central Leduc well was likely a dry companion.

The independent oil market went to hell in a basket. Leduc Consolidated was hurt worse than any other stock. And it hurt me to watch it. Phillips, the promoter, had had about a million shares of it; not that much to start with but he had added on margin to the maximum of his carrying capacity. Instead of selling a million dollars worth of stock or half a million, he held on and bought more. By the time he got around to selling, the market was falling right out from under him. Any sales of 100,000 shares or more would have knocked the market into a wastebasket. He had to hold on to hope for Consolidated Leduc No. 3. But alas bad news likes to follow bad news. The third Leduc Consolidated well blew salt water. The Leduc Consolidated stock went to nothing; down to about 50 cents in the first week after, then down to a quarter, then in two or three months down to a nickel a share. The last I heard of Mr. Phillips was that he was running a service station in northern Alberta. It made me feel very bad.

Meanwhile, we moved into our new house and I had learned a very important lesson. There is no such thing as a sure thing or as my broker put it to me, "Nothing is more unsafe than a lead pipe cinch." And the event that looks to be absolutely incomprehensible, impossible, fantastic, still can happen. Complacency in the market can never be enjoyed, can never be indulged in.

I had been a little worried after I had sold all my stock that it still might go to $20, but now living in the house we were mighty thankful people. Leduc Consolidated had made us a house - something I had been sure that I would never be able to own. How could I, on my wages, ever save enough money to buy a house?

If I couldn't own a house, of course I could never own a car - not feasibly a brand new car. A car of the caliber I would like would cost about $3,000. How would I, on my meager earnings, make the money to pay the living expenses of a family, the clothes, the rent, the payments; how could I possibly save enough to own a car? Perhaps by the time I was 50 - at the very best. Yet, in the year 1948 I became a proud owner of a brand new cream colored hydromatic Pontiac straight eight. What a car! What a beautiful piece of technology. Besides the electric windows and the electric windshield washer, it even shifted the gears for you - by itself. And all this one year after we had bought the house.

In that year I'd had a close shave in becoming a youthful millionaire. It was just a close brush with fate. It could have gone one way or it could have gone the other.

In those days the Canadian Pacific Railroad had the mineral rights on millions of acres of land in Alberta. The railroad had been given these rights as a reward for pushing the rail line across Canada. The railroad was mainly interested in having the land drilled and collecting royalties on production. For that reason it sold off its leases very cheaply and they went very quickly to the big companies.

But in 1947 when all the fluster was Leduc in mid-Alberta and the Devonian reefs, people had begun to forget about the great sedimentary field at Turner Valley and the huge oil and gas traps that had been demonstrated as possible in the geology of Western Alberta. I found that there was 65,000 acres of Canadian Pacific Railroad mineral rights northwest of Calgary that had never been drilled on and of course not near any known oil field. I also found another 35,000 acres of land in the Taber area to the south where this drilling was shallow at about 3,000 feet and where certain gas fields had been found. At ten cents an acre I put together a syndicate to buy up all of the remaining Canadian Pacific Railroad mineral rights. This was called the South Alberta Syndicate. I had about a twenty percent interest in it for putting it together. I think the cost to us was about $30,000 a year which I raised by interesting half a dozen of my friends and associates. The next thing to do was to sell these leases to somebody who would drill a well on them and to retain a producing royalty. That was the way to make money in those days - real money.

But alas the fever of Leduc that had swept the public had also swept the oil industry. I had always claimed, and I still claim, that the big oil companies are like sheep. If one moves in a certain direction and starts leasing land another will follow. Millions of acres will follow one upon the other by the various major companies. At the time there was no interest in the Canadian foothill areas or in the Taber gas area. This works in reverse too.

I took these leases to nearly every large company headquartered in Calgary, and by now most of the major companies of the United States did have Calgary offices. No dice. In the 65,000 acres north of Calgary they all claimed the drilling was too deep. Agreeably it would be down into the seven or eight thousand field range. Every oil company had the same damn answer. They were interested in chasing coral reefs, not anticlines in expensive deep drilling areas.

Finally just before our next year's leases were due I did make a deal on the 35,000 acres in the Taber gas area. I remember it well. I remember my wife and I driving back from Great Falls, Montana, two or three days before Christmas just as that well was reaching the critical horizon where it would be hitting the gas zone - if there was one. After crossing the border we turned off the main highway and sped eastward toward the well. I could see the high tower 20 miles in the distance and the closer we got the dryer it looked. Of course you really couldn't tell from the appearance, but if I ever believed in vibrations I believed in them then and these were very dry vibrations. When we pulled up to the well we found no one there except the geologist in his trailer. I went to the door and got him out and instantly I had the news. They had struck the expected gas zone but they had got a rise of 2500 feet of salt water in the hole - and that was that.

I said to my wife, "Well, there goes my last chance to be a millionaire. It's a flop. Might as well forget it forever."

However, I could well afford to forget it. I had sold the 35,000 acres of leased land for a payment to the syndicate owners of about $5,000 each. I had personally made $20,000 from the sale of my interest in Alberta Syndicate. Had the well been a producer I would have retained a lifetime royalty on its production of either gas or oil.

Meanwhile, no one would have anything to do with the 65,000 acres north and west of Calgary. Nor could I get my partners to put up the money to hold the leases for another year. The due date came and went and the leases lapsed back to the Canadian Pacific Railroad Company.

I found soon after that they had been swiftly picked up by the Home Oil Company. A year later Home Oil drilled a well on this leased land and found a brand new oil field. The Harmatten Oil and Gas Field was one of the best of Southern Alberta and had we been able to hold onto it and save a royalty, there would have been millionaires among us. Certainly I would have been a multi-millionaire. But I wasn't.

Many fortunes in Alberta were made on deals just like this. You could be lucky or unlucky. Some of the millionaires that arrived didn't have a brain to back it up with. But they did have a jackpot full of luck. Some of them were smart enough to keep their money and go on and to create large oil companies. Others soon lost it all. Those were the last opportunities that I ever had to become a very rich man without much work. The dice never rolled over again.

* * * *

In November 1947 we'd had our first child, our daughter Norma. They were great days and though millionaire status had escaped me I had done better than I had ever dreamed I would do. We were even able to buy furniture for the house we had purchased on the strength of Leduc Consolidated. My idea of having a lot of money did not coincide with most people's idea. I recall that when my wife came home from the hospital with Norma I planned to greet her with a great surprise. It was near

Thanksgiving and I remembered that on the farm we had made pumpkin pie at Thanksgiving from the pumpkins in the garden. So I went down to the grocery store and bought a beautiful big pumpkin and put it on the counter. Alongside this pumpkin I had a case of grapes so that she could make grape jelly. To me this was a fine sign of affluence. In my farm days we had never been able to afford grapes in such quantity, but my wife failed to appreciate the wealth. She was not a bit pleased, arriving back from the hospital to be faced with a huge pumpkin. So later on I gave her a vacuum cleaner for Christmas.

After a year or two more of marriage I got educated to the point to where my mind went to flowers and jewelry on Christmas and birthday occasions. I recall on one occasion walking down the street and looking at a beautiful ring in the jeweler's window and going in and plunking down $1,000 right on the spur of the moment, proudly putting a flawless carat diamond on her finger. That is about the nicest way to buy a gift - when it comes as an inspiration. A thousand dollars at that time would amount to ten thousand dollars today, and I doubt I would be quite that impulsive in these advanced years.

After a couple of years in the new house at Elbow Park we got onto the track of an old home in Mount Royal, the famous residential area of opulent by-gone days of Turner Valley explorers a quarter of a century earlier. By some break we were able to purchase this twelve room brick house perched on the hill overlooking the whole city for $10,000. It was in bad repair but we fixed it up with new wallpaper throughout and some other more expansive contributions and inside six months we were offered $27,000 for the house. We didn't take it. I often thought afterwards that's what my dad would have described as "the day when two fools met." The one fool who was crazy enough to offer the price and the other fool who was crazy enough to turn it down.

We lived in that house four years. Our son Richard was born in 1950. By this time Muriel's son Brian was almost eight years old and Norma was going on four years old. I noticed right away we had stopped being a family. Norma was playing with a certain group of children and Brian in his play hours was never at home.

I was strong on a cohesive family, the kind where my roots had been set and I persuaded my wife that we ought to buy a place in the country, build our own house and have our family together. And that's what we did. We bought 27 acres on the highway about ten miles south of the city limits and in the next summer constructed a new house at a cost of about $45,000. The place later sold for about $250,000 and I believe the Elbow Park place changed hands a few years ago at $100,000. But money wasn't on our minds in any of those transactions. They were purely done for the quality of life. We lived in the house at Mindapore south of Calgary from 1952 until our home was raided by a squad of income tax goons in 1974 while my wife was incapacitated with a serious illness in the hospital - and even afterwards for two more years.

Our idyllic life had lasted from 1947 to 1952. With the move into the country, for some reason everything changed. Nothing would ever be the same again.

Chapter Twenty

DOMESTIC STORM CLOUDS

When the leasing contract finished in 1951 I got work almost immediately as the oil editor of the *Albertan*, Calgary's morning newspaper in competition with the *Calgary Herald,* independently owned by Max Bell.

Mr. Bell was a youthful magnate. No older than I, he was the sole owner of the *Albertan* and a member on the boards of many of Canada's important corporations, including the Canadian Pacific Railroad Company, the largest corporation in Canada. Max Bell followed the oil industry with intense interest and became one of its most active participants. He knew at once whether an oil writer was worth his salt, and I had his support throughout my tenure at the *Albertan*.

Not long after taking up my new job I came across a fraudulent oil promotional deal. I exposed it in all its horrible detail. The deal was structured to take advantage of the investing public through false claims and false literature, and fraudulent stock manipulation. It broke as a big story in the *Albertan* and was prominently headlined. The promoters were named.

I got my first legal shock about a week afterwards when the *Albertan* and I received notification of a million-dollar lawsuit that would be brought jointly against us.

Of course I didn't have that kind of money. I was still just a working stiff. But they could, if they won, get the money out of the *Albertan* and take whatever I had. On the morning that our notices were separately received Max Bell called me into his office

170

and I wondered whether this was indeed the tragic end of a promising career. To my surprise Bell wasn't the least bit shaken. He said, "We've got the facts and I personally know a few more things about these individuals. There have been complaints about them in the United States. And I want you to see the Securities and Exchange Commission in Pittsburgh, Pennsylvania, and then go on to New York and see the SEC officials there. There will be a lot of background information which we can make good use of."

I was gratified to know that my boss would stand behind me. I had in the meantime, with the great growth of the Canadian oil industry, persuaded the *Albertan* that I needed a helper in my job. I had engaged a young lad by the name of Earle Gray without any experience to come in with me. I left him to do routine stories while I took off for Pittsburgh.

I found that the authorities in Pittsburgh had been trying to get their hands on "the culprits" for quite a long time. But they had fled to Canada before an extraditable claim could be proved against them and the securities laws in Canada were not yet sufficiently formulated to deal with this kind of crook. But there was a barrel of evidence; one of the trio, in fact, had been sentenced to a lashing in one of the states, I forget which, and I forget nearly all of the details associated with my quest. I added to them through interviews of the authorities in New York City. And I had my chance to see New York for the first time in my life.

Not many years earlier I was dead certain that I would never get to see these large centers, especially not New York or Hollywood, California. I was simply stunned by the city of New York. Walking down some of the streets with skyscrapers hundreds of feet tall on either side, I felt like a small ant, a gopher in a concrete jungle. I was a gawky kid from the farm again. I was just as unfit for New York as I had been, as a fourteen-year-old boy, bewildered by the traffic of the small prairie city of Brandon, Manitoba. Out on the street, I was immediately lost, once more a country hick. But I got the job done. And I returned to Calgary with my bag of ammunition for the libel suit defense. What I had gathered must have been pretty potent stuff. Whatever Bell's lawyers did with the material I don't know. But never again did I hear a word of the threatened lawsuit. And I think my story in the *Albertan* must have served as a red light to the various fraudulent promoters down in Toronto, which was notoriously crooked. It served as notice that if the *Albertan* ever found out about any rankly dishonest deals the culprits would certainly be exposed.

Our son Richard had been born in May 1950 when I was 38 years old, and I had been writing for about six years. When son Richard was two, we built our country house from the bottom up without ever a mortgaged dollar against it from the time of its foundation until it was sold a quarter of a century later under the most stressful circumstances in 1976.

It started out well enough on the "ranch." We became a family again almost at once. Norma, age six, and Brian, age ten, trotted off every morning to the country school. Norma started a riding career at age six that took her for a period of more than twenty years to the top of the equestrian sport in high jumping competitions ranging from Madison Square Garden through Cleveland, Chicago, Florida, San Diego, Los Angeles and finally as a Canadian team competitor in the Pan American games in Mexico City in 1974. Norma and her horse flew 4,000 miles to Mexico City and returned safely with the Canadian bronze earned at the games. Neither of the boys took to riding but one way or another they reaped enjoyment and health and individualism out of our life in the country. We put in a swimming pool and I have always credited it with saving the life of our youngest son, John, born in 1957 and suffering tremendously from asthma. He became very strong, the largest-chested member of our family.

But a sad note, a bad omen for the future, had begun creeping in in those first idyllic months, imperceptibly at first and ruinously later on.

Have you noticed among your friends and acquaintances that those who have to struggle the hardest are often the happiest? Have you noticed that when the struggle is largely behind them and when they have most of all that they want, that when they get two cars, a fine house, two or three beautiful children, when they can buy T-bone steaks in place of hamburger and with utter abandon, have you noticed that these people often at this point become tragically unhappy? Just when the battle seems to have been gloriously won a period of misery, and sometimes tragedy, begins?

The husband and wife will work like a team of Trojans together but when the mountain has been climbed and the obstacles are behind them, they suddenly find that their mutual trust, their love, their enduring confidence begins to weaken and the troubles, from there on, multiply.

I see some young people who today have everything, fine homes, Porsche cars, and I worry that the peak of their happiness may be already behind them. Is the man developing an eye for younger and prettier women, forgetting what his own wife has been through with him? Is the woman beginning to lose her trust in this man who was her Rock of Gibraltar through all their tribulations, the birth of their children, the new swimming pool? If there are weaknesses in the structure of the marriage **here** is where the cracks will start.

In my case the great struggle for the occupation that I had wanted above all occupations was solved. I was recognized and no one could take that away from me. Our wants were fulfilled. We had the two cars, the two garages, money for our annual trip to California, money enough to engage household help. If we weren't rich it was darn sure that more money wasn't going to make anything better. And right here is where the flaws began to show in both of us.

More than I ever realized, I know now that my wife was dreadfully insecure. Not by the fear of the loss of our money or our home but fear for the loss of love. She was in her family the third and last child; her mother had been a wheelchair cripple from the time of her birth. From the beginning she played the part of a baby instead of a child. When other girls were wearing silk stockings she was required to wear wool stockings to school to make her mother sure she wouldn't catch cold. It was a fearful world out there and every precaution had to be taken to ensure safety.

Whereas my strong father had given me enduring confidence, Muriel's parents had instilled in her fear and timidity. The result was that she relied upon me completely for our safety and that meant of course that if I should ever abandon her or ever love someone else, the end of her world would be upon her.

It's strange that I can tell and understand this now but that I could not tell and understand it when it was needed.

The move to the country was the trigger for a different kind of life for us. Whereas I used to come home every day at noon without fail, I now never came home at noon. There was a whole blank day in there when she could not know what I was doing. Maybe it was natural for her to begin to wonder.

But to me this was not natural at all. I resented it when she doubted me, and the more she doubted me the angrier I became. There was a total failure in understanding, a breakdown in communications was at hand.

The first early symptom of trouble brewing occurred in the big Mount Royal house as the new country house was building. I was away from home much more as I often went out to the building site in what spare time I had. We had always been moderate drinkers. We had been only social drinkers, and I never gave the slightest thought to alcohol as a potential problem. But in those days she did begin to drink some in the afternoon and often had a drink with me at suppertime.

The house was building during the spring and summer of 1952. My job at the *Albertan* was going very well. The oil industry was forging ahead at an astonishing rate in Canada and I was the best oil writer on the patch.

Max Bell had a very attractive secretary and her name began to increasingly enter our conversations. She was a fine young lady whom I shall not name, and quite beautiful besides. Muriel got to thinking in her numerous probings, and judging from my remarks, that I was developing a great interest in Mr. Bell's secretary. It was complete nonsense and when she let this cat out of the bag I was nothing but disgusted. She received no comfort, no reassurance from me. I felt that this rubbish should not be allowed to enter our lives. That only increased the distance growing between us, although at this time it was small.

Then one time, unknown to me, she invited the young lady up for a drink after work. I was surprised to find her at the house and just a little bit ill at ease, perhaps because of what I knew about Muriel's suspicions. I was scared to death that Muriel might bring up the question of a relationship.

One day I said to Muriel in great anger: "You must be crazy. Helen (I'll call her that) is the confidential secretary of one of the richest men in Canada. She has beautiful diamond rings, she wears a very expensive fur coat, she drives around sometimes with the boss in the Cadillac, and do you think that in all common sense she would be likely to be interested in a working stiff like me? I'm no more than another work horse in Max Bell's stables."

Reason made no difference. Muriel remained frightened of the prospect, which I believe in her mind was that someone else would steal my affection, and she would be left out on a lonely desert, deserted, abandoned, alone.

The fear increased her use of alcohol, and the increased alcohol increased the fear.

One night in the late summer of 1952 I hurried through my dinner and went out to the house to work. I was shoveling gravel, leveling it in the basement when all of a sudden there was the rush of an automobile and squeaking breaks. I looked up to see Muriel standing in the basement door demanding; "Who is it? All right, where is she?" I began to laugh.

"Where is who?" I asked.

"You will not lie out of this one," she said. "I saw you driving down seventeenth avenue in your Lincoln with somebody along."

I invited her to come down into the basement and look around, or look around anywhere she wanted. At the time I thought it was very funny and that this would prove once and for all to her that she was off on a wrong tangent.

It does not work that way. An insecure spouse needs a response of love and assurance rather than anger or ridicule. And that's practically all that's needed, although it may be needed every day.

Muriel never got that from me. Looking back, these years later, I feel so badly now. I have had time myself to learn in this last decade or so what an unbearable weight insecurity can be. The yearning that arises out of insecurity cannot be matched by any other yearning I know. But back in those younger days I was simply disgusted with weakness in any of its manifestations. I felt that insecurity was a weakness which with a little common sense, could be easily wiped out.

My impatience with insecurity may have also been a contributing factor to the failure of my first marriage to Amy and the nervous breakdown that put her finally into the mental hospital. When I was searching for my career in earlier years there had been plenty of reason for insecurity. Unfaltering loyalty to me weakened her ties with her family. In the end her loss was doubled.

Once she was committed to the mental institution, her family dumped her. In her ten years or so in Penocka I think she was visited only once by a sister. The others, including her mother, never came. It began to look like she would die there. During those years she had become well enough to leave, but the authorities would never release her into a strange cold world she no longer knew. She needed support, and where was that to come from?

A strange conjunction of circumstances provided the answer. Muriel's bout with alcohol had landed her into the same institution. I was on the outside alone and I had two wives on the inside alone. Amy's reaction to Muriel was at first hostile. She called her, "The rich Mrs. Myers."

Incidentally, I had scored another first; I was said to be the only man in the country who ever had two wives together in one institution at the same time. There may have been some substance to a casual remark about my sanity; "Myers won't go crazy, he just drives other people crazy."

In support of that they could cite the fact that a roommate of mine in Brandon College had also been committed. Actually he was diagnosed as a manic depressive.

True or not, Muriel's detainment of little more than a month was a lucky break for Amy, because as soon as Muriel recovered, which she did very quickly once she got out, she became deeply concerned about Amy's future because nobody on the outside would help her back on her feet.

Muriel was out in the fall. The drinking stopped as abruptly as if she had turned off a faucet, and near Christmas she came to me with a most unusual suggestion. We would take Amy out; she had talked with Dr. Mickey, the superintendent of the hospital, who had assured her that Amy was ready to go if she could get some help on the outside. I agreed. Muriel found a highly reliable nurse that was willing to live with Amy to help her. After two or three weeks at our home, over Christmas, Amy along with her companion, moved to Vancouver, British Columbia. She made a remarkable adjustment. Within a year she was on her own. She attracted a "boyfriend" of moderate means and substance. They spent many years together.

I have often said that I believe today Amy is the best adjusted of the whole Myers' clan on both sides of the family.

This episode is typical of Muriel's humanitarian qualities, for which she was widely admired. For Amy it must have been next thing to a miracle.

Chapter Twenty-one

FROM EDITOR TO PUBLISHER

Meanwhile, on another track, my career was forging ahead.

I knew what widespread readership I had in the oil industry and I was tempted to capitalize on it. There was in Calgary at the time a publication called *The Daily Oil Bulletin*. But this was daily news. Nowhere could one find a summary of the week's activities in the oil fields. There was a magazine called *Oil in Canada* which bought its material from *The Daily Oil Bulletin*, but it was in my view a non-magazine. It was published by the largest publishing house between Toronto and Vancouver, a stretch of some 3,000 miles, and it was a magazine that only went through the motions of being a publication. There was no meaning in it, there was no continuity in it. The editors would take handouts that came as news releases.

I had the idea that if I put our daily stories together in classifications in a Friday night publication that would hit the oil industry Monday morning they would take careful note of it and many of the executives, especially, would be grateful to see the whole week's activities there in front of them in easy form to find and read.

One Friday, while still at the *Albertan*, and borrowing with Mr. Bell's permission use of their multilith machine, I ran off a hundred or so copies of the actual product I would offer the industry. I distributed this to important personnel and was more than gratified with the resulting enthusiasm. It looked like a hit, no doubt.

178

So within two or three weeks I had rented separate quarters, bought a couple of typewriters, engaged Earle Gray and a couple of stenographers. From the very first day the subscriptions came pouring in by phone, mail, by telegram. We were off instantly to a great start. The price of such a publication which carried no advertising was quite high. I don't remember exactly what we charged but I do know that it was lucrative.

One thing leads to another and when I saw the instant success of this memeographed sheet I began to visualize a full-fledged oil magazine competing with *Oil in Canada* and two or three others who were patterned for advertising and who were taking in huge incomes compared with our small subscription income. I knew we were better and the oil industry knew we were better, so I reasoned we wouldn't have very much trouble in supplanting our competitors.

That was a big mistake in judgement. What I didn't do in my mind was to separate the advertising section of publishing from the editorial side. I thought it was simple. If you had the readers in the oil industry surely the advertisers would want to be in the magazine that was most widely read. What I didn't realize was that the advertisers really had no idea of the worth of a trade publication. They didn't understand the industry and they could care less. The agencies only would tell their clients that most client money was being placed in the **leading** magazines. Their greatest reference point was not editorial value but where their sales competitors were doing their advertising.

Now when you have an entrenched publication that has had the field to itself and has corralled all those advertisers who are interested in reaching the oil industry, you have an enormous job to convince the advertisers that the decision makers in the industry are reading your paper and have quit reading the other one. For instance, if you went to the advertising agency for the Bank of Montreal for a contract in the fall they were very likely to tell you that their competitors, The Royal Bank, and The Bank of Nova Scotia and all the other banks were running their ads in *Oil in*

Canada. Why should they go in your magazine. Obviously their competition unanimously thought *Oil in Canada* was the place to be.

This mistake in judgement very nearly cost me every cent I had as well as my home and the well being of my family. I entered into a slugging match with the odds stacked overwhelmingly against me.

I had started the magazine in early 1956. By year's end I saw that we needed something very BIG to change our image from that "new publication by a **lad** from the West" as our competition phrased it.

In Canada they have an auditing board, privately run, that will offer to guarantee your circulation and the circulation by categories to the industry. This board is highly regarded and advertisers depend on it. They are prepared to give an audited guarantee of circulation by classification of the magazine's recipients. For instance, they will guarantee that it is received by so and so many engineers, so and so many geologists, so and so many managers, etc. and throughout the classifications of the industry. These do not have to be paid subscriptions. In other words, the magazine can make up its mind to send a publication free if necessary to as many engineers as there are in the business, and so on. *Oil in Canada* had an ABC circulation. That meant paid circulation by categories. One expected that to be much lower than the CONTROL circulation where you sent to the numbers of people you wanted to.

I thought this out as an opportunity to get out in front with some of the advertisers and so we revamped our circulation and made sure that *OILWEEK* went to all of the bona fide engineers, geologists, geophysicists and drillers. We were able to get those names without too much trouble, and by simply paying the fee for the audit, the circulation would be accredited.

Of course ABC circulation speaks a lot louder, and the competition can argue convincingly that the "control" means nothing. **"It doesn't mean that anybody reads it.** It means they get it. They also get lots of other mail they don't look at," ran their argument.

But I thought that being an accredited member of the Circulations Board would give us a boost. In fact I was on a high about it. We would have the biggest circulation of any trade magazine in Canada.

I was so oversold that I approached my old friend, Barney Jones, the one who had to have about $25 to get his northern job about ten years earlier. I offered him $500 a month, which was at that time pretty good pay, and in addition a share in the magazine when it performed. I don't remember how big the share was, but I do know that I had nothing to offer him **UNLESS** the magazine performed. Of that I had little doubt.

"But nothing is so uncertain as a lead pipe cinch." This was another one of those. There was no doubt about the readership. There was no doubt about the great editorial superiority. There was no doubt about the numbers in the circulation. It all added up to no doubt. But afterwards you could add it up to say no doubt **except for one thing.** Without that it was all doubt. The one thing was **advertiser acceptance**.

I knew Jones was a good salesman. I figured he was about as good as they come, and with all we had going for us, it would be a great future for him and me both.

Everything was geared for the advertising season when the big agencies and corporations give out their advertising schedules for the coming year. The season came and went. All the good contracts had gone to other magazines. We were left with a few crumbs. We could pick up a little advertising locally but not enough to pay any substantial part of the costs.

I had been publishing the magazine through a print shop in Calgary. Soon after our CCAB acceptance I saw that we could not afford these bills. The printing bills were eating us alive. Unless costs went down or the advertising came we were headed straight for catastrophe. I got cost quotations on a printing machine that was big enough to do our job, and some other equipment. With that equipment I figured we could do the printing for about half the price. It was a German press. I forget its name. And I hope I never hear it again. We'd set up our print shop in the basement and such a God-frightening mess you never saw. The magazine was printed in sections of eight pages, four on the one side and four on the other. These had to be carefully made up ahead of time because sometimes page eighteen, say, would come next to page four in the paste up, and so on. We had one or two bad issues that way and I nearly had a fit. But apart from that the printing press turned out to be one of the seven horrors of the world. I could give you the other six if you were interested.

On Fridays I would come down into the print room and it was so fully stacked with crumpled pages of eight all over the floor and over the sides of the machine that you nearly had to paw your way in. What a mess!

I remember that in one issue we had been lucky enough to get a double page spread of a two color ad. These were facing pages. In producing this the printer has to print twice. He prints the colored section (in this case yellow) and then he runs it through and overprints the black section. Of course the negatives have to exactly match.

In this particular instance they had got the double page color on the wrong printing form and when the magazine came out some editorial copy was covered with blobs of yellow color all over it. On the other hand the copy for the two page color ad appeared without any color in it and where the color should have been there was nothing but glaring white space.

This wasn't very good ammunition with which to persuade the advertisers to give up the books they were in and to come with *OILWEEK*. All the competition had to do was get a few copies of our magazine and take it around and show it, asking potential advertisers if they would like some of that.

An unspeakable disaster!

Our biggest obstacle, however, remained what I have mentioned before, advertiser acceptance by the competitors. All of the advertising competitors were already in the other magazines. None was with ours. When could we expect to get some who were strong minded to go with a book because it claimed to be editorially superior?

The months passed on through the winter into spring and to summer. My resources were used up. Jones completely unaware of my financial situation, continued to do his best, but for some reason his best did not put the advertising in the book. The advertising which should have borne all expenses hardly paid for Jones' wages. We were coming to a desperate end. And something very big had to take place.

I fought these demons alone. I never mentioned these mortal dangers to my wife or to anyone at all. Jones knew nothing about the upcoming disaster. I sat down with it all alone. I knew we had the product. And I knew sooner or later truth would triumph. I knew quality would triumph. But could we survive until that day sometime later?

In the first place I couldn't afford to pay an advertising man $500 a month - at least until the advertising started to come our way. In the second place the quality of our book had to be improved to be the equivalent of the major media - as good as *Time* or *Newsweek* - or any other. Thirdly we had to produce this quality consistently, week in and week out.

The ultimate meaning of those conclusions was fairly simple.

Firstly, I couldn't afford to keep Jones. I already had taken every cent of personal resources including a $2,000 mortgage on my Lincoln which had been fully paid previously. I had to continue to pay my editorial help or we wouldn't have a book. I wouldn't take any money myself, but I had gotten used to that. I had earlier socked away a small personal fund for food and the minor essentials.

Even without Jones I was going to need money and I didn't know where to get it. I was also going to have to get in a new printing press, one that was proven and I had to get a man in the printing department who really knew his business if we were to get complicated four color process ads and do them ourselves. I would need quite a lot of money.

I remember the bitter turning point. I can never forget. It was the first day of the Calgary Stampede, and according to custom all employees were released to go down the streets to witness the Stampede parade. I sat alone in my office and looked at the mistakes in the previous book and pondered the absolute dearth of advertising. The only thing I could find that looked any good was the editorial content. And yet editorial content is the very heart of any magazine. What we were up against was some kind of a technicality that surely could be overcome - if we had the stamina to hold on. On this one of the blackest mornings in my life the telephone rang and the printer advised me that they could not typeset the magazine this week because the Stampede was on and everybody got off on Citizens' Day, Wednesday afternoon.

I remember sitting at my desk with my head on my arms and saying aloud twice, "God, I can't make it." And I actually cried.

But of course I had to make it. I had been in a hole **too deep** when I was a small boy and never had things looked blacker to me than they did that day. Now as a grown man I had unwittingly stepped into a hole again **"too deep."** I didn't have my dad to call on this time. What resource did I have?

In reality, I had the strongest resource of all. I had the best editorial content in Canada and probably a better editorial content than the big U.S. oil magazine, *The Oil and Gas Journal*. The question was not what I had but how to use it.

That afternoon I made the decisions. They were the major decisions of my lifetime; one personal and one business. On the one hand the business decision could save everything. On the other hand they could kill my future as an oil writer forever.

Chapter Twenty-two

BIG BOYS DON'T FOOL AROUND

The following morning I had to call Jones into my office. I had not faced a worse day in my whole life. Jones was my closest friend and I was about to fire him; I couldn't tell him the reason. It was cold-blooded murder.

To tell the truth, though, with the facts starkly clear, it was the best thing I could do for him. In another couple of months or so we would be out of business. We wouldn't have the dollars to pay the printing bill. Jones' job would be gone, so would our jobs, including my own. Jones would not be helped in finding a new position if he came from a magazine that had just gone bankrupt because it didn't have enough advertising to keep going. I knew all this. But he didn't, because I dare not let him know.

I know Jones would have been most sympathetic. But where was sympathy going to get us? When he went home he would have had to tell his wife the reason he was being let go. In their own self-defense, and even in my defense, they would be forced to say that Myers tried, but he just didn't have the funds to keep going. The other thing he could say was that Myers was a rotten son-of-a-bitch, had fired him without ample reason - that he didn't know why he had been fired. He was going to have to say one thing or the other.

I believed it would be more beneficial all the way around if Jones really thought I was a rotten son-of-a-bitch and presented it that way to the world. It would be better in the long run for him, and it would even be better for me.

Oil in Canada had been spreading the rumor that I was about to go broke. But their song was getting kind of thin after we had persevered month after month beyond our prophesied bankruptcy. If it happened now the little advertising we had would fall into their lap and we would be through. The last thing I needed was somebody to get out there and say, "Myers is nearly broke. It's doubtful if he can pay for another three or four issues." No, I could not let Jones know that!

So when I had steeled myself I asked him into the office. I had to tell him that he wasn't cutting the mustard, that I'd have to get somebody else in the advertising slot.

I don't want any more days like that one. Maybe MacBeth agonized at having completed the foul deed, and his wife never got over washing the blood off her hands. I don't think they felt much worse than I, as Jones left the office, pale and shaken.

My next job was to get some money. We had to have money and quite a bit of it if we were going to carry on until we could get the advertisers in. That was not a pleasant prospect either. All I had to offer was a stake in the future of *OILWEEK*. Over and above that, my reputation as a writer; anybody and everybody in the business would give me that. Yes, my biggest asset was my reputation. That was the route I had to go. So in the afternoon of that day I took a giant step. I put in a call to some people who were known in the East as fast operators.

In fact the principal operator, (I'll call him Henry Oaks) was rumored to be behind a murder in the Waldorf Astoria in New York City. There had been a bitter proxy fight over the ownership of a company and the man that got killed in the hallway of the hotel was the main competitor of Henry Oaks. Nothing was ever proven and nothing came out in the papers about it. But Oaks won the proxy fight.

Henry Oaks, through an aide of his, had told me on two or three occasions that if I ever needed any help be sure to call him.

I said to myself: "I guess the day has come. Here goes!" I got Henry Oaks' aide on the phone. One seldom got to talk to Oaks himself. I had met the aide before. I told him my dilemma and I told him frankly I needed money and that if I didn't have it the magazine would fold, and very soon. I told him I was prepared to offer a substantial equity of the magazine in exchange for capital and that I believed the necessary capital now, would repay the investment several times. The aide listened politely and I suppose intently because his first question was, "How much do you need?" I said: "Fifty thousand dollars."

Without an indication one way or the other, he said, "I'll get back to you."

I tell you these guys do business in a hurry. Within an hour this guy was back to me. He said; "We'll be glad to help you out on this and to supply the capital for you. Don't worry about the stock in your company. We are not interested in acquiring your stock."

Well - there was the money - right now. But what would be the price? If it wasn't stock - what? It wasn't any of my material belongings. In those days $50,000 was worth a quarter of a million dollars now. This was very substantial money. My mind was turning over at a high rate of revolutions per minute.

I recall now that Howard was the name of the aide. Howard continued, "Mr. Oaks thinks you should come down here to Toronto and we'll talk it over. We'll pay your expenses and reserve you a room at the Royal York for the day after tomorrow if that would suit you."

I needed some fast action but this was moving a little faster than I liked. I felt I didn't dare at this stage decline and I couldn't see how going down there would put me in jeopardy. I had to get the answer. I was up against it.

I hedged slightly. "Can you give me some kind of an idea of what you will want from me?"

"Well - I really don't think we should discuss this over the telephone. Mr. Oaks believes that we ought not to rush this arrangement but sit down together and kick it around. I want to stress with you that you will be under no obligation. Mr. Oaks thinks very highly of your publication and your ability. He wants to help you. What about day after tomorrow - that will be Thursday - can you make that?"

"Yes," I said, "I'll make it."

When I put the phone in its cradle I found I was trembling ever so slightly. I was on the verge of a very big step. It could be my salvation or my damnation. The promise of such a sum of money, available that swiftly, scared me, and if I gave it much thought it scared me a lot more.

I hurriedly got enough material ready for a small magazine that week and left Earle Gray and the others to fill in the blanks. I offered no explanation as to where I was going or why.

As we deplaned in Toronto I was met by a man carrying a placard boldly spelling out the name Myers. When I stopped he told me he was Mr. Oaks' personal chauffeur and he was driving me down to the Royal York Hotel. At the desk I found the room was already assigned to me and there was a note saying that Mr. Oaks and Howard Statsky would like to have dinner with me at about 7:00 P.M. and if this was not satisfactory to advise them, and it gave me the phone number.

It was one fine room. I was getting the red-carpet treatment, and it was happening too fast; I didn't know what to make of it. It was going to cost me. I felt pretty lonely in this world.

Oaks was a good looking man, a powerful man in his countenance, though only of moderate size. Probably 5'10". He had solid character lines across his forehead and deep horizontal lines down his cheeks. Those lines hadn't come from laughing. But I was struck at once with his magnetic personality. Howard Statsky was what you would expect him to be, a pale reflection of the man at the top, obviously the assistant, obviously a good one too, obviously secure.

At dinner we spoke generally about the oil situation in Western Canada, some of the great plays that had been made up there, some of the great discoveries, prospects for many more, and in what areas the prospects might lie. I found them both well read, intelligent, and on top of all the latest information. I knew that Oaks as a professional promoter had been in serious trouble with the Ontario Securities Exchange. There was big suspicion, but **no one** had been able to pin any wrongdoing on him to this point. Yet it was known back in Calgary, or at least believed, that Oaks had made millions out of shady deals in mining and in oil.

After dinner, in their suite, we sat down to talk around a bare table. Two other men joined us and in a corner at the back of the room next to a telephone sat a secretary with a shorthand book.

I had never experienced anything like this and I was baffled at the treatment. And increasingly apprehensive. As we talked, however, the apprehension began to disappear. Oaks laid his cards squarely on the table. I had a feeling he was shooting straight.

"I might as well tell you, Myers, we expect to make money out of you, and in the same breath I want you to be assured that we will not ask you to do anything you don't want to do. We'll put up your $50,000 the moment you need to set your publication on its feet. We're buying leases in central Alberta and we expect a company of ours will join the exploration on a very interesting tract near the Stettler Oil Field. You have already written very favorably of the prospects in this. All we will ask of you is that you write of these prospects just as you would write of them had you not known us. You will have the money, but if you don't believe in our prospects you don't have to write about them at all. You can wait until we have a prospect that you do believe in. We're in for the long haul."

"You know," I said, "that sounds almost too good to be true. I have to tell you that while I have the largest circulation of any oil magazine it is not a **paid circulation**. Many of these copies are sent out free and audited by the Canadian Circulations Audit Board. These people are all industry people; not many invest- ment people. I don't believe what I would write would be a great use to you in promoting your company - even if I liked it."

Oaks said: "That isn't quite the plan. We want you to

produce an investment newsletter that can build up a large circulation, and you can use this newsletter any way you want, and we do not want any of your stock in payment. We do want a friendly vehicle that will carry our story, written up as favorably as possible, according to your own judgement. Do you find any difficulty with that?"

"No, I don't find any difficulty," I said, "and I can see where under the conditions, where your promotion will get the boost you need in order to put up this kind of capital for me. I can see the place for a new publication as an ADVISORY on oil stock investments. But it would take a long time to get a letter started and build up enough circulation to do you very much good. Frankly, I'm puzzled to know where you're going to get your value out of it when you hand over $50,000 to me."

"Just a minute. We're not handing anything over to you. We are merely advancing this money and we have the faith that you will do well enough that you can pay every cent of it back. If in the meantime we can be helped with our own business along the road and if we can also profit, I don't think you or anyone else can find objection to that."

My God, I tell you I was sweating; not on the surface but underneath my skin. I knew the reputation of these boys. Out West I had been told "these guys play rough." And not being able to find signs of the roguishness attributed to them unsettled me. What was I getting into?

"The only thing that bothers me," I said, "is the time it would take to get an influential circulation of a couple of thousand readers at least."

"Myers," said Oaks, "we expect you to have at least 5,000 readers and maybe double that! That is where we come in. We will get you the subscribers. We have experience in that line. Is there anything wrong with that - as you see it?"

How could there be anything wrong with it? But if they were going to get that kind of circulation surely they would demand a big interest in the *Investment Letter*, if not in *OILWEEK* itself.

"But you'll have to have a very large interest in the newsletter?" I asked.

"As a matter of principle, we don't want to take ownership positions in any publication. We are contented to do what we can with the success of our companies, for the benefit of our shareholders, and we are contented to have you keep the profits from your writings. You're a publisher and we're promoters. We like to keep that separate."

I noticed the secretary had picked up the phone and now she put it down and came over and laid a piece of paper in front of Mr. Oaks on the table. Oaks turned to her and said, "Send this message right away, fast wire. 'We accept your offer for our purchase of the mineral rights in the south half of section 21, township 22, range 10, west of 4th. Funds will be wired to your bank upon our receipt of wiring instructions from you.' "

The steno asked, "For your signature, Mr. Oaks?"

"For the signature of Roger Carson. You just wire it out over Carson's name as president of Midwestern Petroleums.

"Myers, you'll probably want to think about this. Why don't you have a good night's rest and we'll meet tomorrow for lunch. If we can make an arrangement that will be beneficial to us all we'll go ahead with it." Oaks turned to his men, "Don't you think so?"

Of course they all thought so.

I didn't get the sleep I had intended. The stakes were big for me. My whole past and future were tied up in *OILWEEK*. I didn't want to get in a mess, down another hole. My dad wouldn't be around to pull me out of this one. I was scared but I had no other way of getting the money. How could Oaks have such a bad reputation? The impression he made on me was very good. Was I being sucked into a whirlpool? I was just a kid from the farm, a greenhorn. I opened the window of my room and I felt a chill with the wind. But I would have felt the same chill if the wind had been warm.

The next morning at breakfast I made up my mind that I would go along with any proposition that didn't require me to participate in something crooked, or that didn't require me to tell anything but the entire truth as I saw it. Under those terms I would go forward, and perhaps save the life of *OILWEEK*. I would make those terms quite clear.

As we entered for the meeting at one o'clock, Oaks looked at his watch and said, "I'm sorry. I only have about half an hour today. Howard, will you order a quick sandwich up. What will you have, gentlemen?"

When they had ordered Oaks looked at me, "Did you come to any conclusions?"

"I've come to the conclusion, Mr. Oaks, that I will be willing to work with you if I am not asked to write anything I would not otherwise write about any prospective oil territory or about any particular company. That is my only reservation."

Oaks stood up, "Then we have made a deal," he said. He thrust forth his hand, "In front of these men as witnesses, I guarantee your condition. And I believe we will have a mutually happy association and one that is highly profitable to us both, and profitable to the people who will read your new publication. I think we should agree on a name, maybe say; *'Myers Oil Investor'*?"

I was on the spot. Almost without my knowing it we had come to a deal. I had made the offer and asked for the guarantee and he had responded affirmatively and guaranteed the guarantee. I had to either shake hands on the deal or withhold my hand and kill the deal. On what grounds could I do that?

I shook hands. "We've got a deal."

Oaks came around to my side of the table, then put his hand on my shoulder, "This will work out well for you. You're a great writer and we're happy to be associated with you. But I believe it best, and I'll make this my overall condition, no word or mention in the slightest form of any arrangement between us should be breathed to anyone. That will be better for you, and it will be better for us. Look," he said, glancing at his watch, "I've got to go. Howard, you better come with me. The rest of you fellows, finish your lunch there and give Mr. Myers any assistance he needs, make the arrangements to wire $50,000 from the Y account to his bank in Calgary."

Oaks left. I couldn't eat any lunch. I asked to be excused on the basis that *OILWEEK* was going to press and I had to make a call.

When I got into my room I sat down at the desk looking out the window at the towers and said out loud, "Jesus Christ!"

Chapter Twenty-three

HONEST CROOKS

When I got back to Calgary I made things happen in a hurry. The first thing I did was to engage a first class print shop foreman by the name of Cliff Petley. I never had a man who knew his job better. Petley was a printing wizard. When I once heard in later years that there was a flood of counterfeit money on the market I said facetiously, "Look for Petley. If there's anyone in the Canada that could do it, it would be Petley."

Not that Petley was involved, I'm sure. But what a printer!

He soon had us set up so we could do four color process ads with the fully equivalent appearance of *Time* magazine. In swift order we got a printing press, a linotype machine where we could set our own type, a collating machine which had about eight stations on it and on Fridays there would be one girl at each station shifting batches of *OILWEEK* into the next batch, and finally when it ended the magazine would come out with the cover on it stapled and ready to cut.

We had to order an expensive cutter, but with that we were ready to go. All we needed now was the advertising.

We were set up in ample new quarters of about 2,000 square feet on the basement floor. First off we installed a Swedish Chief printing machine and a few months afterwards a second Swedish Chief. Ever after that when *OILWEEK* came out it was professional to the point where it could match any production in North America. We did it by offset photography in which the type is transferred from the linotype into proofs and these images are photographed and then burnt into metal sheets which then fitted onto the press. Since sometimes there were two or three runs of color on the same form they all had to match within about a thousandth of an inch. Just to look at the book when it was finished was a lift in itself.

I think our first issue under the new setup must have been a dreadful shock to *Oil in Canada* who had been whispering that *OILWEEK* was soon going to fold. Now they got the backlash. Advertisers, picking up the new book, remarked; "It doesn't look to me much like this book is going to fold." That didn't put us over the hump but it sure made a good start.

Additionally, I started the financial paper called *Myers Oil Investor*. It was a pretty good hit of its own accord as in those days there were thousands of people in Canada and the United States interested in investing in the Canadian oil picture. Of course I didn't have a large circulation because I didn't know how to get to the crowd and I didn't have the money for that kind of promotion. Anyway it was a secondary issue with me.

My own staff hardly knew what to make of the change. I guess they came to the conclusion that I had decided it was time to put my full assets behind the future of *OILWEEK*. They never knew that I had a hard-up moment through the whole process.

Early in the game my friends in Toronto phoned to congratulate me on the new paper, *Myers Oil Investor*. They believed my stories had been excellent . My analysis of the different oil plays had been right on and my recommendations on investing in different corporations in the oil industry had been perceptively keen.

I now boosted our *OILWEEK* classified circulation to about 9,000. It was a hot book because by using the offset process I was able to include news up to the last moment. The full magazine was prepared Thursday night except for an eight page green section that would be four pages in front and four in the back. These green colored pages were typewritten pages with the urgency of a Kiplinger Letter. The first page was called the "Oilgram" and I always wrote that myself, bringing into focus the events of the full week. On page two we had the late news and, although we mailed starting Friday noon, we could include these Friday morning stories. In the back of the book we had the new locations in the oil industry throughout western Canada right up to Friday noon. We were able to do this because of the offset process. I pioneered the printing of a slick paper magazine by the offset process in Canada. There was no other like it. Today scores of magazines are printed on slick paper by the offset process.

We began to get a swell in local advertising soon after our revitalization and reorganization. This early improvement came from advertisers who understood the oil industry and who knew that our readership among the industry was far out ahead of anything else.

To prove this I had a trust company make a random survey of 2,000 names which they themselves picked out of oil industry personnel names with questions which oil magazine do you read, *Oil in Canada, The Western Oil Examiner, OILWEEK, Canadian Oil and Gas Industries, or the Oil and Gas Journal* out of Tulsa. Please rate the magazines by your preference.

From the very first the *Western Oil Examiner* fell way to the bottom and the *Canadian Oil and Gas Industries*, which was a technical book, took a fall. There was also another small book called the *Roughneck* and it took a fall. But in overall readership the *Oil and Gas Journal* of Tulsa, Oklahoma was still first. It was the virtual bible of the oil industry all over the world. In our early surveys only the *Oil and Gas Journal* and *Oil in Canada* were in the same territory with us. In about a year the surveys would show that *OILWEEK* had climbed way ahead of *Oil in Canada* and was now close on the heels of even the *Oil and Gas Journal*. Within a year the *Western Oil Examiner* had gone belly-up.

Canadian Oil and Gas Industries was a thick monthly magazine carrying loads of full page colored advertising. It was a job out of Montreal. Its essence was the technical papers given by the various technical groups in the oil industry in Alberta, including

196

papers on drilling, geology, engineering, oil completions. This magazine, called COGI for short, had the technical end of the industry pretty well tied up. They had come into the game early and they had gone around to the various technical societies and offered to publish their papers free if they could have the exclusive right to publishing the papers. By the time I had got *OILWEEK* on its feet COGI had a monopoly on all technical papers. This was important because the technical people in the oil industry were also the people who made the decisions such as what drilling company to use, what seismic company to use, and right down the line. I tried but I couldn't break in.

I knew we had to get in there if we were going to be the complete book for Canada and I devised a way. I found out that during the war the Germans had had a covert taping device. The device was in a small case which I could place in my breast pocket and it was connected by a cord down the sleeve of my arm to my wristwatch. This was however, not your ordinary wristwatch. This wristwatch was the microphone. I would get a seat right close to the speaker presenting the scientific paper and then bring back the tape to the office. It was on very fine wire and the steno had to be most careful with it. But by this time I had two excellent stenos. I was amazed to find out that they were able to get every word out of these technical papers. I got a new sensitive camera to take pictures of the maps and graphs as they were projected on the screen, which I produced along with the text in *OILWEEK*.

COGI was the next magazine to get a shock. They never could figure out how I got the papers. The authors of the papers denied they had given them to us. But here they were appearing every week, the most up-to-date, the most technical information in the oil industry. In all its years *Oil in Canada* had never got a smell of that material.

Here was COGI publishing this magazine once a month and most of the papers were about a month behind, basically because COGI didn't have to be in any rush. Now here came *OILWEEK* publishing the papers within a few days. If a paper had been given on a certain week it was in *OILWEEK* by Friday. COGI had come to the end of the line. It came out with the same papers that *OILWEEK* had published, six weeks to two months later. I believe that before the end of that year COGI folded. Somewhere along in there also the *Roughneck* folded.

In our next batch of surveys we had passed *Oil in Canada* by a wide margin and we were right neck in neck with the *Oil and Gas Journal*. I think most of this happened in 1958. In the fall of that year I personally took over the advertising responsibility.

I knew that in order to get the Bank of Montreal in Eastern Canada, or Goodyear Tire or many of the other accounts not strictly related to oil, I would have to get the prestige advertisers in oil. In order to get to them you had to get to the leading agency which was Rives Dyke and Company in Houston. In time for the fall budgets I made my first trip to Houston.

I had arranged ahead of time to get an interview with Mr. Rives, the president of Rives Dyke. As a man of his word, he received me personally when I came in. I got to the point pretty fast.

I had with me our recent issues of *OILWEEK* and the corresponding issues of *Oil in Canada*, and I had the latest annual review of the oil industry in *OILWEEK* and the latest review of the oil industry by *Oil in Canada*.

Mr. Rives was the most knowledgeable oil advertiser I ever met. I could talk to him about anything and he understood what I was saying. I showed him the reader surveys, but I realized that the surveys in themselves were not quite good enough. So I went into comparison of the two books. I compared them story by story and the result for *Oil in Canada* was awful; they were so pitifully behind us they weren't even in the running. Then I showed him the annual review of the two books side by side and even to my own surprise I found that a lot of the material in *Oil in Canada's* review was from the year before. I had these all marked in both books and I believe the story was an avalanche. I decided to give it both barrels.

Mr. Rives had listened intensely without saying anything. I was ready to make my closing statement. I said: "Mr. Rives, I know it's considered to be poor policy to run down one's competitor. But the truth is the truth, and the truth for you is that you are sitting here confident that thousands of dollars of your clients' money are getting the best results possible. The truth that you have to ask yourself is; who is reading this magazine?

"I don't care what they say about me, I know you didn't get these clients just by being a nice guy. You got them by your ability to pick the potent media. And I have shown you a story here that I don't think you will ignore or even that you can afford to ignore. This is the book, Mr. Rives, that the oil industry is reading and I think I have proven it to you. I'm sorry to say this but you might as well be throwing much of your money away as putting it into *Oil in Canada*. And that's the TRUTH! I'm sure you recognize that what I have shown you today **is the TRUTH!"**

Mr. Rives had remained mostly silent throughout the interview with barely a question to ask. Now in a manner of some relaxation and he said simply, "You've sold me."

He called in the account executives of Hughes Tool, Reed Roller Bit, Schlumberger, and a great number of other leading clients in the American oil industry. He said to the account executives, "Mr. Myers has gone over his book with me and I am convinced that this is the book we should be in up there. Make your arrangements with him for most of our advertising up there and reserve as many covers on the magazine as you can."

That was music! The covers were the big paying thing. A page in *OILWEEK* cost $185 but a cover cost $500 and if it was two or three colors it could cost $700. More important was this fact: **BIG NAME ADVERTISERS had come into *OILWEEK*.**

We didn't make it all in a single year, but when the big ads started coming out January 1, 1959 our competitors must have had a heart attack. They were still carrying more pages of advertising than we were in 1959, but this had been like a panzer thrust in the Battle of the Bulge, the difference being that the

Germans ran out of steam but we picked up steam.

Meanwhile, during this course of about nine months or so *Myers Oil Investor* had been going along quite smoothly with nothing very much exciting happening. Then I got a call from my friends in Toronto and Howard Statsky, Mr. Oaks' top aide, said he was coming out to see me. I thought, "Uh-oh, now we're going to find out what I have to do!"

I had an indication a few days before his arrival what it was about. Midwestern Oils had announced a wildcat well nicely located on the Western side of the Stettler field. Stettler was a good field, it was a coral reef field. It had good quality oil and Gulf Oil had been the explorer to drill it. Before Howard Statsky ever got there I had a story in my desk on this stepout. Midwestern Oils had the mineral rights on three-quarters of a section. If the well were successful it would be **very** successful. Of course no wildcat is ever a guaranteed success and if it were not successful it would be a story similar to Leduc Consolidated.

Howard filled me in on their coming announcement, including the fact a drilling rig would start making hole in about two weeks. He said if I thought it was a good prospect this is the one they would want me to write up and recommend.

There was no doubt about it. This was a part of our deal and now it was my turn to deliver. Howard asked me if I looked upon this prospect favorably and I said of course I did. He said, "We're expecting to announce in about ten days and we are interested in the timing of the announcement and we'd like this story of yours to come out in your next issue." Actually that was giving me about ten days. He asked me if I had any objections and I said I had not.

I asked Howard when he expected me to start paying off the $50,000. He said he hoped I would make enough on this deal to nearly cover it. The stock was selling at 75 cents a share; Howard said they were offering me an option on 100,000 shares at that price. If things worked out well they would sell them for me and give me the difference. How could I complain? He said he hoped I would make money over and above the $50,000. They'd settle up after it was all over. I admit that in my mind there was a pretty big question mark.

Howard looked closely over our plant and the story went out to my employees that Howard was an efficiency expert from down East and that I had engaged him for the purpose of streamlining our operation.

The day came; Thursday prior to Friday publication of the investment letter. I got a call from Howard and he said he wanted us to run off some extra copies. They, of course, would pay the cost of the printing and he wanted us to send the copies fast air freight. I readily agreed. "How many?," I asked.

"Fifty thousand copies," said Howard.

That took my breath. Where in the world would they ever send 50,000 copies. And to think of the cost, even the postage involved!

Now I understand how they were able to do this. These people had lists or had access to huge mailing lists, including the names of people who were known to have invested in oil stocks. If such people got sold on what seemed to be a top-rate speculation they would start buying; there was only one way this stock was going. It depended largely on the strength of the writing. The promoters had huge blocks of escrow stock to unload.

"One more thing," said Howard, "we would appreciate your permission to print copies of your letter ourselves if we like the story."

I agreed. "How many?"

"Don't know. Could be substantial. Maybe a hundred thousand or so."

As I hung up the phone, I heard my own voice as if it were someone else's voice as it involuntarily said in a loud whisper, "Jesus Christ!"

* * * *

That was the beginning of some exciting days.

The announcement was made on schedule. I wrote it up and

it was published in *Myers Oil Investor* and we printed 50,000 copies and sent them to Toronto. On the following morning the announcement hit the tape and the market on Midwestern Oils started to move like nobody's business.

I know now what happened; I was somewhat naive at the time.

As soon as the sponsors had the letter which they knew would serve as their promotion to 50,000 known oil investors they began buying their own stock which of course put the market up, about 25 cents the first day. The next day it went up again and about a week later when the newsletters hit, large volumes started to come into the market from outside. Obviously the buying was widespread. Obviously my story had been a wringer although I had not written it for that purpose.

The well was spudded soon after and now the operators would have about two months to play with the stock; that is it would have periods when it could go up and go down and I felt quite sure that when it went up dramatically they would sell it down by selling from their own treasury's stock and if the market started to lag they would start buying and inject new adrenaline. Reports came in about the well's progress, its depth and so on and this was carried in my weekly *Myers Oil Investor*, but there was nothing either way, favorable or unfavorable in these reports.

I did keep readers posted as to where the payzone would be if there was a payzone and as that grew closer the price took off further. I had thought in my innocence that promoters would not want to sell such huge amounts. What if the well came in a real gusher? Now I realized they were going to win either way. If the well failed, which is always most likely with a wildcat, they would come out of this with very high prices for very big blocks. If the well should come in a gusher they would probably get the drilling reports before the press would get it and they would probably manipulate the market by selling, to put the stock price down, and then they would buy large quantities back again. This was supposition on my part and still is.

Then a shocking thing happened. It would be about a week ahead of the well's final answer in the Devonian zone. The stock started to tumble. It dropped from $1.80 to $1.35 in two or three days. Then a friend of mine came to my office and closed the door and said, "Boy, you should hear what stories are going on about this Midwest Stettler well."

"What is that? What stories?"

"Norm Jakes, the head broker at Carlyle and McCarthy said to some fellows there this morning, 'My God, I would never have believed it. Myers is in bed with Oaks.' Somebody asked him to explain and he said, "This is a typical Oaks' deal. Huge volumes, going up on rising prices and then when it gets to near the climax huge sell-offs involving hundreds and thousands of shares. This is an Oaks' deal if ever I saw one.'"

That left me speechless. There was nothing I valued so much as my reputation. And I had not said an untrue word. But I had unwittingly allowed myself to be used. And there was no way back out. But the well still had a week or two to go. As soon as my visitor left I picked up the telephone and I got Howard; I insisted on talking with Oaks himself. Remember, Oaks had the reputation of being a tough hombre and a damn dangerous one. I didn't know, and I still don't know, if I was putting myself in danger. But I was where I had to stand, come what may.

When Oaks came on the line I said: "Mr. Oaks, the story is going around Calgary and it will soon be in Toronto that you and I are in cahoots on a shady promotion on Midwestern Oil. I know that you have sold very large amounts of shares at very high prices and that now you are dumping off the remainder of your treasury stock on a promotional manipulation that is forbidden under the law. Now, by God, I'm telling you right now - you better reverse this market. If you don't, I'll publish this whole story. I'll announce your participation from the start, and my own participation as well.

"When I publish this story *OILWEEK* may go down the tube, and me with it, but I'll tell you one thing, you will go down the tube with us.

"And just in case - you should know the story is written up and is in my safety deposit box - if anything happens to me it will be in the next issue of *OILWEEK*. I expect to see that stock moving up by noon, Mr. Oaks." I hung up.

My office door was closed. I couldn't hear anything from outside, but I could hear my heart thumping. Oaks was no ordinary Joe and I didn't know how he would take it. But I know now why they had to take it. And why they had not wanted to own any shares of any publication; they didn't want their names on record. Couldn't afford it. I knew that I was on strong ground with my ultimatum because I knew they were in bad standing with the law in Ontario.

My call went in at about ten o'clock in the morning and within fifteen minutes of my call the Midwestern Oil stock started to improve. It rose 35 cents a share by the end of the day.

It was obvious that they had thrown money into the market now and that they had at least delayed the harvest they intended to reap. Throughout the week the price of Midwestern Oils continued to improve by slower amounts until it got back over $1.50. I was satisfied with that. People who had bought into it had seen it rise 100 or 200 percent in value and they had had their chance to sell out. They knew they were dealing with a wildcat and I had pointed out to them quite squarely that every wildcat is a gamble. Within the next couple of weeks the well was abandoned and the whole deal was over.

I wondered if I would ever get the cash difference in the options that they had set aside for me and the price at which they had sold those shares. I made up my mind I didn't care; I had come through with my obligation as I saw it. There was not a dishonorable word in all of my writing or an untrue word and I never heard another word or rumor connecting me with Oaks. The comeback of the stock had swept all that away.

After about two weeks I got a call from Howard, suggesting that I come to Toronto to settle up. I really didn't know what to expect, but I had to see it through. Just before leaving I got another call from Howard asking me to meet them instead, in Montreal, at the leading Montreal hotel. It was just one twenty-four hour party. Full meals were brought to about three or four rooms all adjoining, drinks flowed freely. Pretty young ladies trapsed about. There was song and laughter and not much of anything else.

Oaks did not come to the party, but three or four of his men were there. Howard confided to me, "We didn't bring the money up. There are too many crooks in Montreal." So they asked me to come down and meet them in Toronto the following day at a remote hotel. It was a good enough hotel, but it was not well known. I didn't know whether to regard this move with suspicion or confidence. Maybe Mr. Oaks wasn't taking my riot act with complacency. Maybe there would be a price to pay for that.

After I had checked in they phoned to say that they would be up after dinner about eight o'clock to settle up.

Almost on the button of eight Howard and an assistant knocked at the door. Howard was carrying a large briefcase which he laid on the coffee table. He said, "I'm going to give you an analysis of what took place."

I can't remember numbers, but I do know that whatever number of shares (I think it was 50,000) that they had set aside at 25 cents a share was represented in this accounting. They gave it to me item by item, sale by sale, date by date, including the exact moment of each transaction; so many shares at 85 cents on such and such a date, so many shares at $1.05 on such and such a date and time, etc. and throughout. They had the calculation on each line of figures and they showed it to me.

As I remember it came to about $95,000.

"Now," said Howard, "you owed us $50,000 on the equipment. The difference is $45,000. Do you agree with these figures?"

Of course I agreed with them. I had no way of knowing any different, but I will say their accounting seemed to be meticulously honest. When Howard saw I could find no fault he opened the briefcase on the table and there were the bills in the briefcase. He counted out the $45,000. They left as abruptly as they came. I found myself alone in the room wondering what in the hell had happened.

I wondered whether I would get knocked off before I reached an airplane and the money would be taken away from me. I advanced my departure date by a few hours for the following day. I put some chairs up against the door of my room. All of this made me feel very foolish because I thought it was superfluous but still I knew this was one tough hombre.

When it came time I got a taxi, traveled uneventfully to the airport, got on the plane and the next thing I knew I was getting off in Calgary and I was home for supper.

Chapter Twenty-four

OILWEEK - A NEW VIEW

Following the Toronto operation the future of *OILWEEK* was secure.

By 1960 the new readership surveys showed *OILWEEK* now ahead of the bible of the industry, the *Oil and Gas Journal*, out of Tulsa, and so far ahead of *Oil in Canada* that it was no longer a race. I still wanted something to put us far ahead of the Tulsa book and I felt I knew what would do it.

At the time OPEC (the Organization of Petroleum Exporting Countries) was in the formative stages. All of the excitement centered around the Middle East where oil was pretty well in the hands of the big majors, Texaco, Shell, Esso, Mobil, Gulf. That oil was selling on the world markets at around two dollars a barrel but those companies were able to find it and produce it at between five and ten cents a barrel, whereas the exploration cost in Canada was one dollar a barrel and exploration cost in the United States was near two dollars a barrel. North Sea oil had not yet been found and neither the fields of Mexico. I felt that there was a great need for an evaluation of how successful this new exporting group might be. If they could really get together there was no doubt in my mind that they could raise the price of oil steeply by withholding surplus deliveries. The conventional oil industry, both in the U.S. and in Canada, was to laugh the subject off. People said the Arabs can't get along among themselves for an hour, let alone get together on a cartel.

My next move was to arrange for a trip throughout western

Europe and as far as the Middle East.

I think my first trip may have been in 1960, the World Oil Show in Frankfurt and then the oil personnel in the Netherlands, where North Sea gas was just coming into production, and on to Rome; then to Beirut where many of the oil executives of the large companies were headquartered, then down to Cairo in Egypt and back through Libya which was then just coming on the scene as an important producer and finally back home.

Every successive issue of *OILWEEK* for some time carried these exclusive and highly comprehensive stories about what was going on in that part of the world. I had concluded that OPEC was a real danger and that they would form a pact along with Venezuela, which I had visited on my way over, and would strip the major oil companies of the United States of their ownership of Arab oil. They would let them share but this was going to be a new ball game; they were no longer willing to permit these foreigners to skim off their riches in return for peanuts.

These articles made a tremendous hit with the industry. They also made a hit in the United States for not even the *Oil and Gas Journal* had ever bothered to make an indepth report on the events in the Middle East. This gave *OILWEEK* a prestige that it never had before and could not have got in any other way. It was an exclusive bombshell. I don't think *Oil in Canada* knew what hit them.

Meanwhile I tried to make our magazine editorially better. I never judged the volume of editorial content by the amount of advertising. In the game you will see formulas laid out like two pages advertising one page editorial, and so if they only have twenty pages of advertising they will only give ten pages of editorial. I don't mean these as absolute figures but that's the way they work it. My policy was completely different. We would have all the news in *OILWEEK* if we didn't have one page of advertising and I developed the slogan

IF IT HASN'T BEEN IN OILWEEK IT HASN'T HAPPENED YET!

I was 48 years old. The future of *OILWEEK* was a foregone conclusion. But now with a fresh outlook, I saw that my time could not be permanently devoted to advertising. I had a big job to do as publisher. Constant innovations were needed, so I called in young Leon James for a memorable interview in my office. I asked Leon if he would like to become advertising manager.

Leon is a character hard to describe. He was then nineteen years old. He had come with me from being a busboy at the Palliser Hotel. At the time I was starting my first weekly publication I had a small job opening running the multilith. That is the machine that would print the typewritten sheets on a daily basis and on a weekly basis. Several young fellows came in to interview. I didn't know how to pick one. I developed this question for them all. "Tell me, do you really want this job?"

Leon's answer far excelled. He left no doubt in my mind that he wanted this job as he had never wanted anything. He was a refugee from Czechoslovakia and he had to get going on something that would offer a future in this country. He totally convinced me that he would give any job I gave him his utmost effort, and I also read in him a probable loyalty which I did not often see in the early stages with anyone else.

Leon did a great job on the printing and soon I had him writing some formula development well stories. That is, I would construct a sentence announcing a new well and all he would have to do would be to use that same sentence every time substituting the new locations, the new names, the new interests and so on. It got to where he was writing up all the development well stories. Later he graduated to writing the wildcat well starts. Wildcats were much more interesting than development wells of course. They held out promise of a new field. Everyone watched the wildcats and so there was more to say, and those writeups required a little more editorial know-how. Leon never had outstanding editorial ability, but he had the utmost ability in accuracy. He was so conscientious that I began to develop a faith that whatever I asked him to do he would do well.

One time when my mother was having a hard time getting a driver's license I asked Leon if he would go up with her to the testing office and see if he could help her get a license. I asked him to take her around the block a few times and tutor her.

I never expected my mother to get a license. Most of the time she drove like she was out in the middle of a quarter section. She would stop at a stop light but only so long as she thought was necessary. When she thought it was time to go, pedestrians scattered like chickens. On one occasion, reported to me by a friend, a cop stood at a criss-cross intersection in Calgary, red lights on both sides. After a little while my mother just drove through. The cop's jaw dropped, as he stood there, motorists transfixed by the spectacle.

Leon returned, and by God, my mother had a driver's license. I couldn't believe it. However, Leon let me know that there was a very nice briefcase in one of the stationary stores that he had been admiring. I was so amused that I bought him the briefcase.

One other time on the occasion of some domestic trouble Leon approached my wife in the car outside the office and asked her how things were going at home these days. I was furious when I heard about it and I called him in. I said, "Leon, I hear you're very concerned about my domestic situation."

Poor Leon! A beet is red but never as red as Leon in those few seconds. He seemed to be gasping for air when he left the office. He got hold of my editor, Earle Gray and said, "I'm sure Mr. Myers is going to fire me."

Leon was operating smoothly in his job in the editorial department when I called him in about advertising. We had had so many advertising men that the mortality rate was legend. At the moment we didn't have anyone because I had been riding herd on that for some months myself. I felt all we needed now, since we had the prestige advertisers, was a very hard working and determined person and I thought Leon could do the job, although I'm sure by most people's judgement he would never have been offered the job as advertising salesman.

Leon changed color for the second time that I knew him, first a little pale, then pink. He said in a subdued voice, "Mr. Myers, either you are joking or you are getting ready to fire me."

I assured him that I had no intention of firing him, that he was one of the best people we had, and that I really believed he could work himself into the slot as advertising manager. I think my confidence in him did a lot for him. And I never regretted that day.

He told me later that on his first trip to Toronto he passed the glass doors on one of the skyscrapers five consecutive times before he got the nerve up to go in and see those captains of ivory advertising at the top. Many clients were amused at Leon, but mostly they gave him their business. After I sold *OILWEEK*, later on, Leon went on with Maclean Hunter who had bought the magazine and became the publisher eventually of its largest trade book in the electronic industry. He's still there.

One day Leon came in very upset. He had heard that *Oil in Canada* had made a complaint to the Canadian Circulations Audit Board that our circulation reports were unreliable and that we had hood-winked the board into figures which we did not have. In another day or two I got a communication from the Audit Board that we had been suspended. More serious news at advertising budget time could not be imagined.

I never will know just what *Oil in Canada* used to convince the Audit Board that we were hood-winking them. But it was absolutely untrue. We stood behind every name on our circulation list. I had to go to Montreal to attend a meeting of the top members of the board authorities to convince them of the error of the reports they had received and to once again support every circulation figure we had published. I got them to agree with me and after a couple of months which had been very serious for us I was able to send a telegram to all of our prospective advertisers, between two and three hundred, "Audit Board suspension lifted today."

I had been in touch with the advertisers anyway but I sent this wire with a great deal of relief. That is until the next morning when

I began to get telephone calls from seemingly everywhere. "What on earth does this mean?" a few of the big advertisers asked. "Audit Board suspension listed today."

I said, "Listed?"

"Yes," he said, "Listed."

"My God," I said, "it's a telegraph company mistake. The 's' should be an 'f'."

They had already known we were suspended and now this telegram was telling them that the suspension was listed today. I had to send out repeat wires to all of the clients saying the telegraph company had made a typographical error and the suspension in fact had been completely lifted. That is, cancelled.

It was a pretty horrifying experience and the last time *Oil in Canada* was ever able to do me much harm. From then on it was cut and slash to the bitter end.

Chapter Twenty-five

AFRICAN SAFARI

Before leaving this phase of my life, I feel I should write a brief account of a period of a few weeks which qualify as one of the most pleasurable periods, a release from the seemingly unending battle.

My work since the inception of *OILWEEK* had brought me to a state of exhaustion. Maclean Hunter, which is the Canadian reflection of the huge American publishing company McGraw-Hill, had been pestering me to sell *OILWEEK* to them. As their bids got higher my resistance declined. It was reaching the point where while it was something I didn't want to do, it was creating an internal conflict because of the increasing size of the offers they were making. I didn't want to make a decision. I just wanted to get away from it.

I was many years this side of my father's death and I knew now that I had become a man. No one stood between me now and disaster, material or spiritual. Nowhere in the world was there a protector, or would there ever again be a protector, to pull me out of the hole. I was now the protector. I would have to live with my mistakes, and my decisions were irreversible. I faced alone all the fears, the imagined fears and the dangers that bedevil us from the womb 'til we enter the grave.

We are launched in this arena of life without our permission. We are thrown on the vast sea; the only options we are given are sink or swim. We didn't ask for life, but we have to deal with it. We keep on swimming until we can't swim any longer. Then we sink. Whether our swim has been notable or notorious or a thing of little consequence, one way or the other, is measured by what we leave behind us.

What we leave is sometimes measured solely by material things, the money, the securities, the houses, and the automobiles. These material residue are generally not an impressive mark. In fact when they are all totaled up the swimming seems hardly to have been worthwhile. A man can make a billion dollars and if that is all that can be said of him, his place in history will be very small, if indeed there is room eventually for even his name.

My father left little in the way of material things, not enough to matter. But as a person, as a father, he cut quite a swath. His integrity, his simplicity, his forthright nature, and his ability spiritually to stand against all storms were among the highest values that we can strive for. His enormous common sense against all the tempests of nonsense, against the madness of fads and fashion, translated into security, long years after he was gone. It was now my turn to fill those shoes. But I was very tired.

Luckily, I had some money. In the fall of the year when *OILWEEK* had undoubtedly turned its final corner I took off on a safari to Africa. I took my younger brother with me. Richard was about 30 years old. I think this trip showed better returns than any other investment I have made.

The trip to Africa was a trip backward in time. At least I felt we were seeing the human race at a time much nearer its beginnings. We traveled by truck both in Zambia and through the veldt of Mozambique. I'd had visions of teeming thousands. I was totally surprised at what I found. Miles and miles of uninhabited lands and then occasionally here and there a village of thatch huts. Not a village as we envision it, mind you, just thatched huts.

There was no store in these villages, no meeting halls, no schools, nowhere ever a hospital. Doctors, other than the witch doctor, had hardly been heard of, much less used. Each hut housed a family which could easily number eight to ten. There were no partitions, no rooms. Thatched grass served as bedding. The floor was dirt. There was no evidence of any fire having been kindled in any of the huts. The climate was warm enough to make it unnecessary. Here and there the odd pig. How they shared the pig, and who was lucky enough to get some of the meat, I never understood. For a living they grew maize. With a kind of a horizontal hatchet blade the women chopped up the ground, sowed and reaped the maize. I never saw the men do anything. I did learn that they poached animals when they could. Once in a while they would get an elephant. Their method of shooting an elephant was to shoot him in the knee with a shotgun. This would bring the great beast down. Then they would dive in with their spears.

Wrapping paper was a novelty to the children, even brown paper. But the glossy metallic like paper used as wrapping for cigarettes in packages was an absolute novelty and a marvel. In all those journeys I never saw a girl. I saw children up into the age of 12 or 13. Any girl that age or over was pregnant or already had children. Africans I met were irresponsible. They could not usually be counted on. If they quit it was often at a crucial time.

One day the hunting party came across a herd of elephant. The elephant is about the only animal in Africa to strike fear into the heart of a white hunter. Many have been killed by elephants. The elephant is the only animal that will rise up in defense of its kin and even take revenge. We were moving along through heavily wooded country and on the track of elephants, numerous elephants. Their spoor was fresh and in their wake they had knocked down great trees.

All of a sudden in front of us, a barrage of shooting. I believe the white hunter himself had lost his head. I'm not sure. But all of a sudden a great many elephants crossed in front of us. They were moving very fast and I saw that if I was going to get an elephant in Africa I would have to take what I could. I fired and hit a medium sized animal, evidently in the lungs. At the time I couldn't tell that I had hit anything. The beast just kept running with the rest. They were moving forward around one of those giant anthills, which in Africa can be over 15 feet tall. We stopped momentarily. Then all of a sudden the silence was broken by the wildest sound I ever heard. The trumpeting of a charging female elephant. She charged our party three times before she was finally silenced.

We moved forward cautiously around the anthill and there lay the female elephant, head to head with the elephant I had shot. My elephant had been hit in the lung and had bled profusely. The female, which turned out to have been pregnant, in protection of her kin had turned on her tormentors. Now she raised her head and tried to stagger to her feet. At that moment the white hunter's gun bearer, who had been given the care of the gun when the shooting was over, took off for the high timber. I'm sure the ground he covered in a few seconds would have given him a gold medal at the Olympics. He had the gun with him. The white hunter was left with just his hands.

Of course there were enough of us and we had no trouble with the wounded elephant. But it was an emphatic lesson and in some ways makes understandable the whites' reluctance to put blacks in positions of utter responsibility. What could be more important to a hunter than his gun in the jungle?

Some days later I had a similar experience. I had been tracking an eland. That is the biggest antelope in the world. My gun bearer was with me, but I had held onto the gun myself, and finally I got a shot at the eland. I was heaving from exertion so heavily that the gun wavered terribly. Nevertheless I fired and missed. When I turned it was to face two lions who had been in the bush not more than forty yards to the side of my track. They had been mating there and it's rather amazing that they didn't attack me.

Instead they took off running through the high grass. I fired several shots at the male lion, but missed every time. The party, hearing my firing, knew that my gun was empty and knew that we were in lion country. They came racing across the veldt, the truck bouncing and banging and thumping. My wave to the white hunter was a huge relief to him, I'm sure. A while later after the lion pair had split we got the male lion. I can see him yet sitting up like a huge dog, glaring at us. It was as if to say, "What the hell are you doing here?" That night there was a great native celebration, an habitual ceremony with drums and dancing whenever a lion is killed.

We were gone for over a month and got one of most of the animals we had licenses for, including Cape buffalo, wildebeest, hartebeest, sable antelope, eland, wild boar, zebra, and two or three other more obscure type of antelopes.

We got those all in about two weeks, our first effort having been aborted when we found out I had been taken in by a pair of crooks in the original contract and they had led us into Zambia to an area where there seemed to be no game whatsoever. We discovered the hoax in time to make an issue out of it by luckily catching a panel of justice authorities that visit these villages at long intervals. The crook, posing as a white hunter, terribly embarrassed, promised to give our money back. I made him tell us the name of his bank and the address and forced him to send them a wire directing them to pay us the something like $5,000 that he had. I wrote the wire.

We made extraordinary fast time from Zambia to Salisbury in South Rhodesia and were there promptly at the opening of the bank. A minute later we were in the office of the manager as he opened the telegram he had received the day before. Hardly had he done so than he received a wire from the phony hunter cancelling out his first. We told the manager our story and luckily for us he agreed the first telegram had precedence and that it had been acted upon as soon as he received it in our presence.

That made it possible for us to go on another safari under a well known white hunter in Mozambique headquartered at the Port of Beira in Mozambique, Portugese East Africa about 500 miles from Salisbury. His name was Alleregua; they called him "one shot Alleregua." He was very upset to find a story in the paper a few days after we got there headlined "One Shot Alleregua Shoots Lion in Foot." Apparently on one of his hunting parties either he or someone in the party had actually shot a lion in the foot. Alleregua was not amused.

Getting to the hunting spot was not uneventful. We drove with our travel agent about 180 miles from Salisbury, Rhodesia to a place called Umtali near the Portugese border. We successfully caught the train out of Umtali bound for Beira in Mozambique. Unfortunately, after we had gone down the side of a winding mountain track I couldn't locate my passport. The Portugese Immigration man couldn't understand a word of English. It seemed like the only English words he could speak were, "You back Umtali." My brother wanted to go back with me but I urged him to stay on the train and get us settled in Beira which was about another 300 miles on and and I told him I would be there the next morning. It didn't work out just that way.

I felt that the passport which had been in my back pocket had slipped down in the seat of the car the travel agent had used to drive us to Umtali. If I could reach them I would have it somehow sent on by hired messenger.

When they threw me out of the train at Umtali it was pitch black and there were some kerosene lanterns on a long station platform and a few blacks who didn't speak English loitering around the lanterns. A freight train puffed up and slowly snorted forward in the opposite direction, and they all motioned toward the freight train and shouted at me. I ran as fast as I could. I caught the freight train. I was on my way back up the mountain.

I found myself in a semi-enclosed car as the old engine belched heavy smoke and soot and it was nearly midnight when I got back to Umtali. At the platform I had seen a telephone and somehow I had managed to unearth an operator in Umtali. I asked them to have a taxi for me at the station in Umtali to meet the freight which would be coming in. I didn't know who I had on the line but I must have spoken very convincingly for when I got off the freight train and started to hike down a lonely railroad track towards the station I was overtaken by a black man shouting and gesticulating wildly. I figured this must be the taxi man that they had sent. So I showed him money and somehow I got it across to him that I wanted to go to every hotel in town. I thought I might still contact the travel agents.

As luck would have it, of course, they had already gone back to Salisbury. I got a room in the hotel but they told me I couldn't phone out. The switchboard would be closed. I made a little personal arrangement with the operator and for some dollars, I don't remember how many, I arranged for her to leave the switchboard connected with my room. I couldn't remember our travel agent's name but I thought it was Brain. By about two or three o'clock in the morning I managed to get the Salisbury operator to put me in contact me with a Mr. Brain. Man, was he mad! Mr. Brain had never heard of the travel agency.

But early next morning I got a phone call from Salisbury from the wife of the travel agent in Salisbury and she said, "Mr. Myers, did you lose your passport? This is Mrs. **Blaine**."

Mrs. Blaine said she had taken the passport down to the train station and that the conductor would give it to me in Umtali that evening.

I was there at the station in good time to meet the train from Salisbury bound for Beira. The same immigrations agent was on the platform. I was smiling and in pretty good spirits. I thought, "This will stop him."

But when we got going down the mountain again and the agent came in, and I showed him my passport, he kept saying, "Not valid," and again "Not valid!" He said "You back Umtali."

Then I understood. The passport had already been used to go into Portugese East Africa when we went into Zambia on the aborted trip. Now he was claiming it was only good for one entry.

Another ride back on the freight train?! Thereupon - whether he could speak or understand English or not - I flew into a rage that would probably beat my best record anywhere in the world up until that time, gesticulating that my brother had passed through the night before. I think at this stage he understood that he had let my brother through also on a passport that had been used once, and in the excitement of my own missing passport had let it go. Now he stood to be in trouble if we chose to make trouble for him for having passed my brother illegally. Anyway, he decided to let me pass and the next morning I arrived on time in Beira. After that the animals came thick and fast and what we had expected to get in four weeks we easily completed in two weeks. The weather was about 115 in the shade when we left. It was so hot at night that, having exhausted every other device to keep cool, I would take off my ring and lay it on the table.

It was a great trip. One time I remember walking about twenty miles in a day in the heat, and I remember sleeping on some roots of a tree waiting for elephant, which we never got. I remember hearing some wild shrieking by natives when they went down to the creek to get some water and came across a small elephant that had just been killed by a lion. But I do not remember of having thought once of *OILWEEK*. The greatest marvel was that the name of *Oil in Canada* never crossed my mind.

I did think: If I hadn't been a nonconformist long ago I wouldn't be in Africa now.

But the African trip had been a fine oasis. I felt rejuvenated, fresh and eager now to finish the job, meaning to obliterate my last competitor. And I learned something from the trip as well. Don't take yourself too seriously, and above all don't take your investments too seriously.

A very good friend of mine had always had the dream of going on a hunting safari in Africa. I urged him to come along with us, but after long thought Sam declined. He said he just had to stay home now and look after his investments. It seemed like a critical time in the market and he felt he would be irresponsible if he just up and left. Sam was one of the first I saw on my return. He said, "I guess you were right, Myers, I should have gone with you."

What had happened was one of those big unexpected reversals in the market. Prices of many of the stocks had hit the skids. Had Sam had sold out, he'd have had the trip and returned with more money than he had on the day I saw him after our trip. His dream of a lifetime was lost.

On the other hand, I sold anything I had before I left because of my upcoming absence, and as a result avoided the losses I would have had if I had stayed home. In one way of thinking I got the trip free. Because I was irresponsible, maybe.

Chapter Twenty-six

SALE

I came back from Africa refreshed. The future stretched before me like a smooth green highway; the harrowing past had been swept away. There was no question that *OILWEEK* now was on its way to complete dominance in its field. I was hitched to a future of satisfaction, success, perhaps wealth. How could I guess that in the longer term I was headed straight into the mouth of hell?

How could I guess that there would ever be a time when I would be descended upon by not one, but by two governments with all the spite and vengeance their bureaucracies could muster? That the family unity I had tried so hard to build would be blown up?

When I got back, my business life quickly expanded and prospered. The *OILWEEK* lead became so great that MacLean Hunter, the Canadian image of the huge McGraw-Hill redoubled its effort to buy me out. By the fall of 1963 *Oil in Canada* had descended to where it was about to give up the ghost.

The story got around that I had used one wall of my office to create a crypt, commemorative of my slain competitors, each magazine in a picture frame with a fine black velvet backing and room enough for the big black and white letters stating "DEATH ISSUE." Into the frame of each of these would go the last issue of the slain competitor. A special empty frame was set up, so it was said, obviously reserved for the competitor still not dead, the intended crypt for *Oil in Canada*.

It didn't quite happen, so the cemetery was never really

complete. What happened was that MacLean Hunter stepped in, and with successively higher bids made my continuing position of refusal increasingly uncomfortable. At one time they had wanted to buy my publication for $50,000. Finally in the fall of 1962 after I had taken another trip through the Middle East, gained again overwhelming prestige, they came on with $350,000. I was not ready to sell at that price but it was big enough to command sober thought.

No one in my family was in a position to take over in my place. Should I get killed or die, I felt that the publication would probably end up being bought up at a fire sale price. Still, I resisted until finally one day in late September I decided to kill this thing or cure it. I would up the price $100,000 and if they were ready to fork over the money I'd let *OILWEEK* go. So I sent this fateful wire:

"An offer to purchase *OILWEEK* for the sum of $450,000 cash and your transmittal of $50,000 cash to seal the deal will result in the sale of *OILWEEK* to MacLean Hunter as of this date. The deadline is 12:00 noon tomorrow."

I remember feeling very happy the day I sent that wire. And I began to gather our forces for a strong fall campaign. I thought surely MacLean Hunter would not unequivocally meet those terms, and anything less would set me free.

I was mistaken. By 11:00 A.M. the next day the fateful confirmation came to my desk. The money had been wired to my attorneys. It was my darkest day.

* * * *

Those days are so charged with emotion that even now a quarter of a century later I find it hard to write about them objectively. I find it hard to write about myself objectively. This watershed in my life can only be described by others. I have to let other people speak.

I have in my hand the copy of *OILWEEK* published one week later, September 30, 1963. It carries the banner **OILWEEK SOLD** and my farewell to the industry.

More importantly it carries a capsule assessment by a man in a good position to know, Earle Gray, my editor of thirteen years.

How we see ourselves often differs from the way others see us. Most of what Earle Gray said in his final "Tribute to the Founder" was surprising to me. I was deeply touched, profoundly grateful, and very sad. I had never seen it that way, but if it is the object of an autobiography to faithfully relay an outside, presumably objective view, I shall here quote generously from the Earle Gray summary, a piece of very fine writing, I think, and maybe one of his best.

"The business world, in the mind of OILWEEK founder C. V. Myers, is a jungle where only the strongest survive.

"In this jungle there is no room for friendship with your competitor. Such friendship is at best a luxury that self-survival cannot afford, at worst sheer hypocrisy. In Myers' world of the business jungle, a cold, controlled dislike for the opposition is the key prerequisite. I once heard him tell a man who seemed about to become his competitor: 'No, I'm not mad at you, yet. I'm just getting ready to get mad.' Because of these views Myers developed a reputation as the most ruthless predator in this jungle world, a man with the soul of a dollar.

"I first met this ruthless predator when I was little more than a cub reporter looking for a job with the Calgary Albertan . . . That was 13 years ago, and about the two best things that ever happened to me were to spend this time writing oil news, and working with C.V.

"That was in 1950, when we stuck pins in big wall maps and watched some of the most exciting oil fields in North America grow. I tried to learn about the oil industry, and in 13 years of writing and studying have only learned how much there is about this industry that I do not know. But I learned, perhaps, a little more about C. V. Myers.

"I learned a secret: this ruthless man has a heart as soft as butter and as big as Pembina. For his staff, he was a soft touch. If anyone was in a tight squeeze for money, he would underwrite a loan at the bank. Sometimes he got stuck. He hated to fire anyone, often delayed doing so longer than was prudent, then only did so as a last resort.

"I learned that he is demanding. He demanded I give to the job everything I had in me, and he got out of me more than I knew I had in me. It was the same for the rest of the staff.

"I learned that he is no less generous than demanding. If one day he had me on the carpet till I bled, another day my income was raised.

"I learned that he had a sense of the dramatic and an ability for clarity and vividness of expression that bordered on genius.

"I learned that he had an ability to crystallize a complex picture, to strip it of all non-essentials until it stood stark naked and as simple as a grade school problem in elementary logic. In his writings he dealt only with the heart of the matter, and nothing else really mattered. Thus his reporting has been criticized as prone to exaggeration and oversimplification. When Pembina had less than a score of producing wells, when it was thought no more than a small pool, he reaped criticism for describing it as the first field of its type in Canada, the largest oil accumulation in the country, a field with a billion barrels of reserves. It took nearly a decade before "accepted" estimates confirmed the billion-barrel figure, and no one yet has found another as large as Pembina.

"I learned that he could make mistakes. And that he was always the first to admit them.

"I learned that he was probably the best salesman in Canada. He sold advertisers on the virtue of OILWEEK, and his staff he more than sold, he inspired. He was able *to sell, to inspire, because he himself was completely sold on OILWEEK.*

"I learned that if ruthlessness was a part of his formula for success, there was a much larger part. The larger part was a driving determination to make OILWEEK the best, and to make it excel. To do this, no steps were too big. To make it the best magazine he travelled for stories to Washington, Venezuela, England, Holland, Germany, Italy, North Africa, Iraq, Kuwait, Saudi Arabia and Egypt. He sent his writers to cover oil stories from Ottawa to Mexico.

"For eight years he poured his heart and soul into OILWEEK. To him it was sheer drama, and he loved every moment of it.

"In the end it was his success which caused him to sell. Never for a moment did he want to sell, because this was his life. For three weeks the pressure to sell mounted while he resisted. Finally, the end came with sudden impact and it was as though a heavy gate fell closed with a loud clang, and shut off part of his life.

"But then he had made it. By every conventional yardstick that business can be measured, this ruthless predator in the business jungle had won.

"And then he did a strange thing, this ruthless man with the soul of a dollar. He wept."

By Earle Gray, OILWEEK Managing Editor.

* * * *

As I look back on those days I have to ask myself the question: Is this the kind of a person you would expect to hatch a devious plot, to weave a scheme complicated to the extent of setting up a company across the ocean and holding money in hidden bank accounts in Switzerland? Did Judge Holmes know the man whose fate he was sealing and whose family he was condemning when he ordered the maximum jail term for me in March 1976? Or was Judge MacDonald who had acquitted me completely of these charges in 1976, more realistic? Was I the complicated crook that Prosecutor Bill Major made me out to be? Did I really deserve to spend two years behind bars in the company of the toughest criminals (minor crimes draw less than two years and are served in easier jails). Or was Earle Gray all wrong?

Maybe the story of C. V. Myers is worthwhile, for perhaps the reason that it's not so much the story of one man, as the story of a social order and a system. Maybe it's a portrait of justice. Is justice always justice, or is it sometimes the sadistic expression of bureaucratic spite? Maybe this is a reflection on our bureaucracies in North America, the fierce and repressive tax collection machine on both sides of the border which in widespread instances have emulated the mentality of pitbulls.

And at the risk of being tedious I will call upon a witness from another source; these words from an October 1963 issue of *Canada Month,* a magazine I had no connection with.

Which verdict is the more just, that of our justice system, or our press? Here are the excerpts from *Canada Month.*

"Canada's oil business, today slightly less exuberant than it was in the late '40s and early '50s, is still served by the liveliest, most exuberant, and fightingest trade paper in the land: OILWEEK.

"For years - since 1957 in fact - OILWEEK has campaigned insistently and noisily for a crude-oil pipeline from Alberta to Montreal.

"Recently, continuing the thumping, OILWEEK was earnestly interviewing Dr. Juan Pablo Perez Alfonzo, petroleum administrator of Venezuela. A large part of Venezuela's national income comes from its crude oil exports to the U.S. (which has a quota restricting oil imports) and to Canada. OILWEEK wanted to know what Venezuela would do if Canada went ahead and built the pipeline to supply Montreal refineries with Canadian crude oil. The question alarmed Alfonzo; was Canada going to do that, really? The OILWEEK interviewer said his question was only hypothetical; but what would Alfonzo do? Alfonzo apparently wasn't reassured. Within hours he was on a 'hot line' to Ottawa, then he called Washington (which hopes Canada will keep itself open to oil imports even though the U.S. doesn't). For a while, everybody was pretty stirred up.

"The interviewer, then on his second long-range junket round the oil world, was the publisher and editor-in-chief of OILWEEK, C. Vernon Myers of Calgary. He is an old hand at keeping things well stirred up. But he, like his magazine, is above all else a competitor.

"About a year after he had started the raucous OILWEEK, Publisher Myers was interviewing a young candidate for the job of advertising manager, a job that Myers was to throw five people out of, one after the other, before he filled it with the astounding choice of one of his junior editors (who has ably held down the job ever since 1957).

"Myers and the young man were talking about others in their business - publishers, editors, but mostly advertising salesmen. Some of them were good, some not so good. It became clear that the young man thought most of them pretty nice fellows, competitors or not. In fact he was surprised at the older man's ruthless assessments.

"Myers was genuinely astonished: 'But this is the jungle. You just can't. . .' The young man didn't get the job.

"Myers is a man who can't like a competitor. To him, this really is "the jungle", and he lives the life of a classical businessman. Competitiveness is the very stuff Vern Myers is made of. Even today, when he has clearly beaten all the competitors he has had in Canadian petroleum publishing, he never fails to denounce Oil in Canada, the 'other weekly' as he calls it in his promotional literature. One gets the feeling Myers may have started in business just because those people at Oil in Canada made him so *mad. . . .*

"Along the way, Myers became the first publisher of a national magazine to print by offset rather than letterpress, encountering a hornet's nest of technical problems that seemed for a time to guarantee that each issue was going to be more of an ugly mess than the one before it. But he got it licked, and won the competitive advantage that offset printing affords: it is cheaper, and it relieves his advertisers of the necessity of preparing costly printing plates. Today other national magazine publishers have followed Myers into this revolution, including Time and Canada Month.

"It is characteristic of Myers (and perhaps not that different from what many small-business geniuses have done) that he started into offset printing because he mistakenly believed that the colorful weekly news magazine he was patterning OILWEEK on, U.S. News & World Report, was printed by offset. Had he known in advance that he was wrong he might never have done it. . .

"The competitive spirit abides in a man who earned a BA degree in geology at 19.

"He never practiced geology, but there could have been no better background for a man who was to find his way to oil-rich Alberta to practice journalism while the industry's renaissance was waiting in the wings. . .

"Last month Myers decided to turn down a bid for his publication from MacLean-Hunter Publishing Co. Ltd. . .

"Did Myers think the Toronto publisher might now simply turn round and buy up that devilish Oil in Canada, intending to make mincemeat of him? He is somewhat concerned about the financial power the easterners can pour into a magazine: 'I'm gambling they won't but . . .' he adds, remembering that he has successfully taken on and licked everyone else who's tried it, 'we're ready for them if they do!'"

Chapter Twenty-seven

STARTING A FINANCIAL LETTER

Following the sale of *OILWEEK* I had looked for other things to do. First off, I made a mistake that is common to so many who have carved success out of a stormy career and proved their success with a big chunk of money. They leave something they thoroughly understand to start something they know nothing about. Usually it results in heavy losses. Sometimes it results even in bankruptcy.

I escaped the last of these but when I sit down to think of it I am compelled to wonder how, in spite of heavy losses, here and there, I have managed to remain solvent. By means of a maybe some mysterious gift I have retained an ability to make money; I have ended up with my financial security intact, at least to this point.

That's despite reverses in the stock market, substantial losses in the cattle business, mountainous legal bills, and huge taxes to Uncle Sam of well over a million dollars; I don't know how much over, and I don't think I care to know. But I believe it must all be honest income because Uncle has audited me twice and so far found nothing wrong - except to claim I made too much money, and instead of taking it out in wages, it should have been paid out in the form of dividends, which would have meant increased taxes for Uncle Sam. The original cost here was about $200,000 or $250,000 which we finally got down to $60,000, by the expensive method of spending nearly $100,000 in lawyer fees.

After a retirement of four years in 1967, in pursuit of knowledge about financial conditions in general, and monetary matters in particular, I attended a conference in New York City under the tutorship of the well known Franz Pick. Pick had one message: paper equities are no good. All paper promises throughout history have been repudiated and this time it is no different. Bonds, shares, mortgages, bank accounts - they will all go down the drain. What people call securities, he said, should be called **insecurities**. Like, "How many insecurities traded on the New York Stock Exchange today?" Bonds, he said, were guaranteed certificates of confiscation. Pick said that only in precious metals would value endure.

Pick was obviously an extremist and if you followed him too closely you would have been a heavy loser. He had been preaching gold already throughout the early 1960s and the price of gold did not go up at all until 1971. In the course of ten years a given amount of wealth would at least double its size by compound interest - no effort expended. Pick was basically right but a little early about the "certificates of confiscation", U.S. government bonds, etc., which are still circulating at face value.

But I will say that Pick has been proven two-thirds right. The value of the dollar is now less than one-third what it was in 1967. Through inflation we have suffered unconscious confiscation. Had I taken my $450,000 and set it aside in 1966 it would be worth less than $150,000 today and maybe less than $100,000, which with compound interest would have made only $200,000. The confiscation has been more or less "**invisible**" because it is still called, $450,000.

At any rate I saw the basic truth of what Pick was trying to get across. And I came away completely sold on the idea that my assets or a large portion of them ought to be in something **real**, something I could hold in my hands, or at least look at, as for instance a gold coin, a piece of property, a silver bar, a diamond, a rare painting.

Basically the core idea was: reality versus unreality, or

something real versus a promise. Pick said all paper, even the currency you carry in your pocket, is a promise. Today it doesn't promise anything, as it once did in silver or gold. Even in 1967 it was only printed paper; the dollar bill promised to pay one dollar in legal money of the United States. When I wrote to the Treasury and asked them to make good on this the best I could get was exchange for another dollar.

Later on I expanded on Pick's idea of the poor worth of promises with regard to government bonds which promise dollars. If you are a child, I said, and your mother promises you an ice-cream cone, no matter how much you trust your mother, no matter that she has never fallen down on her word, still it's better to have the ice-cream cone than your mother's promise. After all, she might fall down and break her leg. Being promised something and having it in hand are two quite different things.

When we got down to specific statistics in 1967 I realized with a shock that, my God, we are already broke. The country is broke and not one in a million knows it. I arrived at this conclusion simply; the United States at that time guaranteed to redeem foreign held dollars at one ounce of gold for every $35.

Pick showed us where the outstanding claims against the U.S. were something over $30 billion and the entire gold hoard of the United States as of that time was under $27 billion. In the previous couple of years the United States had passed the boundary between the comfort of solvency and the insecurity of insolvency.

From there on, I developed my own philosophy, my own line of thinking and my own line of planning for and during insolvency. In doing so I became an analyst and I started a newsletter, not so much for the reason of selling subscriptions. I really didn't need a newsletter for income. I started it because I was mad. I was mad at the government's coverup of the insolvency, at the propaganda emanating from the U.S. Treasury, the "all is well" syndrome. Not to worry, we are in the early stages of the greatest prosperity in the history of the world. It has hardly got started yet.

I named my newsletter *Myers Finance Review*.

I returned from New York flush with excitement over the new project. I would write a newsletter loaded with shocking facts, facts that would set the investment community on its ear, the shocking TRUTH. I decided that my slogan would be: **LET THE TRUTH BE TOLD**. Now twenty-two years later it is still on the *Myers Finance and Energy* masthead.

I prepared a list of some 18,000 people comprising the entire establishment in Canada, general managers, chairmen of the board, presidents; 18,000 of the most influential people in the country. I waited eagerly for the first returns. I envisioned it as a repeat performance of the maiden issue of my oil report a dozen years earlier.

The first few days produced no returns at all. Then in the next few days there was a dribbling of two or three returns. The total response was eighteen, one out of a thousand, willing to pay $25 a year for such a newsletter published weekly. It was not a good omen.

But I was confident that I was right and people needed to know the inside story. I went on week by week, although my subscriptions by fall still remained well under one hundred. In October I went to the conference of the International Monetary Fund (IMF) in Rio de Janeiro where bankers from around the world, the big money managers of the globe, huddled together for four days to talk about their idea of world finance. I was amazed. I couldn't believe it. I, the boy from the prairies of Alberta, the country hick, among world sophisticates, listened to them talk about this panacea "PAPER GOLD" and saw plainly that they were nuts. We had run out of gold so now we would take special pieces of paper and on it we would print "GOLD." Then we would dignify paper - gold money with a new name; "Special Drawing Rights"; and that would make it pass for gold. I wished my dad could have been there so I could have observed his response to this nonsense.

In my newsletter of September 27, 1967 I had the effrontery

to write this:

"THIS IS THE FIRST IN A SERIES OF MOVES TO KICK GOLD OUT OF THE BACK DOOR.

The Special Drawing Rights are not being presented as a substitute for gold. They are being presented gently - persuasively - coated with honey - as a supplement for gold. It is stated they are to stand beside gold. They are to be a helpmate of gold. But in the end the Special Drawing Rights, if adopted, will turn out to be the camel that kicked the Arab out of the tent.

At this Press Conference, questions were directed to Mr. Pierre-Paul Schweitzer, Managing Director of the International Monetary Fund. I had only one question:

"I understand, Mr. Schweitzer, that the new Drawing Rights are proposed in order to increase world liquidity. Do you see the new Drawing Rights as a substitute for gold in the near future?"

Answer:

"Yes, they would take the place of gold." Then Mr. Schweitzer hedged: "I would rather say they would not be a substitute for gold but they would supplement gold. They would be an addition to the existing gold. Supplement rather than substitute."

I was not satisfied with the added clarification, and I pursued Mr. Schweitzer at the reception following the Conference:

"Mr. Schweitzer, I was not clear on the distinction you made between a supplement and a substitute for gold. If the newly-mined gold each year is absorbed by private demand — in addition to existing gold reserves — is it your view that the new Drawing Rights would be a substitute for this new gold, and lost gold?"

"Yes, that is a fair way of putting it."

So here we reach the core of the plan.

GRAND CONCLUSION: The Rio Conference is aimed at worldwide inflation on a scale never before dreamed of — because governments have overspent their wealth on extravagant social benefit schemes aimed at getting votes and keeping themselves in power. Now, at the bottom of the barrel, they propose yet another monstrous violation of economic horse-sense to keep the bubble floating.

THIS RIO CONFERENCE IS AN EXERCISE IN FUTILITY, A FARCE AND A WASTE OF TIME.

There wasn't anything wrong with what I said. What was wrong was the lack of anyone to read it or, it seemed, anyone who cared? But at that conference I did get an idea of how people promoted newsletters.

It was much the same principle as old Oaks had used in the days of my crisis with *OILWEEK*. Get lists of good names. The good names were subscribers to other newsletters, or the cancelled subscribers, preferably originating from newsletters that might be gold oriented. I found to my surprise there were two or three agencies that did business in selling lists.

I revamped my newsletter. A new masthead which is the skeleton of the newsletter today; on the right hand, two columns, an editorial piece called "The Quiet Corner", which proposes objective thought. On the left hand side the "Outlook" which is a brief summary of all of the hot events taking place and liable to take place. Inside was my interpretation of the financial news of that week, all topped off by **LET THE TRUTH BE TOLD**.

In late 1967 and early 1968 when I sent sometimes as many as 40,000 promotional letters, subscriptions began to show real life. In a few months I had over 4,000 subscribers, all in time for perhaps the most startling monetary development in a few hundred years. The subject was the price of silver. From my newsletters of that time:

MFR - May 5, 1967: SILVER PRICE SHOULD GO FREE WITHIN ONE TO 60 DAYS. RECOMMENDATION — buy pure silver at once.

MFR - June 1, 1967: In September 1966, Robert A. Wallace, assistant-secretary of the U.S. Treasury declared: "No one should expect to reap a windfall from hoarding either silver bullion or silver coins."

Anyone who believed the Treasury was a sucker.

The financial press shrugged off any possibility of a change in the price of silver. The famed, reliable, revered *New York Times* March 3, 1967, said this: "The Treasury aim is to hold the price (silver) for several years more at least — thus the Treasury would continue to have control over the market for an indefinite period."

Exactly two months and fifteen days later the U.S. Treasury lost control.

In that single day from 10:00 A.M. to 3:00 P.M. silver jumped from $1.30 an ounce to $1.65 an ounce. The profit on my silver holdings was about $250,000; and at that time there was no capital gains tax in Canada. Never before or since have I done as well in an eight hour stretch. Not only that; I was the only one in North America, or perhaps the world, who had accurately zeroed in on the timing of the U.S. Treasury surrender to world market forces. Unheard of, unbelievable, impossible? 'Fraid not. It happened in a single day. It was the first real hard evidence that the U.S. Treasury was beginning to lose world monetary leadership.

No newsletter writer anywhere had come even close to predicting the fall. I had been to New York to visit Pick in March and to my disappointment he was down on the idea. He said, "It's much too early. The silver price won't break for quite a while yet." Pick missed the move completely and so did all his clients.

Disregarding Pick, however, though he was supposed to be the master I decided I would stick with my own reasoning and let my prediction stand. That proved to be correct.

The outlook for my newsletter had made a dramatic leap in the year March 1967 to March 1968.

* * * *

There was tremendous satisfaction in having hit this one, this most unique and important development right between the eyes. And it demonstrates to me how it was that through all my adversities I have been able to make money. The secret is not a secret at all. It is a very simple truth. When you are right be right in a big way. Stick with it. When you are wrong be wrong in a small way or at least be out in a hurry. More than once that has saved my solvency - out in a hurry.

To illustrate I recall that when I was publishing *OIL WEEK* the owners and promoters of Pacific Petroleums and Atlantic Oil Company obtained the permission from the government of Alberta to export gas into the United States. I knew them well, particularly Frank McMahon who was probably the biggest independent oil man in the history of Canada. On the evening of the receipt of the approval of the Alberta government to export gas I was invited up to their offices at the top of the Pacific Building. There was a mood of great celebration, champagne corks were popping. The conversation all centered around which stock to buy. Several were involved including the pipeline company that would buy and export the gas. One of the biggest producers would be the Atlantic Oil Company, all owned by the McMahon group. The general feeling seemed to be that the stock to buy next morning was Atlantic.

On the opening I bought Atlantic. As I recall I believe it was up about a dollar from the previous close and ended the day $1.50 higher. I put everything I had into Atlantic and then I margined it besides. The next day the stock didn't rise. In a few days it began to look weak. I couldn't understand it. Here was a great bonanza. How could it get weak? I had bought it around $8.50. In a few days it dropped to $7.90 and it still looked weak. Large blocks had been trading. I didn't know what was wrong but **something** was terribly wrong. Would McMahon mislead me? I thought not. Still, reality speaks very loud.

When I looked at my position I found that I had lost about half my total capital which at that time was about $50,000. I wasn't a chartist and I wasn't an investment expert. I used what I had always used, just old farm boy common sense. Something is rotten in the state of Denmark - and it's got to be something pretty bad. The next morning I ordered my entire position sold and I lost half of what I was worth. It was hard to take. But I was soon glad I had taken my loss. In a short time thereafter it was learned that this export of gas to the U.S. was no pushover. Acceptance by the United States was not cleared and it was beginning to look like it might not be cleared at all. The stock gradually sank to about $3.60 a share. Had I hung on I'd have lost every cent.

The principal of making money in the market is easy to verbalize, not so easy to follow. It is simply to make the big positions pay and to be in strong with most of your eggs in one basket. The second part of the equation is to get the hell out when the market is going against you in defiance of your reason. You will find later on that it was going down for a reason. Some people knew the reason and the number of people that knew it was expanding. The necessary part of the equation is to be willing to take losses, even serious losses, if you find your position is faulty. Sometimes you will take a loss only to find out that the market turns around and goes up again. That's very hard to take, but in the overall picture you have to take that loss to salvage the rest.

An investor can take quite a number of smaller losses if he makes his BIG POSITION count.

The silver development, when my newsletter was only a year old, was just an introduction to what was going to happen down the line with gold. Silver had launched me successfully and permanently on the financial newsletter scene.

If the silver prediction brought me some fame I was in demand as a speaker and in particular demand with the silver industry in Spokane, Washington and in Idaho. I was asked to come down and address a meeting which was attended by all of those interested in mining of the precious metals in Idaho. The word about my prediction had spread quite a ways to the point where in fact I received in my office one day a very famous client; not so famous then as now. His name was Bunker Hunt.

He paid my regular consultation fee which I think was $200 or $300 and spoke quite enthusiastically about silver prospects. I had suggested that the whole silver market could be tied up by a few rich men. It wasn't like gold where such a scheme would be impossible to the richest of all people in the world, and even to a country. For silver it made quite some sense and I was not too surprised in some later years that Bunker Hunt and his brothers had made that attempt to control the silver market. The main reason they lost was that the Commodity Exchange changed the rules on them in the middle of the game and for a time would not allow any more buying of the metal. So it could be sold and not bought and what happened is just what you would think would happen. The price collapsed. Silver had raced up from about four dollars an ounce to $50 an ounce and now it raced back until this day in mid 1989 it is only $5.30 an ounce. Bunker Hunt was an enjoyable fellow to talk to and I believed he was quite smart and quite perceptive. I smile a little to recall a story I had heard about him not long before.

Apparently he had bought a football team for a million dollars. It was learned then that Bunker had lost the million dollars on this team somehow. So a couple of reporters went to see old man Hunt. They thought they would get really a nice dish of criticism of his flamboyant son. They posed the question to Mr. Hunt, "What about young Bunker losing this million dollars on a football team?"

The patriarch replied, "Well I can tell you this: If he does it 187 more times, he's gonna be broke." So the disappointed newsmen didn't get much of a story.

I guess the moral is; no matter how big you are you can go broke; and no matter how big a country is it can go broke.

That's where we are now.

But long after we're all broke there will still be the bureaucrats.

African safari 1957 - a wild boar bit the dust.

Lion that jumped up in the Veldt - about twenty minutes later.
Brother Richard on right.

Dangerous Cape Buffalo of trophy quality, 1957 safari.

Proceeding to the bank with first $25,000 check, about 1949.

Family at the big house in Mt. Royal, spring 1950, with Brian eight, Norma three, Richard one, Muriel and housekeeper.

Front lawn of our new ranch home near Calgary: Norma, Muriel, me, Richard, Brian.

Bette Mae, Amy's daughter and mine, getting married, me and Muriel.

Sister Ruth, before her winter holiday at Bowden.

On our Chris Craft boat at remote Shuswap Lake: Norma, John, Richard, Brian.

Daughter, Norma, at the outset of equestrian career with her Arabian stallion, "Wildwood Farouk," as appeared on the front cover of a national horse magazine. Off to a good start with seven entries into the ring, and out seven times first.

Off on a holiday a year before the *OILWEEK* sale. Norma, myself, John, Muriel and Richard.

From acorn to oak in seven years, 1956-1963.

With wife Muriel a month before the Revenue Canada raid,
when lightning struck.

Atop quarterhorse registered "Grubstake Jake," in rocky desert
at Palm Springs, early 1987.

Speaking at the National Conference for Monetary Reform, New Orleans, La., November, 1980. Annual conferences were highlights during years of exile.

BOOK THREE

LIGHTNING

PREFACE

The third phase of my life erupted violently. It launched me into an unknown world. None of my experience had prepared me, even slightly, for the hurricane I had to face now. At the center of the storm was **Revenue Canada**. When it subsided I wanted to write about it. The problem was how to treat such personal trauma objectively.

First of all I listed factually the high crimes against freedom as integrated in the bureaucratic system. Canada's tax men may without notice do the following:

1. Simultaneously raid your home, your bank, your auditor, your lawyer and seize all documents relevant to you.

2. Seize and hold without due process all of your property including your car, your bank account, your safety deposit box, your mail and even third party property which might be in your possession.

3. Arrest and incarcerate you without notice and without prior claim.

4. Demand exorbitant bail and, if not forthcoming, keep you incarcerated until you are brought to trial.

5. Prosecute you without allowing you access to any of your assets to hire lawyers for your own defense.

* 6. Try you a second time - if you are at first acquitted on the same charges, using the same evidence, in front of a different judge.

*The Trial deNova, an exclusively Canadian device for DOUBLE JEOPARDY, was expunged from the legal system in late 1976.

7. If they lose - walk away unscathed, uncensored, free of responsibility for the waste of taxpayer money. You as a taxpayer have contributed to your own prosecution.

8. Hold third party property until ready to give it back, and return it with conditions attached.

In 1979, broken and debilitated by the exercise of these atrocities, how could I write about it all and remain objective? I hit upon the device of using third person narrative, thus avoiding a loss of credibility.

The third person I invented was Norman L. Stone. What you're about to read now is to the best of my ability a totally factual, wholly objective account of the stream of enduring events that were kicked off September 19, 1974.

My own first person narrative resumes with Chapter twenty-eight.

UNBRIDLED BUREAUCRACY IN CANADA

By Norman L. Stone

Chapter I

THE BIZARRE CASE OF C. V. MYERS

THE RAID

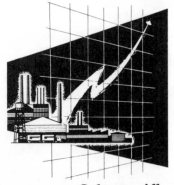

On a fine autumn morning of September 19, 1974 at precisely 10:00 a.m., financial analyst and newsletter writer C. V. Myers stepped out of his country home near Calgary, Alberta to go to his office. At the bottom of the steps two men advanced, each flashing a badge. One showed him a Court Order authorizing the search of his home.

As Myers read the Order a second car came roaring up the driveway and three men got out.

The five men then entered the home, four of them with large cardboard boxes. Each was assigned a part of the house while the fifth, a Royal Canadian Mounted Police plain clothesman was left to watch Myers. This man demanded Myers' keys. He yanked off the safety deposit key and put it in his pocket. He took the other keys out and opened the trunk of Myers' car. Finding nothing, he returned these keys.

Myers phoned his office to learn that five men had also just arrived there.

At the house the men were picking up every conceivable paper, riffling every possible drawer and corner, collecting all letters including those of his grown children, his wife's diary (Mrs. Myers was in the hospital), searching his wife's bedroom for jewelry and picking up her bank books and statements. No nook or cranny was left unsearched.

Disgusted, Myers said he was leaving for the office. They couldn't hold him.

At the office he found a similar scene; four men vigorously probing every cabinet and corner; filling their boxes. By now very little was left in the office. Fortunately the newsletter, **MYERS FINANCE AND ENERGY**, was headquartered in Switzerland, and so it was possible to continue the service without interruption. Myers continued to write his analysis. By sending the copy air freight to Zurich it was immediately published and mailed out to the subscribers with little delay. Interpublishing Company, publisher of the newsletter, had been in existence since 1969.

Simultaneously with the raids of home and office, other investigators had entered the law office of Macleod Dixon; the auditors' offices of Touche, Ross; the Bank of Nova Scotia; and the Canadian Imperial Bank of Commerce. They demanded and received all documents pertaining to Myers, including cancelled cheques, previous income tax returns, working papers and adamantly demanded papers and all data on Interpublishing. Of course the auditors had nothing on Interpublishing because it was a **bona fide** Company operating out of Switzerland, paying taxes in Switzerland, and its records were there.

At the bank of Nova Scotia Interpublishing was holding four million dollars gold bought and paid for by American clients, with the safety box rentals also paid for by the clients. The tax men sealed all boxes as well as Myers' personal safety boxes.

At 2:00 p.m. that day Myers and his attorneys visited A. Manfredi in his Calgary investigative headquarters. Very little was said and nothing revealed. Manfredi's only response was to advise Myers to revise his 1973 Income Tax Return.

At this stage the greatest worry was the Americans' gold of which Interpublishing was custodian and felt responsible for, now sealed and inaccessible to its owners.

Chapter II

THE GOLD HASSLE

Although the tax men had the record of every check which had been paid over by the Americans for this gold, they did not have the owner's names.

It had been illegal for Americans to own gold but most of them believed that the law was unconstitutional, and indeed the U.S. Treasury, although fully aware of multitudinous cases of gold purchases by U.S. citizens, seemed reluctant to pursue this matter in the courts. Loss of the case would have upset the U.S. International Monetary policy and it was a risk they did not care to take.

Gold ownership was fully legal in Canada. Myers had started buying gold for his clients at first as a service for them. He said, "We don't care if you are Chinese, Burmese, Russians or Americans, gold ownership is legal in Canada; put the money on our desk and we will buy you the gold. Your account will be numbered but your corresponding identity will be kept secret in Switzerland."

There was nothing illegal in all of this.

But it gave the tax men an ideal opportunity for blackmail. If the Americans couldn't come forward to claim their gold, it could be held hostage to any assessment the Tax Department might like to issue against Myers or Interpublishing.

The hope was that mounting pressure from the gold owners would force Myers and the Swiss Company to pay the assessment - right or wrong. Myers likened it to a high-jacking, the only difference being high-jackers held third party **lives** while the tax men held third party **money**. Without the names of the gold owners made available to them, tax men could not be accused of violating third party immunity, although they knew full well by the check information that at least great numbers of innocent third parties were involved.

They were sitting pretty. Myers went to the hospital with a severe attack of pancreatitis.

Chapter III

BAD BREAK FOR TAX MEN

Then an unlucky thing happened. U.S. gold ownership became legal December 31, 1974. This meant that owners could come forward. But it meant much more. It meant that if the claimants identified themselves, the Tax Department, having all the documents and all the keys, had automatically become the legal custodian of the gold, and fully as responsible as Interpublishing had been to turn it over to the owners on demand.

The safety deposit keys and the identification list had now been air-mailed from Switzerland and turned over to the Tax Department. They had the gold . . . Now they had everything, including the responsibility.

At this point they were holding a hot potato. With rentals on safety deposit boxes coming due at the Bank were they going to bill the clients as Interpublishing had been doing, or were they going to pay the rentals themselves? Or was the Bank to demand that the boxes be emptied if not paid? And what if an owner sent in an order to sell? They were legally obligated to sell it for him and send him the check. Like it or not they were in the gold business.

Non-plussed for an answer, they did what all bureaucrats do - nothing. The job of going down to the Bank, opening boxes and making and insuring special shipments of gold to the U.S. was something for which they were unprepared. Furthermore, if some gold turned up missing who would be responsible? They had been holding **third party** property in order to extract (or extort) taxes arbitrarily assessed against Interpublishing Company, whose records they did not have. Their assessment was a calculation and an extrapolation of what the earnings should be.

They had no bank accounts, no statements and no record of invoice.

Myers advised all clients to write A. Manfredi of Revenue Canada demanding that he deliver up to them their wholly-owned gold.

Typical Gold Owner Reaction

Mr. A. Manfredi
Dept. of National Revenue Taxation
205 - 8th Avenue S.E.
Calgary, Alberta, Canada

Dear Sir:

On Jan. 19, 1975, I mailed a letter to your department concerning th ownership of 26-20 oz. goldbars, which you confiscated in a dispute with th Interpublishing Co. So far I have received a form letter, but no satisfaction c release of my property.

In today's papers we read about hijacking, political executions (as th U.S. Consul in Argentina), the abduction of the Mayoral candidate in Berlir — those are all acts of terrorism against innocent third parties. Those action are decried and condemned by the whole civilized world.

But is not your action against third parties in your dispute wit Interpublishing Co. in the same category?

To me, this is almost an act of gansterism, not something I would expec from the Sovereign State of Canada . . . in Chicago perhaps, or in Africa, i Kenya or Uganda . . . but never in Canada.

I have always believed Canadian justice to be equal to English justice which has been unassailable throughout history, but it seems, I am mistake in that assumption.

We, the owners of the confiscated gold, (I assume the others feel th same way) have invested our savings in Canadian gold, to preserve the swea of our labor from inflation. As the situation now stands, we were able t achieve this, only to have it confiscated.

There must be other and legal ways and means to settle your clain against Interpublishing Co., Ltd., instead of using the properties of thir parties as pawns.

Hoping to hear from you.

Yours truly,

Name Withheld

Things were getting too hot. The gold owners had to be answered.

For starters, a huge counting operation was arranged, including a representative of Interpublishing in Calgary, the Calgary lawyers of Interpublishing, Tax Department men, officials of the bank, and one or two security guards. All boxes had to be opened. Each owner's gold had to be counted and recorded. **FOUR MILLION DOLLARS WORTH!!**

When the count was finished it was found that every claimant's gold was separately wrapped. Not a coin was out of place, not a coin belonged to C.V. Myers or Interpublishing.

Clearly that could amount to a wrongful withholding. The law of precedent is that a wrongful withholder must pay the claimant the highest price at which he could have sold, had he not been prevented from doing so. Clearly, also Revenue Canada was the custodian. If not - who was?

Falling prices spurred American owners to action. Through the Calgary law firm of Jones, Black, they launched an action against the Department and the **individuals**, whom they claimed had acted beyond their legal authority in withholding from them their rightful property. If proven, the individuals, Mr. Manfredi, Mr. Robertson, Mr. Schwendmayer and the Deputy Minister would be on the hook for damages not only for the price loss on four million dollars worth of gold but also possible punitive damages. It would be very difficult for the government to stand behind them if they had exceeded their legal authority. This time it might mean that **their homes** would go on the auction block in a dramatic turning of the tables. A wild scramble to get out of the mess brought top brass flying from Ottawa to negotiate a settlement. Their offer was this: We will give you back your gold if you will sign a commitment to hold us free from all harm as a result of our having withheld the gold to this point.

The gold holders, anxious only to recover their property with the least pain, inclined to agree. The offer by the Tax Department went out to the gold owner list. Most signed it.

Had they refused to sign, tax men would have been faced with their greatest disaster to date. What court costs and damages the individual officers could not pay, the Department would have had to pay. Their resulting image would have been mud in Canada, because the offer in itself was proof of their recognition **of the ownership by the foreign nationals.**

To get his own gold, every owner had to sign the following form - admitting that Revenue Canada had given him a **consideration** by returning his own property.

General Release

IN CONSIDERATION of the release from seizure of my property, which property was stored in the name of Interpublishing Company Ltd., and identified as follows:

Key No.:	Account No.:	Gold Holdings:
471	176	57 Krugerrands
1208	176A	18 Krugerrands

and which property is under seizure by the Sheriff for the Judicial District of Calgary pursuant to Writs of Execution against Interpublishing Company Ltd., the undersigned **hereby remises, releases and forever discharges Her Majesty the Queen in the right of Canada and in the right of the Province of Alberta and all their employees, servants and agents, including the Sheriff of the Judicial District of Calgary and his bailiffs, and all employees of the Department of National Revenue Taxation** from all actions, causes of actions, claims or demands whatsoever which the undersigned now has or hereafter can, shall or may have for or by reason of or in any way arising out of any cause, matter or things whatsoever existing up to the present time and in particular, without in any way limiting the generality of the foregoing, by reason of or in any way arising out of the seizure of the said property as aforementioned.

The provisions hereof shall endure to the successors of Her Majesty the Queen in the right of Canada and in the right of the Province of Alberta and to the executors, heirs and successors of their employees, servants and agents, and shall be binding upon the executor, the legal personal representative, the heirs and successors of the undersigned. *****

IN WITNESS WHEREOF I have hereunto set my hand and seal this _____

day of _____ A.D. 1975

SIGNED, SEALED AND)
DELIVERED in the)
presence of:)
)
)
_____)

Witness

*Emphasis ours.

Chapter IV

WHAT THE JUDGE THOUGHT

The Court had previously registered its impatience with Revenue Canada. Here is a reprint of part of the tongue lashing they took from Justice F.H. Quigley in a preliminary hearing as it appeared in the *Calgary Herald.*

FROM THE *CALGARY HERALD*, MARCH 22, 1975

$4 million in gold

Evidence asked to back seizure

Federal tax officials were warned in Alberta Supreme Court Friday to quickly produce e v i d e n c e to support their continued seizure of over $4 m i l l i o n in gold claimed by about 100 Americans.

Mr. Justice F. H. Quigley asked if the tax men had evidence which would justify holding the gold "or are they just sitting back with a big stick putting people to a lot of trouble."

The judge was highly critical of the tax department after lawyer Bill Major said he did not have substantive evidence to support the federal position that the Americans do not own the gold.

"They (the tax department) move with their great power but they haven't seen fit to state under oath what their position is," he said. "Surely they must have some material relevant to back up what they assert."

TROUBLE..

"If they haven't they should be in a lot of trouble, in fact, they will be in a lot of trouble. They're not like a private citizen who moves around with ignorance of the law."

He said the department has all the facilities and manpower necessary to move ahead with its case and suggested: "They want to go on a fishing expedition. They aren't ready to move. . ."

The gold was seized along with assets of Interpublishing Co. Ltd. last September- after the Swiss firm was investigated for non-payment of taxes. The firm published an energy and finance newsletter written by Calgary analyst Vern Myers.

One of the services they supplied to subscribers was p u r c h a s e and anonymous safeguarding of gold, most in t e r e s t i n g to U.S. citizens since they were prohibited by law until last Jan. 1 from owning gold anywhere in the world.

The action by the Americans seeks damages against a number of tax officials, members of the sheriff's department and bailiffs who seized and sealed the gold in Bank of Nova Scotia vaults on 8th Avenue where it was kept.

Mr. Major argued the Interpublishing was not a regis tered Alberta company and was acting as a "blind" for another corporation. Mr. Justice Quigley said that claim was only a "red herring."

"The nominee (applicant) could be Al Capone and that doesn't enter into it at all. The question is, who owns the gold?"

He told Mr. Major the tax department was g o i n g to have to present more than "a suspicious mind."

He warned that "unless something magical happens, you have a pretty clear indication which way I'm going to go."

* * * * * * * * * *

The capitulation left the tax men red-faced, angry and vengeful. Talk among the personnel in the Department was funneled back: **Get Myers!**

The full story had broken in the national press. The loss of face was, for an organization which relies on "voluntary returns" unacceptable. They were further angered by Myers' comments published in his newsletter, **Myers' FINANCE AND ENERGY**:

> *"This offer to the Americans is like saying; we recognize it is your gold. We have no legal claim on it. We are going to give it back to you on the **condition** that you sign this commitment to hold us free from any harm for having held this gold. The implication is clear. If you don't sign we won't give it back to you at all."*

Not only did the Americans give up all rights to collect damages, they also assumed the expense of a special agent who would be required to make a separate counting together with a tax official, and to move the gold for them to another bank or to somehow return it into their hands.

Revenue Canada, except for loss of face, got off scott free. Foreign nationals - completely innocent of the tax situation - had been heavily penalized by Revenue Canada - no apologies.

But this bloody nose they had received and the published comments about them proved too much to swallow. Within days of the Government capitulation Myers was arrested.

Chapter V

THE ARREST

Soon after the raid of September 19, 1974, Revenue Canada issued an assessment of $878,602.67 for taxation years 1969 through 1974 against Interpublishing Company of Zurich, Switzerland whose address they had. However they mailed the assessment to Mr. Myers in Calgary. Myers forwarded the assessment to Switzerland and so advised the Department. No assessment had been issued against Myers, nor had he been approached.

On what seemed to be a normal May morning in 1975, Myers drove into his parking lot, steps away from his ground floor office. But this was no normal morning. As he opened the car door, two armed plain clothesmen blocked his way. "You're under arrest!"

Myers was stunned. He wondered if he had hit someone on the way to work. "What for?"

"For the evasion of taxes. I must warn you that you do not have to speak, and anything you say may be used against you." The officer handed Myers a document charging him with evasion of exactly the same taxes as had been assessed Interpublishing Company almost eight months before.*

The officers demanded that Myers get into the police car at once, but he had some cleaning in the car and he persuaded them to let him take the cleaning to his office. He told his secretary, "Get my lawyers. I am under arrest and I'm on my way to jail."

It was just as well because when Myers got to RCMP headquarters he was not allowed to make a call. He was stripped

---

*Later, during the trial they would increase these charges by $400,000 for a total exceeding $1.2 million.

of everything in his pockets and relieved of necktie, matches and belt, then fingerprinted and put behind bars. The lawyers had received a message and within an hour and one-half two of them were meeting with Myers in the cubby-hole barely large enough to hold them.

"Do you know how much bail Major (the prosecutor) wants to let you out of here?"

"How much?"

"One-half million dollars."

This sum seemed fantastic on a tax case which had been in the hands of the Department for nearly nine months, and in view of the lack of any previous effort to collect. In view also of the fact that alleged murderers and even terrorists had often been released for less.

The attorneys hurriedly arranged a meeting in court and at 2:00 p.m. Myers was released on bail of $100,000.00, still an enormous sum considering the nature of the charges. The Judge expressly directed that Myers be allowed to travel to the United States to appear as scheduled three days later on the Merv Griffin show in Hollywood.

Most people react with disbelief to the statement that the Department had never tried to collect preceding the arrest, for collection is precisely the purpose of the existence of Revenue Canada. Also such an arrest without notice and without claim seems to have never taken place before either in Canada or the United States (to our knowledge). To put any such doubts to rest here is a photocopy of that portion of the transcript in the first trial dated January, 1975.

Myers' Defense Attorney, Sheldon Chumir, is cross-questioning tax accuser Schwendmayer.

Q Now, was Mr. Myers ever advised, or were his legal advisors ever advised that you were contemplating a charge of evasion against him?

A I do not remember.

Q Do you remember that there wasn't? You don't remember at all?

A I don't remember at all.

Q You don't remember that there was?

A No, and I don't remember when it was.

Q If I told you there wasn't, you wouldn't deny it?

A I wouldn't deny it one way or the other.

Q Did you ever advise Mr. Myers that you were going to t him on this income, you were going to include this inc on his hands?

A No.

Q You never told him that?

A No.

Q Did anybody from Special Investigation ever say, Myers we are going to tax you on this income that relates to Inter and come in and explain?

A No, not that I know of.

Q Was he ever assessed on any of this income?

A He's not assessed yet.

Q He's never assessed a penny in these prosecution items from 1969 to 1974?

A No.

Q Not a penny, and he's never been asked to come in and explain?

A   No.

Q   So you have never had an opportunity to sit down with Mr. Myers, or his advisors, and find out what the circumstances were surrounding this transaction?

A   No, I didn't.

Q   You just charged him on May 5th?

A   Yes.

Q   And arrested him?

A   Yes.

Here is a photocopy of the cross examination with regard to Interpublishing.

Q   And, then you receive a letter from Switzerland with some explanation?

A   Yes.

Q   And, then there is no further approach from the Department, there is no evidence of anything further from the Department on that, correct?

A   Not with respect to Inter Publishing as I recall it.

Q   Now, the next step, the next official document from the Department is September 24th of 1974, and you assess Inter Publishing. And, lo and behold Inter Publishing sends in the proper documents, Notices of Objection, and says we want to -- here's our position on it, let's discuss it and nobody contacts Inter Publishing. Now, each and every time, that you've ever sent anything to Inter Publishing or to Mr. Myers you've had some response, isn't that correct?

A   Yes.

Q   And, you've had lawyers involved sometimes, correct?

A   Yes.

Q   And, you've accountants involved sometimes?

A   Yes.

Q   And, notwithstanding that you've never asked Mr. Myers or

     Inter Publishing for any explanation with respect to these

matters from the time you seized the documents to the time

you laid the charge on May the 5th, 1975 and threw Mr.
Myers in gaol, isn't that correct?

A   Yes.

     MR. CHUMIR: I believe that's all the cros

     examination I have. *

Chapter VI

THE OFF-SHORE COMPANY

The arrest simply ignored the existence of Interpublishing Company. From the very beginning the Tax Department had tried to proceed on the pretense that no company really existed, that it was all a crooked deal and that the company was merely a name - a sham - therefore not worth talking about.

They even refused to recognize Jones, Black & Company, one of the oldest and one of the three largest law firms in Alberta, as representatives of Interpublishing Company of Zurich, Switzerland in the gold case. Jones Black attorneys were furious. They had received a retainer of $20,000.00 from Interpublishing, Zurich, and they had the Swiss government registration giving it full recognition as an operating company in Switzerland, including records of its officers, directors, and tax payments to the Swiss government. This high-handed attitude on the part of the tax men and their prosecuting attorney was quickly put down, and Jones Black pursued the gold question to its successful conclusion as the appointed attorneys of the fully **bona fide** and fully recognized off-shore company.

It was surprising then when after having recognized Interpublishing in court, Revenue Canada simply brushed it aside a second time in assigning Myers the full responsibility for the income of the company, especially in view of the fact that he was not a director of the company.

Off-shore companies are perfectly legitimate and necessary units within the structure of the international economy. They have become so big that in the United States they are known as "multi-nationals." These large firms have subsidiary companies in many lands around the world. These subsidiary companies are completely independent of the United States government and do not pay taxes to the United States government. Taxes are paid by the American mother corporation only when profits are returned to them in the form of dividends from their off-shore subsidiaries.

The basic monetary criteria for a legitimate off-shore company is that its income derives from a foreign source and comes to rest in the foreign headquarters of the company.

In Canada the classic example is the Canadian Pacific Railway Company (practically synonymous with Confederation) and its wholly-owned off-shore company, the Canadian Pacific Steamship Company, operating out of Bermuda.

The Canadian Pacific Steamship Company is one of the four largest in the world. It does some business in Canada but the bulk of its revenue is derived from foreigners. The income is deposited in Bermuda banks, the expenses paid there, and the residual profit retained there tax-free until such time, or in such amount, as may be declared as a dividend to the Canadian Pacific Railway Company in Canada. No one has any doubt that the Canadian Pacific Railway with full ownership calls the shots on how the shipping company should be run.

There is never any argument about this, nor is the CPR considered even to be unpatriotic in having its Steamship Company based in the tax-free haven of Bermuda.

This is the reason that innumerable shipping companies fly foreign flags such as Panamanian, Greek, Liberian, etc. This is universally recognized as a legal form of tax avoidance. It would be foolish and irresponsible of the executives of a Canadian company whose income is foreign to incorporate under a Canadian charter. No one is expected to oblige the Tax Department with revenue that it cannot legally collect. Many large Canadian corporations have foreign subsidiaries, not taxable in Canada. The tax men have better sense than to try to challenge such operation. An individual though is a different matter. He is fair game.

Interpublishing Company received - and in court it was fully admitted - nearly all of its income from the United States. There was some from Europe and a small amount from Canada.

Canadians, it seemed, were not interested in reading the financial analysis of C.V. Myers, his recommendations to buy gold and silver, to distrust both the American and the Canadian currencies and to convert those funds, when they were surplus, into Swiss francs or German marks. Anyone with such preposterous ideas back in 1969 to 1973 was obviously a crackpot.

This was pretty well clear when Myers started his newsletter in early 1967. He sent out 18,000 free copies to presidents, vice-presidents, general managers of all of the larger corporations in Canada. From this massive mailing he got 18 subscriptions at $25.00 each. But when he began mailing to American lists the response was electric. It attracted so much attention that in early 1968 the United States Securities Exchange Commission sent him a letter demanding that he cease mailing letters to the United States. If he wanted to do so he must register with the Securities and Exchange Commission in Washington. Myers ignored it.

Later on a sharp letter from the Securities Exchange Commission told him that he was breaking American law and if he didn't stop mailing the letters immediately or register, he would face criminal charges in the United States.

Myers reacted with a blistering refusal. He told the SEC essentially this:

"I live in Canada. For your information it is a sovereign nation. I have all I can do to keep up with the laws of Canada. I abide by them. I do not abide by the laws of China, Russia, France, or United States. I have a deal with the Queen. This deal is that if I put sufficient postage on a letter and drop it in the post box here in Calgary she will deliver it for me to anywhere in the world. I suggest you take your complaint to the Queen."

This resulted in a summons to Myers to appear to face charges in Baltimore, Maryland, May 29, 1968. He was served officially in his office in Calgary, Alberta.

Myers told the SEC that he regretted he was unable to attend the trial because he was busy at a horse show that week. Nine years later Judge Holmes would regard this as just another sign of basic lawlessness. The following is a true excerpt from the March 1st, 1977 conviction, by Judge Holmes.

> *On May 29, 1968, that agency obtained an injunc-*
> *tion ordering Myers to stop sending his newsletter*
> *into the United States of America. He disregarded*
> *the injunction which was made by an American*
> *Court at a Hearing he refused to attend.*

In Baltimore the trial took place on the appointed date and the SEC received an injunction which prohibited Myers from any further mailings into the United States of his newsletter. The U.S. judge allowed as how it would be difficult to enforce the ruling.

Myers' attorneys however advised him that it would be wise to abide by the injunction. If he continued to mail newsletters, and if at some later date he should visit the United States, he might be picked up for having broken the injunction. Their advice was that he form a corporation. Thus the **MYERS FINANCE & REVIEW** as it was called then ceased immediately to be a proprietorship. It was taken into a company Myers owned called Bar C.V. Ranch Limited registered in Alberta. Henceforth the company collected all revenue, paid all expenses, including the wages of the staff that mailed the letters and the postage. Myers became the writer on a salary. He personally **never** mailed another newsletter to the United States. (He did not disregard the injunction, his Honor's statement above notwithstanding).

The attorneys however were not comfortable with this arrangement because of the enormous influence that the U.S. could exercise in Canada. They felt a foreign incorporation would be better. The company could still do all the business, invoice the subscribers, collect the money, pay the expenses, pay Myers a salary if he liked, and retain the earnings until such time as Myers should decide to take them as dividends or in some other form. Even the printing could be done in Canada if paid for from abroad.

This was done and in early 1969 the Myers' Newsletter bore the Swiss mailing address and the bills were sent from Zurich and the subscription fees were deposited in Zurich. All of the expenses in Canada were paid from Zurich. During the next four years Myers took a salary ranging from $16,000.00-$18,000.00 a year. He did not need to take more because in 1963 he had sold his OILWEEK magazine to Maclean-Hunter for about $450,000.00. At that time there was no capital gains tax in Canada and he had from 1963 to 1971 to further enhance his net worth without tax. Myers had been retired between 1963 and 1967 when he started his newsletter and was in no need to work.

The off-shore company operated smoothly and without protest from the tax department for four years. During all of this time it processed his returns, was aware of the publication of the newsletter in Switzerland, gave no indication of dissatisfaction until out of the blue it staged the now infamous raid of September 19, 1974.

Myers had no doubt that the tax men had learned of the large gold deposits held for Americans in the Bank of Nova Scotia. There would be no problem for them to find this out because the Myers' Newsletter openly offered to buy gold for the Americans and to keep it for them free of harm and anonymously in the Nova Scotia Bank. But the existence of this large amount of wealth held under the name of Interpublishing offered tax investigators an opportunity of seizure which would place the company in an impossible position - in view of the fact that Americans would be very unlikely to come forward and claim their gold. Under those circumstances the off-shore company was really a sitting duck.

During the first two years the Myers' Newsletter had not bought gold. It had been recommending silver, predicting that the U.S. Treasury would lose control of the silver price, which it duly did. Importantly, the gold had absolutely nothing to do with the SEC complaint, which preceded Myers' gold recommendations by nearly two years.

Nevertheless, Judge Holmes in his double jeopardy conviction would erroneously state:

photostat of judgment

It was Myers' counselling of Americans to defy United States law that brought him into conflict with the United States Security Exchange Commission.

But we are getting ahead of ourselves.

Chapter VII

THE FIRST TRIAL

The first trial lasted four months, consumed 25 trial days, used 240 exhibits and 20 witnesses, none of them from Switzerland where Interpublishing records were headquartered.

Except for mail lists, subscription lists, Calgary expenses, and a pile of shorthand books, the prosecutor had little to go on and nothing which was in itself conclusive. **It was the first time an accounting problem had to be solved by the use of circumstantial evidence, on the face of it a mathematical impossibility.** It is a cardinal rule of accounting that if you don't have the full record you really don't have any record at all.

For instance an investor might make 18 transactions on which 16 might profit him $50,000.00. But if the other two transactions are unknown the net result could be anything from $100,000.00 profit to a $50,000.00 loss or anything whatsoever. The reverse is also true; apparent losses might on full record become profits.

It was impossible for the prosecution to claim they had the whole record. They made deductions from shorthand books and used their imaginations with as much discipline as possible, but under the cloud of numerous and hefty assumptions. They had nevertheless assessed a specific amount — $867,642.67. Now they set out to prove not only that this amount was correct but that Myers had personally and willfully evaded the paying of the taxes on this off-shore company.

The main thrust of prosecuting attorney Bill Major was to make out that Interpublishing was a joke even to the point where a highly competent lady who handled the Interpublishing affairs in Zurich was suggested by Major to be a "belly-dancer." Major had concocted this idea from a personal letter in which the lady director had addressed Myers by his first name, called him "boss" and referred to ballet lessons which she took twice weekly as a hobby.

Major spent a large part of his effort in painting a complexion firstly of a sham operation and secondly the picture of a man of obviously devious character, who would advise clients to have bank accounts in Switzerland to purchase gold against **American** law, and in his newsletters to call tax department operators "snoops."

One of Myers' attorneys pointedly remarked that judging from the **quantity** of the evidence required, it wasn't surprising to see deficiency in **quality**. In the middle of the trial Major introduced another assessment of $422,000.00 as a personal tax bill against Myers therefore accusing him in the trial of evading taxes exceeding $1.2 million. This gave the trial the dubious distinction of being the largest tax evasion trial in the history of Canada.

But when all of the fluff had been stripped aside the case rested basically on the following questions:

(1) Was Interpublishing a **bona fide** Swiss corporation?

(2) Was the Interpublishing income mostly foreign to Canada?

(3) Was it legitimate for a Canadian to own an off-shore company?

(4) Was Myers personally responsible for tax as an income from the off-shore company?

(5) Did Myers personally receive profits from the off-shore Interpublishing Company? That was really the key question of all questions.

The first question had passed all doubt. Copies of documents registered with the Swiss government established that.

The second question was also easily answered in the affirmative by the addresses which appeared on the subscriptions lists. As to number three, there was Canadian Pacific Railroad.

As to number four (personal responsibility) defense attorney Sheldon Chumir quickly put that to rest. Here is a true reproduction from trial transcript on that particular portion. Mr. Schwendmayer, who is in charge of the case for Revenue Canada, is on the stand.

No Personal Tax Liability

Q *Now, Mr. Schwendmayer, under our system of taxation, is it not true that a Company is taxed separately on its earnings, and that the shareholder or owner of the Company is not taxed on those same earnings until such time as they have come into his hands?*

A *Yes.*

Q *Is it not true that this applies, regardless of whether the Company is incorporated elsewhere, or a foreign entity, or a Canadian entity? In other words, let me give you an example. Supposing I incorporate a United States Company and that United States Company carries on business in the United States and earning $100,000.00, now, that $100,000.00 or let's assume - let's change the facts. Let's assume the United States Company is carrying on business here in Canada and earns $100,000.00, isn't it accurate that that United States Company would be taxed separately on its earnings and I as a shareholder would not be taxed until such time as they came into my hands?*

A *Yes, you are correct.*

Q *Supposing I had a United Kingdom Company and that United Kingdom Company carried on business here and I was a shareholder and it's earned $100,000.00, it's taxed on those earnings and not me until I get them, isn't that correct?*

A *Yes*

Q *Supposing I have a Swiss Company and it carries on a business in Canada and it earned $100,000.00, the treatment is exactly the same, the fact that it's a Swiss Company is irrelevant, it's a corporate entity and it's taxed separately and not the shareholder?*

A *Yes.*

Q *Is that correct?*

A *Yes.*

Chapter VIII

"NO DIRECT EVIDENCE"

But the fourth question was really Achilles heel of the prosecution which, up to this point, was estimated to have spent already over $500,000.00 in its work. Did Myers receive the money?

Here is the transcript on that. Schwendmayer is on the stand:

Q   Now, Mr. Schwendtmayer, we've seen that $878,000.00 of unreported business income has been included in the charge against Inter, and then the identical amount of $878,000.00 has been included in the charge against Mr. Myers. And, we've also gone through the principal that a company is taxable on the income which it receives, and a shareholder or an employee or whatever, somebody related to the company, is taxable only in respect of funds which come into such persons hands, correct?

A   Yes.

Q   And, that could be by way of dividends for example is a common way, correct?

A   Yes.

Q   And, it could be by way of appropriation where somebody takes it personally for their own purposes, correct?

A   Yes.

Q   And, it generally wouldn't include just a simple loan, would it?

A   No, it would not include any loans.

Q   Now, in 1969 Mr. Myers is charged with having unreported
     business income in the amount of $105,731.53 which is the
     same amount as for Inter. What do we have to indicate that
     that money came into Mr. Myers' hands in 1969, the year
     in respect of which he has been charged?

A   The reason why this was included is the set-up of
     establishment, the documents which we found in Mr. Myers'
     personal possession with respect to that set-up, the
     articles and additional information which we obtained in
     respect of the establishment. Furthermore there was at
     least evidenced before the Court with respect to an
     apparent purchase of sixty percent, and also the ownership
     of the rest of the forty percent spelled out in letters
     to Dr. Hinderling. This is the reason why we did it for
     the year, sir.

Q   You don't have any proof or any evidence that Mr. Myers
     received $105,731.53 in his hands in 1969, do you?

A   No, not direct evidence.

Q   You don't have any evidence?
     MR. MAJOR: Surely this is getting argumentative,

THE COURT: He's already answered that
question, Mr. Chumir. He said, "No direct evidence."

   MR. CHUMIR: Okay. Now, for 1970, do you have
   any evidence that Mr. Myers received the amount of
   $126,679.00 which is stated to be unreported business
   income, and is identical to the amount for Inter Publishing?

A   The same answer applies, Mr. Chumir, that I have no
    direct evidence with respect to this.

Q   Now, for 1971 the amount is $141,129.00?

A   The same answer applies, Mr. Chumir, that I have no
    direct evidence.

Q   And, 1972, $128,936.97?

A   As of November 30th, Mr. Myers owned at least sixty
    percent, but there is no further evidence that he received
    the full amount.

Q   No evidence that he received it?

A   No, sir.

Q   And, in 1973, the amount is $145,542.00?

A   With the exception of the letter of the sixty percent and
    forty percent you are speaking of, I have no direct evidenc

Q   And, in respect of 1974, the $219,582.00?

Q   In the Will he said he owns Euro and he owns Inter, and
    this is the reason why I concluded that amount.

Q   So, you have no evidence that these came into his hands?

A   It could be in Swiss bank accounts, I don't know.

Q   You have no evidence that they came into his hands? *

A   Personally, no, I don't, no.

Underlining of transcript were made by the attorneys.

In about two hours Chumir had knocked the heart and substance out of 20 days of prosecution, thereby laying waste to the valuable time of the Department's chief sleuth, A. Manfredi. Although Manfredi was in charge of all of southern Alberta he found time to attend the trial almost every day from start to finish, demonstrating the anxiety surrounding the case.

The trial closed late March 1976; Judge D.M. MacDonald put the decision over until April 30th. On that morning all assembled in the Courtroom which, by the time the gavel hit the desk, swarmed with men from the Tax Department accompanied by an R.C.M.P. officer to take Myers away if the cherished conviction should be issued.

The Judge's verdict: NOT GUILTY.

* * * * * * * * * *

Actually Myers' attorneys had anticipated the verdict. In the beginning they reasoned that if the Tax Department had a real strong case they would have moved aggressively with their evasion charge long before they lost the gold. They had picked up the records in September. Not until their gold capitulation in May, eight months later, did they move with the street arrest. The attorneys' guess was vindicated.

Unfortunately that was not the end of the story.

Chapter IX

FAST FOOTWORK

Humiliation in a court of law following the bad press on the gold case could mean harm to the Tax Department approaching national proportions. Loss of face across the nation surely would spell deterioration of respect and with it probably substantial loss of the **voluntary returns** by taxpayers which is the key to the revenue of the country. This was now verging on a NATIONAL matter. The verdict would have to be appealed.

But an appeal would have little if any chance of success. Grounds for appeal are limited to showing that the judge has erred in fact or in law.

Judge MacDonald had simply issued an acquittal and left it at that. There was nothing for them to hang their hats on. To go to the Court of Appeal with the complaint that the Judge had shown poor judgment would get them nowhere.

However, there was a loophole. Back in homestead days the government had introduced what was known as trial **de nova**, i.e., a new trial. That was for the benefit of some farmer or rancher who might be brought before a local magistrate of a remote community. The magistrate might be the town banker or even butcher with little knowledge of the law. Trial **de nova** gave the convicted party the right to seek a new trial before a competent court. It was never intended that trial **de nova** should be utilized as a device to exercise double jeopardy, or indeed at all for the benefit of the crown. Gradually however it worked into the system and was occasionally used to try an acquitted party again. Its use was rare.

But trial **de nova** was the only option open to Revenue Canada. Their battered image had to be repaired.

And there was another problem. If Myers should be acquitted by Judge MacDonald he would be free to leave the country immediately — as free as the Judge himself the moment the "not guilty" word was uttered. The tax men would only have thirty days, in the event of an acquittal, in which to serve MYERS with **repeat**

Investigator Manfredi
Service at the elevator.

charges. If he were to leave immediately after the trial, as he was legally entitled to do, their last chance — the trial **de nova** — would have evaporated. They might obtain one, two or even three extensions but if Myers should stay away for 90 days or more the war was lost.

And there was a difficulty in serving him. Proper service requires the signature of the clerk of the court. The clerk could not sign such a notice ahead of the verdict. The Courthouse where the clerk operated was at least one-fourth of a mile in downtown Calgary from the Court of Judge MacDonald. The fastest foot-work could not possibly deliver **bona fide** service in less than 20 to 30 minutes. There would be no legal way to hold Myers during that 20 minutes, and once he was gone service couldn't properly be delivered.

The problem suggested its own solution. Immediate service. **That had never taken place before** but it could be done with the direct consent of the Minister of Justice. Sometime before the April 30th court session for sentence, the prosecutor made contact directly with the Justice Minister in Ottawa and obtained his authority to serve Myers immediately upon acquittal — if that should happen — by-passing the Clerk of the Court.

With service papers already prepared and copies in the hands of several, tax men placed themselves at all exits. As Myers approached the elevator none other than A. Manfredi himself whipped out the service from his pocket and handed it to Myers.

It amounted to legal notice and service that Myers would face trial again. The charges spelled out were identical with those from which he had just been acquitted. The whole trial was wiped out, and with it the $50,000 in legal fees it had cost.

Back to square one!

Chapter X

THE SECOND TRIAL

The trial **de nova** — now abolished in Canada — was scheduled to end in 1976. At first Myers' attorneys wondered whether its abolition might prevent the second trial taking place. The exact date of declared obsolescence could not be found out.

It can be surmised that the government through the Justice Department might have obliged the Tax Department by keeping trial **de nova** alive for this **final run**. Later actions by the Justice Minister were to increase the suspicion that this might indeed have occurred.

The trial **de nova** was set for November 1976. In September the Liberal Government appointed a new judge to the Federal Bench in Calgary. R.K. Holmes had been a lawyer in Red Deer, Alberta, the center of a prosperous farming community 100 miles north of Calgary. The defense had hoped that a veteran judge in the Federal Court would be appointed to hear this rather sophisticated financial case, involving as it did international monetary practices and the background of knowledge about monetary affairs. The attorneys felt that would make their chore of getting the meaning of the case across much simpler. **But it was learned soon after the appointment of Judge Holmes that he had been selected to hear the case.** There was no provision for the defense to ask for a different judge. Judge Holmes was, after all, now a fully accredited Federal Judge.

The course of the second trial was as tedious as the first, chocked full of detail and trivia. No new evidence had been added to the records collected in the raid of May 1974.

In the end though, the second trial still rested on the same planks as the first. In fact as it went along it looked even better. A

Swiss lawyer called in by the prosecution from the Swiss Consulate in Washington affirmed the legitimacy of the companies. Myers' attorney (this time he only had one) grew more optimistic as the case progressed.

Myers did not have to attend the trial. Having been judged "Not Guilty," he was free to come and go as any Canadian. In early January he went to Palm Springs for his usual winter vacation. The vacation was shattered by a phone call on the morning of February 3, 1977.

Attorney John MacPherson, himself stunned, minced no words: "Judge Holmes has just convicted you and has set you down for sentencing March 1st."

Myers could not be forced to return to hear sentence. He decided that, whatever the sentence, an earlier return than usual wouldn't change it. The shocking culmination of the three-year battle came by telephone on March 1st.

Again MacPherson: "You've been sentenced to the MAXIMUM — two years mandatory imprisonment. It's the heaviest prison term ever handed down on summary conviction. What's more, I don't think we have a very good chance on appeal; it's such a sweeping judgment."

* * * * * * * * * *

Most of Myers' trial had been in absentia; he was sentenced in absentia, and a warrant was now issued for his arrest. He could not be brought back, but if he ever were to cross the border in his lifetime, he would be walking into a two-year jail term. Because the sentence was a full two years, (not two years **less one** day), it meant he would be in with the hardened criminals. The "less one day" is often used by judges to avoid that environment in cases where it produces an additional harshness. Judge Holmes had not seen fit to do that.

* * * * * * * * * *

Transcript of the second trial is not quoted here because no transcript exists. It would have cost $10,000 to get one. Since both trials were based on the same evidence, collected in *the raid of September 19, 1974, there was no compelling reason for this expense. Also, the points made in the first trial stood up in the second trial. The judge simply went behind all that to the question of* **Motive***.*

Chapter XI

THE AFTERMATH

If the verdict was a shocking surprise, the sentence was a disaster. Myers was virtually in exile. In Roman times a sentence to "exile" was regarded as next to, if not equal to, death. There was no comfort in the thought that Socrates, when given the choice between exile and death, chose the hemlock.

Why wasn't there any chance for success on appeal? For the same reason facing the Crown, had it been limited to the appeal route of the first trial. No chance of showing that the Judge had erred either in law or in fact. The judgment was purely a judgment of motive.

The written judgment did not question the validity of the off-shore companies. As legal entities they stood as solid as rocks. Nor did the written judgment dispute the assertion that Myers had not received any money as yet from the companies. Judge Holmes had out-flanked all that. It didn't matter, according to the judgment, whether Myers had received the money or not. He had schemed to defraud the government in the first place when he set the companies up, precisely for that purpose of evading taxes. Therefore the money **really** belonged to Myers the moment it hit the Swiss banks — companies or no companies.

Judge Holmes simply set the companies aside, thus supporting the view the Tax Department had tried to insist on from the beginning, when it had refused to recognize Jones, Black as the attorneys for Interpublishing, implying there were no real companies. What hadn't worked with Judge Quigley on the gold and what hadn't worked with Judge MacDonald came now successfully to rest in the Federal Court of Judge Holmes.

In the written conviction March 10, 1977 His Honor declared:

"I find Euro (Euro American Publishing Establishment) and Inter (Interpublishing Co., Ltd.) to be "shams" for Myers. *

> The secrecy with which Myers kept the true ownership and state of affairs of Inter and Euro disguised can surely lead to no other conclusion but that he intended those entities to be used as a facade for his own business operations for the purpose of diverting his own business profits into them to avoid Canadian income tax.

Had the "motive" danger been foreseen witnesses could have been brought forth to verify the real motive, which sprang from the confrontation with the Securities and Exchange Commission of the United States, and Myers' refusal on principle to subordinate Canadian sovereignty to American sovereignty.

When Myers, in 1968, had refused to recognize the authority of the SEC to force him to register in the U.S., he called on his law firm for advice. For thirty years Myers had been a client of the veteran Calgary firm, Macleod Dixon. They knew his business exhaustively. In a memorandum dated September 18, 1975, C.A. Rae, senior lawyer with the firm set down the circumstances clearly as part of a ten-page memorandum as follows:

> The writer's recollection of the 1968 transactions
> : that the sale to Bar CV and from Bar CV to a Swiss entity
> s prompted by the SEC injunction. We wanted firstly to
> ve a corporate entity (Bar CV) as the party directly vio-
> ting U.S. laws if a violation was to occur rather than
> . Myers personally - hence Bar CV as owner and CV Myers as
> blisher-employee at a salary. With the Alberta Commission
> rompted we suspected by the SEC) getting into the act in
> d-1968, the newsletter was to be sold to a Swiss entity

Nevertheless Judge Holmes fined Interpublishing ("the Sham") $250,000 declaring it to be a legal entity and therefore also guilty.

before the annual report of Bar CV was filed in 1969 - again to hinder the SEC from their snooping tactics outside the U.S.A.

At no time were we asked nor did we consider tax incidents of (1) operating in Bar CV as contrasted with C. V. Myers personally or (2) operating in a Swiss entity as contrasted with Bar CV. As far as we were aware the motivation had nothing to do with taxes but rather the SEC and Mr. Myers' exposure to arrest in the US if he continued as owner and operator of the publication.

Another point that might have been made was that when Myers set up his off-shore corporations his newsletter was less than two years old. He couldn't possibly have known then that it would go on to become one of the most enduring financial newsletters in North America. Indeed, his advice was laughed at by conventional economists — if they bothered to read it at all, as well as most of the foremost investment advisors in the world, who advanced the questions:

> *Move money to Europe to escape the decay of the mighty U.S. dollar — the most prized currency in the world?*
> *The stock market heading for a disaster, while the best market forecasters could see it doubling to reach 2,000 within a couple of years?*
> *Gold eventually selling for $100 an ounce or more, when the U.S. Treasury had specifically vowed that it would never allow gold to exceed $35 per ounce? And didn't the U.S. Treasury have hundreds of millions of ounces to sell?*

What utter nonsense. And what future could such a publication expect? No doubt if Judge Holmes, in his conservative way, had read the Myers Newsletter of 1969 he wouldn't have paid $1.00 for it; now, by hindsight, Myers had schemed to defraud the government of over a million dollars in taxes from its earnings.

The Newsletter was cited as evidence of Myers' guilt as shown in this sample photocopy from the Written Judgment.

If any other evidence of Myers intentions were needed, one might consider his newsletter of February 28, 1969 (Exhibit 45) wherein he advised his subscribers:

"It remains true that the only sure way out of this dilemma is to deposit your money in a foreign country, preferably one of the Big Three Swiss banks, in the form of Swiss francs. Now once this money is so deposited anonymously, there is no way in the world that anyone can pry information from the Swiss banks. At this point the owner of this money, be he a Canadian, an American, or Sudanese, can direct the Swiss bank to do whatever he wishes with the money. He can direct them to buy gold, silver, General Motors, or South African gold stocks without the equalization tax—"

"It is 100% legal for you to send money to Switzerland in any amount you desire. If it is in large denominations at one time there will be a record that you sent it to Switzerland. Later they might ask you what you did with it after it got to Switzerland.

What you do with it, and what you tell them, is not my business."

He was a consistent advocate of the use of Swiss banks.

His Honor's outlook seems to have been that such facts themselves were tainted. Writing the information was in itself evidence of complicity.

Such an outlook combined with setting up corporations in a foreign country surely required a devious mind. If such a surprising point of view had been in the least anticipated, it might have been headed off. Now it was too late.

* * * * * * * * * *

Now Myers' choice was a painful one. His family were grown and established in Canada. His wife had for some years been in poor health and the doctors on whom she relied were in Calgary. Myers had been reared on a homestead on the Alberta prairie. All his friends were there. His roots were there. If his wife joined him it would be a shared exile, for Myers could never come back.

He became a U.S. resident — a landed immigrant — set up a publishing corporation in Spokane, Washington, and continued to write his newsletter from there.

Chapter XII

JUSTICE TURNS A DEAF EAR

In January 1978, nine months after sentence, Myers came across the following news report in the *Vancouver Sun*. It looked like an interesting parallel.

C 8 VANCOUVER SUN; THURS.,DEC. 15,1977 ****

City Lawyer acquitted of four income tax evasion charges

A Vancouver lawyer was acquitted Wednesday of income tax charges, including evasion of payment of tax on income totalling $576,815.

County court Judge L.F.Cashman dismissed a Crown appeal against the acquittal in provincial court of George Arnold Armstrong, who the Crown alleged set up off-shore companies in the Bahamas as a sham to evade the payment of income tax.

Armstrong was one of several people who made a substantial profit in Pyramid Mines in 1965 and, in partnership with another man on advice of another lawyer and chartered accountant, set up two companies in the Bahamas.

Armstrong was charged with:

In 1967, while stating total income of $90,609, failed to report additional income of $269,643.

In 1968, while declaring income of $59,203, failed to declare additional income of $9,717;

And, in 1969, while declaring income of $27,090, failed to report additional income of $297,455.

A fourth count alleged that, between December, 1965, and May, 1969, Armstrong willfully evaded payment of taxes of $576,815, the total amount in the three other counts.

> *Judge Cashman said the provincial court judge*
> *was justified in finding there was nothing unlawful*
> *about conducting business through off-shore corpo-*
> *rations.*

Reading this, Myers decided to appeal directly to the Minister of Justice.

January 23, 1978

Hon. Ron Basford
Minister of Justice
Canadian Government
Ottawa, Canada

Dear Sir:

This is the identical parallel of the charges that were levelled against me in Calgary for tax evasion. I was acquitted by Judge McDonald of Calgary — after a five week trial, one of the longest — in April, 1976, because there was no evidence to establish that I had personally received any of the money from the off-shore company; and there was nothing wrong with doing business through an off-shore company. . .

Also "evasion" is understood by the teaching of the English language to all our school children to carry a meaning of, "slyness" or "trickery" or at least, "secrecy." But all of my operations were openly published in a newsletter announcing the name of the off-shore cor-poration, together with its address and the fees charged. Nothing could have been more openly done. The tax department visited my offices for two or three years, and never said anything after picking up my books.

But, is this justice? Is this what you want your Income Tax Department to do to people? . . .

I am interested to know whether you, as the Minister charged with the administration of justice, have any reaction to this situation.

Yours very truly,

C.V. Myers

No answer having been received in two and a half months, Myers followed with another letter.

April 10, 1978

The Honorable Ron Basford
Minister of Justice
Canadian Government
Ottawa, Canada

Dear Sir:

I am wondering if I will receive an acknowledgment of my letter of January 23, 1978. . .

Television celebrity David Frost set up a Bermuda corporation to absorb the lucrative earnings of the David Frost Show in the United States. According to an article in the Wall Street Journal, March 29, 1978 (enclosed), British Internal Revenue tried, on grounds of avoidance, to collect the taxes on earnings never remitted to Frost's homeland. It argued that the Bermuda partnership should be set aside because the sole purpose of its creation was to avoid taxes.

I quote from WSJ, March 29, 1978:

> "'This was undoubtedly a tax avoidance scheme,' the High Court of Justice declared recently. But tax-avoidance motives weren't legal justification for setting aside an otherwise valid transaction, the British Court determined."

This stands in direct contradiction to the verdict of Justice Holmes, who set aside the admittedly valid corporations of Interpublishing Company and American Publishing Establishment.

The almost exact parallelism between Frost and myself is striking. Frost's income was foreign and was deposited in an offshore corporation in a third country. The revenue of *Myers' Finance & Energy* was foreign and was deposited in the offshore corporation of a third country. Frost never brought the money back to his native country. The Tax Department agreed they had no evidence that I had ever brought the money to Canada.(I had sold OILWEEK for nearly a half a million dollars in 1963, had retired, and by 1970 was easily independent of the earnings of *Myers' Finance & Energy*.) ...

Yours very truly,

C.V. Myers

In early May Myers received the following reply from Basford. Note that the April date had been omitted. The April 10th letter to Basford was never acknowledged.

MINISTER OF JUSTICE AND
ATTORNEY GENERAL OF CANADA

MINISTRE DE LA JUSTICE ET
PROCUREUR GÉNÉRAL DU CANADA

OTTAWA, K1A 0H8

April   , 1978.

Mr. C.V. Myers,
642 Peyton Building,
Spokane, Washington 99201

Dear Mr. Myers:

I acknowledge receipt of your letter dated January 23, 1978 concerning your recent income tax problems.

It would appear that your case was fully considered by His Honour Judge Holmes and a conviction registered against you on March 1, 1977. I understand that no appeal was instituted on your behalf to correct any alleged errors made by the Court. Accordingly, it would be improper for me to comment on the disposition of a case which has been dealt with by the courts.

Yours sincerely,

MAY 8 1978

Ron Basford.

* * * * * * * * *

Chapter XIII

THE CRIME OF FRAUD

Canada and the United States are the only Western Democratic nations who incarcerate citizens for nonpayment of taxes. The laws of other countries provide for the confiscation of assets and even fines, but never imprisonment.

The reason may lie in the definition of what a crime is and what fraud is. Webster's Dictionary defines fraud as **"intentional perversion of truth in order to induce another to part with something of value. . ."**

Now notice, even if there is a perversion of truth in the incorrect filing of income tax, this nevertheless **falls short** of the key element in **fraud**.

It does not induce another to part with something of value.

And this is the key. If by lies I persuade my neighbor to part with certain portions of his property; if by lies I am able to obtain government property, that is fraud. But when a taxpayer fails to pay his full taxes, and maybe even lies on his return form, he has not confiscated something of the government's property by a lie. He has merely failed to yield up something of his own, something **he produced.** In the case of taxes, whatever it was that remains unpaid to the government, did not exist for **anyone** to own until the taxpayer had exerted the effort to produce it.

That seems to be why most Western countries do not regard tax evasion as criminal fraud.

In Canada tax evasion is quasi-criminal. Tax evasion is not dealt with in the **Criminal Code** of Canada. It is not a crime of moral turpitude. At least it is not included in the list of crimes in moral turpitude which the Canadian Immigration Department uses to screen immigrants into Canada.

A conviction in Tax matters is therefore not a crime of moral turpitude in Canada.

Myers' conviction was a Canadian conviction, therefore not a conviction on moral turpitude. When he entered the States he was asked if he had ever been convicted of a crime of moral turpitude. His attorney instructed him that if he were to say "yes" to that question, it would be, if not a lie, at least an erroneous answer. His answer had to be "no'.

Myers was accepted as a landed immigrant into the United States in April 1977. Shortly thereafter the Canadian bureaucracies began prodding the U.S. Immigration Department in an effort to destroy his landed status and thereby force his return to Canada. The pressure of Canadian bureaucracies is still in progress. While they cannot extradite Myers on the basis of the conviction, they are making a great effort to persuade the U.S. Immigration to deport him into their jurisdiction for further incarceration.

Chapter XIV

JUSTICE PROMISES - THEN RENEGES

A year and three months after the sentence of March 10, 1977 Myers' long time Calgary attorney John Marshall of MacLeod Dixon suggested that while an appeal of conviction was not practical, an appeal of **sentence** might be. The fact that the sentence seemed unreasonably harsh, and the fact that Myers was returning, of his own free will, were very positive points.

Even a one-day reduction would make a big difference, for it would mean incarceration in a provincial jail among inmates guilty of lesser offenses. Parole privileges would be more lenient. Day parole might be obtained in relatively short order.

Marshall retained Hyman Soloway of Soloway and Wright, an Ottawa firm on familiar terms with most ministers and deputy ministers; much used by the government.

The idea was to get the Department of Justice to agree **not to oppose** an application for leave to appeal sentence. Since the 30-day privilege of appeal had long ago expired, the Appeal Court was not obliged to hear any application, but Marshall felt that if he could go before a single judge of the Court of Appeal, stating that **the Justice Department had no objection to an appeal of sentence**, it was likely the judge might allow the matter to be heard. In the fall of 1978 Marshall informed Myers that he had Soloway's confirmation that Mr. Rutherford of the Department of Justice had agreed that if **Myers returned to Canada, the Justice Department would not oppose the application for leave to appeal sentence.**

Following is Mr. Marshall's photostated confirmation:

Macleod Dixon
Barristers & Solicitors

As you are aware, over the last several months Mr. Hyman Soloway, Q.C. of the Soloway, Wright firm in Ottawa has acted as our agent for the purpose of conducting negotiations with the Departments of Justice and National Revenue in Ottawa relating to the possibility of your returning to Canada and entering custody.

Mr. Soloway has reported to us that through Mr. Rutherford, of the Department of Justice, he has been advised that in the event you return to Canada and enter custody and ma.:e application for leave to appeal from the sentence imposed by His Honour Judge Holmes, the Department would not oppose such application.

It was the first breath of fresh air since the conviction of March 1977. Myers told his family on Christmas Day, 1978, in Spokane, that he was going to return, and he advised Marshall that he would turn himself over to the RCMP in Calgary on the morning of January 10th.

On January 9th Myers departed Spokane. At 3:00 p.m., January 9th, John Marshall delivered by taxi a letter addressed to Myers in care of Mrs. Myers at their Calgary home.

This is a photostat from Attorney John Marshall's letter of 3:00 p.m., January 9th. He had just finished talking to Ottawa; a catastrophic change! Justice had changed its mind.

289

In the circumstances, therefore, we are not able to advise you that we have a commitment of any type from the Department of Justice or the Department of National Revenu which would bind them and their counsel not to oppose the leave application.

By this time Myers was already 100 miles inside Canada.

Chapter XV

ILLEGAL SENTENCE

Myers was transferred to maximum security Remand Center in Calgary. Cell Block E was populated by eight inmates convicted on charges ranging from armed robbery to murder.

Marshall's first visit confirmed the worst. Bill Major, the prosecutor, definitely would oppose any application for leave to appeal sentence. Under the circumstances Marshall was gloomy. If Major was going to oppose them, there wasn't much hope.

Next morning Marshall was back. Lo and behold, **the sentence was not on the law books of Canada!** It was an **illegal** sentence. In fact no sentence at all. Technically Myers was being illegally detained.

The fault with the sentence lay in the alternatives that had been open to the judge. They ranged from a "straight-fine" to "imprisonment or a fine," to the most extreme of all — a fine of one-quarter to double the taxes owing and two years mandatory imprisonment. **Two years imprisonment by itself was not an option open to the Court.** Judge Holmes had botched the sentence.

But in his summary the judge had affirmed his realization that two years imprisonment was a very heavy sentence. This should mean then that if a fine had to be introduced into the sentence as well, the time would have to be **reduced somewhat** to compensate. If that were so, Myers would serve whatever time resulted in the provincial jail in the more lax conditions of parole — if indeed he could be re-sentenced at all.

Accordingly Marshall prepared a writ of **habeus corpus**, that is, demanding Myers' release on the grounds that he was being illegally held. Here Judge Quigley wavered. He was reluctant to release Myers and at the same time reluctant to change the sentence Judge Holmes had handed down. He deferred the matter to the Court of Appeal.

But there was a frightening possibility here. The Court might refer the sentence back to Judge Holmes to fix it up. Holmes' remedy might very well be to add a fine of between $250,000 and an astronomical $2.8 million, and if not paid an alternative **additional** six months in prison.

What had looked so promising, now after several days, looked unbearably sour. After much consultation with other lawyers, Marshall came back with a recommendation that Myers had best serve the sentence as handed down, even if it was nowhere to be found in the law books of Canada, and therefore illegal.

The alternative might be much worse. Law or no law, Myers was now behind bars. Judge Holmes' sentence was carved in stone. It was a chilling prospect at the age of 67 — two years in the pen.

* * * * * * * * * *

The botched sentence opens some interesting questions:

Did Prosecuting Attorney Major know that the sentence was illegal? (In view of his zeal in pressing for maximum sentence, it's quite likely he did.) If so, should Major have corrected the Judge then and there? If not, was Major obliged to tell his client, Manfredi, and did he?

If so, did Major and Manfredi advise the top brass in Ottawa, or did they decide to keep silent to avoid the embarrassment of a new and corrected sentence — just to let a sleeping dog lie?

*If Ottawa was informed, did it also decide to let the sleeping dog lie — **to let an unlawful sentence stand?***

Would all of that amount to a cover-up?

The answer will probably never be known.

Chapter XVI

JAIL

A two year sentence, of course, doesn't actually mean two years. An inmate becomes eligible for full parole within a third of the time, that is, eight months; and eligible for day parole within six months. Here is a photostat of those eligibility dates.

File No.: 797496A

Inst. No.: 0255

 Parole Board   Commission des libérations
Canada   conditionnelles Canada

National Parole Board
5th Floor Financial Building
230 - 22nd Street East
SASKATOON, Saskatchewan
S7K 0E9

March 6, 1979

Mr. Charles Vernon Myers
c/o Bowden Institution
Box 6000
INNISFAIL, Alberta
TOM 1AO

Dear Mr. Myers:
In accordance with the provisions of the Parole Regulations,

1. your eligibility date for <u>Unescorted Temporary Absence</u> has been set at July 10, 1979.

2. your eligibility date for <u>Day Parole</u> has been set at July 10, 1979.

3. your eligibility date for <u>Full Parole</u> has been set at September 10, 1979

AR/smf
cc Director, Bowden
cc District Director, Red Deer
cc File

Yours truly,

[signature]

for Regional Secretary

All of this had been known before Myers returned to Canada. It was assumed by everyone, lawyers included, that Myers would be fully paroled within a third of the time. To refuse, the Board must give a good reason. Usually those reasons relate to the danger to society if the inmate is released, and the ability of the inmate to rehabilitate in society, including his capacity for earning his livelihood. None of these standard reasons for parole rejection could be applied to Myers. It had been taken almost for granted that good behavior in prison would result in release in eight months and probably daytime release (returning at night) in six months. Even the lawyers had considered this the WORST that could happen. The prospect of being refused parole when the eligibility date came around was not considered.

After some 21 days in the steel cells in the Remand Center, Myers was transferred to Bowden Penitentiary about 80 miles north of Calgary. His partner in the transport plane (an old two-engine prop job) to whom he was chained, left hand to right hand, freely spoke of the cause of his trouble: "It was for running guns," he said. "We did real good with the 16M automatics (machine guns). We had sold them, all but two. When the cops broke in, my partner and me made it down the stairs to the car and took off. Well, by God, in about 15 minutes we were surrounded by 29 cops; cars on all sides of us. So we jumped out with our automatics and my partner said: 'Will we shoot it out or will we give up?' I said: 'Expletive. . . . there's 29 of them and only two of us — let's give up!"

Myers was inclined to think he was dangerous himself, when at the Remand Center, he was ordered out for X-rays, and was marched through a busy Calgary intersection, legs in chains, his hands chained behind his back, a husky guard holding either arm.

Myers found himself in the company of the criminally elite. No small-time crooks here. Sentences ranged from two years to life. He found himself in great disparity with the prison population — and in every way. About two-thirds of the inmates were under 30. Most of the rest were up to 40. One, a lifetime repeater, was 55.

In age, in background, in interests, in mental stature, in wealth — in every way Myers stood apart — prominent by his differences. Inmates thought of him as a tycoon — therefore doubly deserving to find out what jail was like.

Once or twice there was the smell of trouble; a broken radio in his cell, a plan to "burn him out." In the cells, separated at Bowden by paper-thin walls, turning pages of Time Magazine late at night could bring on a round of abuse. To an inmate high on drugs, turning a page could sound like crashing timber. The ways for smuggling drugs were varied and ingenious — foiling every method of detection — even the body search which occurred every so often. Swallowing a plastic sealed container, brought in by a visitor, and recovering it later was one method. Drugs that would bring $500 on the street would bring easily $2,000 in prison.

But, even here, a support system for Myers developed among the prisoners, who meted out justice in their own way. For example, Myers received a new radio the day after his was broken. An inmate passing him in the corridor whispered: "Don't worry about those guys any more. They won't touch you." Also the "burn out" plot was discovered by new friends and suddenly nipped.

After a couple of months, a growing respect began to develop for "the old man," and the prison population was more friendly than otherwise. Native Indians especially seemed to like "the old man" and often kidded him in mock fist fights, flat races and talk of prowess with the women. And so, "the old man" — the cleaner of the cardroom — after two months never feared again for his safety. There were secret protectors everywhere.

Myers began to see the light at the end of the six-month tunnel. Then the axe fell.

THE LESSON

Does Myers learn a lesson from jail? Does he bring us a message? Yes: Once your freedom is gone, you will endure every humility, obey every order, suffer every indignity without protest. Resistance will make matters worse. To survive you must force yourself to become neutralized, neuterized, nullified. You must sink into a non-entity, a non-person, a breathing apparatus moving on two legs. You must first defend freedom; once the doors close it is too late.

Chapter XVII

PAROLE BOARD AS
TAX COLLECTOR

In March Revenue Canada tried to pin the prisoner down to an interview which they could not obtain if he was on the outside. It was surprising because they had long since seized the last of Myers' assets in Canada — including his Old Age Pension. It was chilling, too, that in his present defenseless position tax agents were now calling on the warden of the Bowden Institution to allow and to arrange an interview with the prisoner.

Myers got permission for an emergency phone call to his lawyer. Marshall drove up immediately from Calgary to see him.

Together they decided that while the issue of taxes was unrelated to the jail term, it might be wise, nevertheless, to cooperate with the Tax Department to the extent possible. But the attorney felt that any discussions with them should be kept on record. Accordingly, on May 1st, 1979, Marshall wrote the Tax Department as follows:

> If you have any questions or suggestions, then I would ask that you set them out in a letter to me so that I can review them with Mr. Myers. He has indicated his willingness to cooperate with the Department in this regard. If you still consider it necessary to interview Mr. Myers personally, Mr. Myers has indicated his willingness to attend such an interview provided that it is carried out in my presence and a tape is kept of the interview.

> Yours very truly,

> John H. Marshall

Weeks passed. No response. Nothing is so intolerable to a tax agent as to have his interview taped for possible future reference. It seemed that faced with a recording, they had given up. Not so. They were merely proceeding by a different means. In late May, via the grapevine, Myers heard that he would be expected by the Parole Board to pay a substantial amount of money in order to realize parole on his eligibility date. The sum of $100,000 to $250,000 was mentioned.

It was incomprehensible. It could never happen! Yes, it could! By word of mouth Myers found himself staring into the jaws of a scenario of horror. **Discussions between the Parole Board and Revenue Canada had been going on since May! Jail as a method of extraction!**

A letter from a friend confirmed all of this:

> At last I have been able to have a telephone conversation with Bob Gillies, Sr. Member of the Regional Parole Board.
>
> Bob tells me that he has had discussions with the tax people

Myers' friend outlined the alternative and there can be little doubt that this alternative had been outlined to him by Chairman Gillies.

> He will expect some concrete efforts on your part to begin repaying what the Court says you owe.

His friend's interpretation was:

The alternative to going the route described is to say to hell with them, pursue your case in court & resign yourself to completing your sentence inside.

Chapter XVIII

DEBTOR'S PRISON

Since a person cannot be put in jail for owing money, surely owing money by itself should not delay his parole. The lawyers had already advised the Tax Department that under incarceration raising of any substantial sum of money was out of the question. Liquidation of assets of this magnitude, even if available and even if they'd been in Canada, would require both time and freedom. As an inmate Myers, like all others, was restricted to three phone calls a month. Hopeless.

It began to dawn that this might mean Myers would have to serve the whole sentence — no parole. It was scary. And he doubted his ability to survive. By June he had already been hospitalized twice and he felt his vitality running down as each endless day dragged into the next.

The problem was that the Parole Board could give any reason at all for denying parole. **They could even say his attitude hadn't changed.** They wouldn't have to use the real reason — the extraction of money. How could you fight that?

Then they made a blunder — they put the reason in writing.

Government Gouvernement of Canada du Canada National Commission nationale des Parole Board libérations conditionnelles OUR FILE: 797496A Mr. Charles Vernon Myers C/O Bowden Instituiton P.O. Box 6000 INNISFAIL, Alberta T0M 1A0	National Parole Board 5th Floor, Financial Building 230 - 22nd Street East SASKATOON, Saskatchewan S7K 0E9 June 18, 1979

Dear Mr. Myers:

During the review of your file, the Board noted that there is an outstanding income tax assessment in the amount of $1,810,000.00. The Board is aware of your lawyer's May 1, 1979, letter to Revenue Canada Taxation; but it is concerned that you have made only minimal effort to discuss this matter with Revenue Canada Taxation and to reach an agreement for payment. As this will be an important factor for consideration during any parole review, the Board hopes that between now and your Parole Eligibility Date, you will take the initiative and try to reach an agreement with Revenue Canada Taxation for payment of the tax assessment.

Yours truly

Norman J. Fagnou
Regional Secretary

Reading the letter of June the 18th at the jail, Marshall was shaken: "My God — it's a debtor's prison. Would the Parole Board demand that you pay off your debt to the Bank of Commerce to get released? I can't believe this!"

Upstairs in the jail, Myers spoke to the Parole representative: "They have become a collection agency for the tax people — they have abdicated their powers to the tax people — they can't do this."

The Parole man's reply: **"The Parole Board can do anything."**

The Parole Board had become so used to doing anything, it had forgotten that the Parliament of Canada never quite granted it the authority to hold people in prison for outstanding debt.

Myers' lawyers were denied the right of representation at the Parole Hearing of July 18th. Nevertheless, they presented a brief which laid the matter out clearly:

> *"It is submitted that the matter of outstanding tax assessment, while certainly related to the conviction, must be regarded as separate from the penalty that was imposed by the Court on the evasion.*
> *"The tax assessments are an entirely civil matter between the Income Tax Department and Mr. Myers as a taxpayer and cannot in any way be regarded as part of his sentence.*
> *"Were it otherwise, the effect would be to re-establish a form of imprisonment for debt — a concept deservedly abandoned long ago."*

They pointed out that under the terms of parole, as laid down, there was no reason to deny parole — except the reason of debt.

But would the Board pay any attention? If it was not openly allowing itself to be used as a collection arm, what was Gillies doing talking to Revenue Canada in May, two months ahead of the hearing?

Marshall believed that if the Board denied parole at the upcoming hearing, the matter would have to be brought to court. It was a poor answer though. Those proceedings could take a year, Myers would still be in jail — that might well prove to be too long.

Boomerang

Myers let it be known in the jail that if the Parole Board turned down his application for parole, he would enter an action based on their letter of June 18th. This evidently scared the hell out of everybody. **Everything suddenly changed.**

When Myers asked his lawyers to seek an interview with the Tax Department and to offer $100,000 as a **token** of intent, the tax men became aloof. They took the position that now they would require $1.8 million full payment or **full disclosure** of Myers' assets all over the world. The lawyers insisted that under incarceration that both these conditions were impossible. No one could be asked to raise this much cash in jail, and as for full disclosure, Myers could say anything. How could it be proved?

The response of Agent Benz was that he required absolute, documentary proof of worldwide assets.

Plainly this was a demand not meant to be fulfilled, for **no one can prove what he doesn't have**. It could always be claimed that there was more money in some other bank in some other country. The conclusion was clear: **Full disclosure meant nothing less than blockage.**

The date of the hearing was drawing near, and since the sum of $250,000 had been mentioned at one time, Myers managed, through friends, to arrange for this amount from jail. Now he asked his lawyers to call the tax men again and to offer them a quarter of a million dollars on condition they would advise the

Parole Board that they were satisfied with this as a **token of intent.** The offer fell on closed ears. Once again, it was the blank wall of **"Full Disclosure."** Whereas at first they had been zealous to break into the jail in an effort to collect money, now they wanted nothing to do with money. Something had scared them off, and it seemed to have been the blunder of the Parole Board letter of June 18th. The Board itself was out on a limb because of this self-incriminating letter.

Myers asked his lawyers to come to Bowden for final advice a few days before the July 18th hearing. The advice was this:

> *We see no point in paying any money at all. There has been no counter-offer by the Department. The conditions for your parole are obviously these: pay them $1.8 million — which you can't do — or give them full disclosure — which you can't do.*

Myers felt himself squeezed between the jaws of a giant vise. The Parole Board was demanding on the one hand that he settle with the Tax Department. The Department, on the other hand, was refusing to talk settlement at all. It was a pretty tense few days. The Board, it was thought, would either issue the parole or deny it. If they denied it, the consequences for them would be a lawsuit and Canadian-wide publicity; for Myers, more time behind bars.

What happened was neither.

On the morning of July the 18th Myers was summoned to the downstairs boardroom of the jail for the long awaited hearing. It lasted for more than an hour. Myers was excused and a few minutes later called back into the room: "We are '**deferring**' your parole." Chairman Gillies stated flatly that Myers should settle with the Tax Department. He knew just as clearly that the Tax Department would not settle. Now there couldn't be a lawsuit. Neither could there be release.

But the carrot was held out, "We'll keep in touch with the Tax Department to see how it's coming along," said Chairman Gillies.

* * * * * * * * * *

Nevertheless the Board had a problem. Under the law they

were required to give a yes or no answer before September. The deferral only bought them time. The purpose of this time was not known. It was soon evident.

A few days after the hearing, a representative of the Parole Board visited the jail and summoned Myers. He wanted written permission to receive the records of the Tax Department's prosecution at the trial. The cat was out of the bag. The Board needed reasons, **other than money**, to deny the parole. The unfortunate letter of June 18th and any consequent lawsuit could thereby be circumvented. With the Board's powers they could give almost any reason except money. Myers strongly suspected something could be found in these records. Certainly nothing good could come out of the **prosecution**. This suspicion was also enforced with the request for copies of Myers' newsletter. Certainly there was nothing in the newsletter that could **help** his case. The reason for a parole denial could easily be: "This man's attitude hasn't changed. Parole Denied!" There would be nothing you could do about it. Not a thing in the world.

The odds seemed to favor full mandatory imprisonment and quite possibly the withdrawal of Myers' right to continue writing his newsletter. **He would come out of jail broke or broken — or both — his voice silenced for good.**

* * * * * * * * * *

Myers had been in jail for six months and seventeen days, and had earned the usual temporary absence which is given automatically unless there is reason to suspect that the prisoner will do harm or misbehave. He had asked his lawyers to set up another meeting with Benz of the Tax Department. The hopelessness of the position was evident in a communication that Marshall sent by a third party to Myers, the day before his temporary absence.

phone message from Jack Marshall's office.   July 25/79

"I spoke with Ted Benz July 24. He had received instructions. Myers' offer of $250,000 in settlement of

his tax liability was rejected. The position of the Department is that they are not able to compromise a tax liability without their first having had full and complete disclosure on the part of the taxpayer of his assets and ability to pay. More important than the collection of the tax itself is their concern with compliance with the Act by other taxpayers."

The June 18th letter was a pretty strong confirmation that the tax men were in charge of the show. The **deferral** supported it. The refusal of the Tax Department to negotiate clinched it.

The 48-hour temporary absence would start at 5 p.m. Friday. Myers asked Marshall to definitely hold on to his Monday 9 a.m. appointment with Benz.

So it may have come as a shock when the authorities learned at 9 a.m. Monday that Myers was no longer in Canada and therefore no longer under the jurisdiction of the bureaucracies.

Congressmen Scorned

On the morning of the parole hearing, July 18, 1979, an important communication reached the Bowden Institution. It was an appeal for Myers' release by ten U.S. Congressmen. Here is the text as it was transmitted to the Parole Board at Bowden:

The National Parole Board
Bowden Institution
Bowden, Alberta

Re: Charles Vernon Myers

Gentlemen:

It is the desire of the following to simply take this opportunity to speak on behalf of and in support of Mr. Charles Vernon Myers.

Without question the Myers' Finance and Energy Report has been and is instrumental in perfectly representing needed facts and insight in those areas of energy and finance today. The research and conclusions which only Mr. Myers seems capable at times to deliver are of great assistance in the shaping of policy on a national level for many leaders.

It is our most sincere desire that he be given the opportunity to continue in his fullest capacity this much needed work.

Yours very truly,
The Honourable Richard Kelly, Congressman State of Florida
The Honourable Bob Stump, Congressman State of Arizona
The Honourable Steve Symms, Congressman State of Idaho
The Honourable Larry McDonald, Congressman State of Georgia
The Honourable Daniel B. Crane, Congressman State of Illinois
The Honourable George Hansen, Congressman State of Idaho
The Honourable Ron Paul, Congressman State of Texas
The Honourable James Collins, Congressman State of Texas
The Honourable Jim Jeffries, Congressman State of Kansas
The Honourable John Rousselot, Congressman State of California

During the hearing before the Board, this communication was not mentioned to Myers, nor so far as he knows were the Congressmen ever acknowledged.

Additionally, literally hundreds of letters of support reached the parole headquarters and the office of the Canadian Prime Minister. This was to no avail, although at about the same time two parolees were released, who promptly murdered two people in Edmonton within the next 24 hours.

Chapter XIX

CANADA'S CANCER

In Canada the Tax Department is a cancer of deep and fast-spreading roots. Their methodology is only illustrated by Myers' case. It goes on all the time, but unfortunately for them, most of the poor victims have no voice. Most of the victims are only too anxious to keep their settlements secret. If they are accused of evasion, they don't want others to know. The victims are like dumb beasts — sheep on the slaughterhouse floor. They suffer the indignities and the illegalities of coercion in silence. Even if they want to talk about it, they have only a few friends to tell. So what!!

This cancer then deepens its hold on the Canadian public. Tax men made the mistake in Myers' case of picking a victim equipped with a megaphone and who wasn't afraid to use it. This brought to public exposure the length to which this tyrannical bureaucracy was willing to go. It covered the following:

(1) The seizure and wrongful withholding of the wholly-owned assets of foreign nationals — innocent third parties.

(2) The final return of these admittedly owned assets by imposing a condition on the foreign owners not to sue the Tax Department.

(3) Vengeance on a verdict of "Not Guilty" by a trial of double jeopardy.

(4) Reversing the Justice Department of Canada on a commitment given that it would not oppose leave to appeal sentence.

(5) Controlling the Parole Board to the point where it was ready to acquiesce to the first case of "Debtor's Prison" since the dawn of democracy.

No wonder James Dines was impelled to write in his newsletter of July 20, 1979, a story entitled **"CANADA'S FIRST POLITICAL PRISONER."**

Chapter XX

CONCLUSIONS

All of what happened to C. V. Myers could happen to anyone. Many of the activities practiced on Myers are being practiced every day on different people by the Tax Department. It just happens that in Myers' case, because of the complications, the Tax Department had to telescope all of its vast powers on one case to win the necessary victory.

The case is merely a MANIFESTATION OF THE SUM OF ALL THE POWERS PUT TOGETHER.

ARREST WITHOUT ASSESSMENT

CONSIDER THIS: If Prime Minister and the government are seriously threatened in an election the Prime Minister calls in the Revenue Minister. "Can't you do something on Joe's taxes?"

"We don't have anything on him."

"You don't have to have — do you?"

"Not really."

"You could arrest him for tax evasion. You don't have to win, do you?"

"No."

"You won't be in any trouble if finally in a year from now you lose this case?"

"No — not under the law."

"He couldn't sue you for it?"

"No."

"Well, you must have some suspicions to go on. Arrest him."

FANTASTIC — you say? Probably it is, but the power is there. Should the power be there?

Remember, Myers, although he was arrested in May, was not acquitted until the following March. By that time the election would have been long in the past — and so would Joe.

No living person has the power to seize property without due process. Should the government have?

No living person — even if he has a judgment against someone — is entitled to intimidate, coerce, and cross-question outside the court. Should the government have this power?

Who is the master and who are the servants? Are we getting the whole thing reversed in Canada? The fact is that we are all, as citizens, in danger from our government and perhaps most of the legal time is spent defending citizens from the government and its regulations.

Already today the huge taxation bureaucracy acts as if it were a law unto itself. Should this be so? Can we let it go on? Our problem is that our elected representatives no longer represent us with any authority. The enormous machine in Ottawa has fallen into the hands of the bureaucrats who survive one election after the other. A new rookie Minister is then "Advised." At first he must accept this advice because he is dependent upon his deputies and sub-deputies. Soon the whole thing becomes too much for him to understand.

The preceding tale illustrates how the tax bureaucracy can dominate even the Department of Justice. **Can Canadians afford to allow this frightening bureaucracy to continue its unbridled advance against their rights?**

Chapter XXI

INCOME TAX ACT ULTRA VIRES

Wouldn't it be strange - a plot worthy of Shakespeare - that if after all this, it should be discovered that the Income Tax Act of Canada is itself illegal?

There's good reason to believe it is.

The British North America Act is the Constitution of Canada. Any law of Parliament that violates that Constitution is null and void. And all the effects of such a law are nullified just as if the law had never been passed.

The BNA Act states in Clause 91: *It shall be lawful for the Queen. . .to make Laws for the Peace Order and Good Government in Canada, in relation to all matters not coming within the Classes of Subjects by this Act assigned* **exclusively** *to the legislatures of the provinces."*

It's very clear from the above that the Federal Government can impose any kind of taxes it wants and to any amount that it wants **except** and **unless** such taxes infringe on the **exclusive** rights given to the provinces under the BNA Act.

Paragraph 92 states: *"In each Province the Legislature may exclusively make Laws in relation to . . . that is to say, -*

"Direct Taxation within the Province in order to the raising of Revenue for **Provincial Purposes."**

* * * * * * * * * *

Income tax is direct taxation.

It is clear that direct taxation for **provincial purposes** is the **exclusive** right of each of the provinces. Exclusive is a word that you just don't fool around with. It means plainly and simply what it says - **nobody else.**

Now it is true that the Federal Government may use direct

taxation for its federal purposes and for good government of Canada. But it is not true that it may collect direct taxes within a province and then spend the money for **Provincial Purposes,** roughly defined as roads, education, hospitals, etc.

The Federal Government is doing exactly that; using direct taxation to collect over and beyond **federal needs,** then returning much of it in the form of provincial grants with strings attached, i.e., if you don't agree to our conditions, you don't get the money.

Through a 1962 collection agreement between itself and the provinces, the Federal government began collecting taxes for the provinces. It simply hands back to each province a percentage of the taxes it collects on a **uniform** basis throughout Canada as the provinces' share.

Myers' law firm, MacLeod Dixon, in an extensive and exhaustive research found that the tax agreement of 1962 had never been tested in the courts. If this needed further confirmation, that is available in a reply by no less than the Provincial Treasurer of Alberta, the Honorable C. Mervin Leitch, Q.C., Provincial Treasurer.

Thirdly, you have raised the interesting issue of "federal direc taxes for provincial purposes". This issue has never been satisfactorily resolved in the courts.

Your question as to the course the Alberta Government would take should the Federal Income Tax Act be challenged, is entirely hypothetical. Any decision to intervene in a "legal dispute" is dependen upon the facts and legal issues in question. Without that knowledge no commitment could be given. Should the issue of the constitutionality of the Federal Income Tax Act arise, the issue of intervention would be care fully considered before any decision is made.

Yours truly,

Merv Leitch

/dcn

In a letter of December 1, 1978, Treasurer Leitch confirmed as follows:

"Payments to Alberta by the Government of Canada are listed by purpose in Table A4 of my 1978 budget address, a copy of which

is enclosed. These are conditional grants paid directly to the Government of Alberta by the Federal Government."

The following is extracted from Table A4 photographically reproduced:

DETAILS OF MAJOR COMPONENTS OF BUDGETARY

REVENUES 1975-76 TO 1978-79

	1978-79 Estimate	1977-78 Forecast	1976-77	1975-76
Payments from the Government of Canada:	(millions of dollars)			
Hospital Insurance and Diagnostic Services	171.0	158.4	230.9	185.4
Canada Assistance Plan	114.7	116.4	101.5	89.8
Revenue Guarantee Payments	7.0	66.3	73.3	42.0
Post-Secondary Education	97.5	60.8	39.0	42.8
Training of Manpower	26.0	23.0	21.5	18.5
Public Utility Corporation Income Tax	—	—	25.5	16.5
Extended Health Care	43.4	38.0	—	—
Other	85.0	80.0	68.8	56.0
Total Government of Canada	544.6	542.9	560.5	450.9

Extensive research by an economist of the University of Calgary has come to show at the conclusion that at least one-fifth of the grants arise out of direct taxation within the province.

The question of the legality of the entire tax setup in Canada is plainly no pipe dream. Also, it is no pipe dream that the government of Canada - in contravention to the BNA Act - is directly taxing the people of Alberta and returning part of this money in the form of grants with conditions attached.

Major rulings of the Courts tend to support the contention that the Canada Income Tax Act is ultra vires. The highest courts have ruled that neither the Federal Government nor the Provincial Government may surrender any of its powers under the BNA Act to the other. When the provinces agreed with the Federal Government to uniform taxation throughout Canada, they surrendered much of their powers because Canada is a large and diverse country. The purpose of the BNA Act was to give each province the authority of direct taxation according to its specific needs.

Another ruling as high as the Privy Council of England has been: Exclusively means excluding all others, it would be ridiculous to think that the framers of the BNA Act would give the provinces an exclusive right, and at the same time give the same right or part of it to the Federal Government. Applied to taxation, this simply says that it is ridiculous to think that the framers of the BNA Act would give the provinces the exclusive right to raise revenue by direct taxes for **Provincial Purposes**, and at the same time give the Federal Government the **same right** or part of it for the same purpose.

But there are very substantial obstacles in the way of an action against the federal government.

(1) The cost could run as high as $100,000 or even $200,000. Intervention in this action could be expected from all quarters. Several of the provinces could be expected to intervene one way or the other.

(2) Cataclysmic repercussions. If such an action were to be successfully brought by Myers, his first response would be an immediate application for the cancellation of the assessment on the grounds of its unconstitutional status, and therefore cancellation of the warrant for arrest which followed it, and expungment of the sentence.

But if Myers didn't owe taxes for the years 1969 to 1974, neither did anyone else in Canada. If the law was ultra vires, it was ultra vires for everyone. Theoretically all those taxes would have to be paid back to the taxpayers. All of the grants paid by the Federal Government to the Provincial Government would have to be paid back, and all of the taxes collected and paid on behalf of the Provincial Governments would also have to be returned.

And if this holds true for the years 1969 to 1974, it also holds true for the years 1962 to the present.

The High Court of Canada would have to sweat a lot of blood to rule in favor of such an action, even if it was plainly ultra vires of the Constitution of the country.

Yet if it were **plainly** contradictory to Canada's Constitution

- so plain that even the public could see - the High Court would risk the loss of integrity and respect for all law in Canada, if it allowed the Income Tax Act to stand.

The question is, which route would the High Court choose?

For sure a ruling against the Tax Act would bring on the greatest constitutional crisis in the history of the country and could mean, before it was over, the disintegration of Confederation. On the other hand, any government which cannot or will not live within its own law, (the constitution) is itself **lawless**, and does not deserve to continue to exist.

There's a great amount of hesitation to bringing this to Court, but the Federal Government probably can never rest easy until the clash between the Income Tax Act and the Constitution of Canada has been resolved.

The desperate urgency with which former Prime Minister Trudeau tried to obtain a new Canadian Constitution is thereby explained.

* * * * * * * * * *

Meanwhile Canada still has the old constitution and a Tax Act that seems diametrically opposed.

Canada's ability to survive as a nation may well hinge on improving its tax machinery and curbing the high handedness of the bureaucrats who run it.

Chapter Twenty-eight

ENTIRE CONGRESS

The entire Congress of the United States, House and Senate, received a copy of the book you have just read. It was sent to them by the late Congressman Larry McDonald. His letter to his colleagues is self-explanatory:

Congress of the United States
House of Representatives
Washington, D.C. 20515

Dear Colleague:

Recently my attention was drawn to a booklet, "UN-BRIDLED BUREAUCRACY IN CANADA." I was so shocked by the contents which demonstrate what can happen to a bureaucracy out of hand that I have arranged to obtain a copy for every member of the U.S. Congress.

The documentation in this booklet leaves me with little doubt about its authenticity. I fear there are implications for the U.S., because the revenue bureaucracies in Canada and the U.S. are similar and their powers are truly awesome.

Although Canada has no constitution as such, we had always been under the impression that fundamental justice looks after itself.

Here we see the violation of the rights of privacy; the violation of the immunity of third parties; the violation of the sanctity of contract; seizure without due process; hostage-

316

holding (money instead of people); tax imprisonment without warning or notice. THEN, worst of all, <u>double jeopardy</u> — a second trial on the same charges and on the same evidence following an acquittal. This violation is frightening because it strikes at the very roots of our social order.

The implication is that the erosion of the power of the people is an insidious process, and unless the representatives of the people are constantly on guard, a Free State may become, by degrees, an Authoritarian State.

The story "UNBRIDLED BUREAUCRACY IN CANADA" may seem incredible to us, yet our bureaucracy, the Immigration Department — apparently at the instigation of the Canadian Tax Department — now seeks to cancel a residence permit issued to this Canadian victim by our Government in April, 1977. In fact, our Immigration Department has set an Exclusion Hearing for Mr. Myers in Seattle, Washington, January 15, 1980.

I think it's important to our form of government that we see what can happen when a government agency goes unchecked. The Internal Revenue Service is far from innocent of some of the practices related here.

I think there is a message in this little book: Our Congress must be a watchdog over all its government bureaucracies since it is a characteristic of these agencies to take for themselves more and more of the Constitutional Rights of our people.

Sincerely,

Larry P. McDonald

* * * * * * * * * *

The hearing which Congressman Larry McDonald refers to was held on January 15, 1980, as will be hereafter related in Chapter Twenty-nine.

Chapter Twenty-nine

BAD DREAMS

You have just read the factual and I hope objective account of what happened to me at the hands of Revenue Canada. We are now ten years beyond January 1979 when I returned to Canada, walked into the hands of the RCMP, and let the prison doors clang shut behind me.

Nothing of the human toll has been related. Out of the human toll rose the fiercest flames in the furnace. For a view of that I am obliged to ask you to step back with me briefly to the judgement and conviction of 1977 and the events surrounding it.

The gold holdings of the Americans were seized in September 1974, released in April 1975; I was arrested and put in jail May 15, 1975. I suffered through a long, dangerous and tedious trial in September and October 1975. I was acquitted by Judge MacDonald on April 30, 1976.

On that very day, within minutes of the acquittal, I was served legal notice that I would face a second trial on the same charges in a higher court. Meanwhile they couldn't hold me. I was legally now "Not Guilty."

Sometime in the latter half of 1976 I bought a place in Spokane, Washington merely as an insurance against conviction. I never thought that could happen, but having learned long ago from the stock market that anything can happen, I acquired the property on the northern edge of Spokane consisting of an idyllic setting flanked by a long stone wall, a beautifully treed back yard including a swimming pool with a roofed-in sun area, two acres of land and a small barn. I thought I'd be ready just in case worse came to the worst. Sure enough!

My second trial started in the fall of 1976. Long before it finished my wife and I made our annual pilgrimage to Palm Springs for the winter. I planned to put the Spokane house up for sale as soon as the trial finished.

The conviction and the sentence on March 2 hit us like a thunderbolt. Our future had been dynamited.

Since income tax evasion is not an extraditable offense. I could remain in the United States safe from the Canadians. But Muriel, who was a native of Calgary, whose whole life had been spent there, could not face virtual exile with me, even though she could go back and forth almost at will. She was afraid we were too far on in life to set down new roots in Spokane, Washington where we didn't know a soul. I had only picked Spokane because it was one of the closest cities to Calgary, within a day's driving distance.

My wife felt that our lives should be lived out together. But her four children, all but one married with families, lived in Calgary. The situation threatened to tear us all apart.

I got in touch with a leading immigration attorney in San Diego who set the wheels in motion for permanent residence in the U.S. His name was MacInerney and he was indeed one sharp lawyer. From the standpoint of immigration the U.S. is divided into districts and all of the districts have quotas. Even if your application is successful you have to wait your turn to get in. The trick is to apply in a district where there's no waiting line. While in some parts that line can be many months and maybe up to a couple of years, MacInerney found out that the District of Montana was no favorite. In fact since no one was standing in line I could get almost immediate acceptance. I would first have to live in Montana. So I rented an apartment there, got a telephone and prepared to make that my home for the immediate future. Meanwhile, I was still in Palm Springs.

After my wife returned to Calgary my sister Ruth from New York joined me. She had only been there one day when

MacInerney phoned and told me I had to get up to Helena right away for an interview with Immigration and for the medical. We started off the next day on the fifteen hundred mile drive to Montana.

My sister tells me that she had never seen anyone so badly shaken, and she had never before seen me shaken over anything. My coffee cup trembled, she says. The full impact of what had happened now dawned on me. In the very best case I would probably have to pay $1.2 million in taxes which I didn't owe. Still cognizant of the lesson I had back on the farm in grade school about standing for the RIGHT even in the face of punishment, I was coming to the conclusion that I would never never go back. That was what caused the shaking. I was 65 years old, all of my friends were in Alberta, the hills of home were there, the roads were there. The roads where I had once fancied myself a mounted Indian fighter or a fierce but virtuous knight of King Arthur's Court. My children were shocked, troubled and apprehensive. The nest had been blown up.

In the Immigration Office in Helena I received my permanent U.S. resident status and I had a green card to prove it. We drove then about four hundred miles west to Spokane where I settled down to my new home and turned out the next issue of my newsletter.

As soon as I'd heard the judgement in February 1977 I closed out the Swiss operation, rented an office in downtown Spokane and engaged a secretary. My newsletter came out on time, preserving the record of never an issue missed, and never a day late. That record was to stand throughout incarceration and it still stands today.

I moved a couple of horses down from Calgary and tried to settle into the new life. With a boat on Lake Coeur d'Alene and occasional visits I managed to survive traumatically through the rest of the year and through all of 1978.

Visits from Calgary tended to decline as time went by. I soon came to understand that visiting people in the area where you live is a trifle compared with arranging any visit of even two or three days when it involves a trip forward and backward and a break in the general routine of life, which flows like a river that sweeps us along, even when we want to duck out for a while. About the only big break I had was attending Jim Blanchard's New Orleans Monetary Conference as a speaker.

This was always a joy; I would see many of my subscribers there and numerous financial writers, even sometimes a celebrity or two. They mattered the least, but what Canadian ex-con gets to speak on the same platform as ex-president Ford and Alexander Haig? That in itself amounted to a reflection on Canadian justice.

Altogether I made many friends; I have them all over the United States; the trouble is I never saw them together at any one place unless it was at a meeting such as Blanchard's, or a monetary seminar of my own.

I struggled through the Christmas seasons of 1977 and 1978 when all my family came to visit. But time, by the mere passing, was eroding me. You can transplant a young tree but if you try it with an old tree, survival is doubtful. The leaves turn yellow, shrink and fall, branches droop and some break off. The tree gives every sign that it will die, even with generous watering, as the visits from Canada were to me. The descent of my spirits continued until I began to question whether the rest of life was worthwhile.

To break uncontrollable depressions, I developed the habit of swimming every morning before breakfast, which I still retain. I rode my horse three or four times a week, pursued and wrote of the financial developments. But there was a huge hole in my soul.

The most painful reminders of the desolation of my life came with the family get-togethers, dinners and celebrations in Calgary. They brought forcibly into focus the life that I was missing, the rewarding substance that was floating past me in the stream of life. Gone, gone! Gone was the event of the admission to the bar of my son Richard, now at last a full-fledged lawyer! Gone the high school graduation of my son John. Gone many of the birthday celebrations of my wife together with all the family and celebrations of other birthdays, gone the priceless family comfort of Thanksgiving together. So many Sundays, so many holidays. Gone and still going.

On nearly all these occasions I was in touch with the family by telephone talking individually to most of them.

But when I put the phone down I felt more than ever my isolation. Worst of all I couldn't see how there would ever be a resolution for me unless I went back to jail to serve out this illegal sentence, this unjust conviction in the autumn of my life.

But the newspaper had quoted me: "I came into this jail under my own power. I left it under my own power. The cops and the authorities had nothing to do with it one way or the other." Hardly a conciliatory gesture.

Sometimes in my dreams I would have a view of a flat and windswept desert and out there on the level sand lay by itself an enormous boulder, smoothed by the eternal winds, always motionless, always there by itself. Then I came to realize that in my dream I was the boulder, incapable of movement, stuck forever.

Simply the idea of being **wanted** by the law, the knowledge that border immigration stations might be alerted, the awareness that if I drove in Canada the slightest traffic violation could put me back in the jailers' hands, was never far from my consciousness. Nearing the end of 1978 I determined that I would take some steps toward re-establishing my life. I would move that boulder if it lay in the power of mortal man to do so.

Inquiries in Canada led me to believe there was a good possibility that upon serving six months in prison I could expect what they called "day parole." I thought long and hard and I felt I could handle that. I said to myself: "Here you are exiled for life, when just for want of the courage to spend six months incarcerated, you might once more be a free man, the same C.V. Myers you had been before 1977. Just for six months!"

But whenever I mentioned this to any of my friends they were, almost without exception, dead set against it. They said, "Once you get in there you don't know how long they will keep

you. They've got it in for you and you may never make it out."
My wife said, "Of all the people I know in this world you're the last
man I can see in jail."

The time allowed for the appeal to the Judge Holmes' verdict
had long passed. My lawyer thought appeal might still be a
possibility, as I have related in the previous section of this book.
Since the government had agreed not to oppose asking leave to
appeal, that became an important element in my decision to take
the risk of going home. Just to be home again - I would give most
of all I had made in my lifetime. But even that wasn't enough. That
wouldn't cure the jail sentence; the bureaucrats wanted jail. Still
the parole board had started following a policy of greater leniency.
Many prison inmates convicted for white collar crimes, even large
embezzlements, serving a two year sentence were being let free
in six months.

I talked it over with all members of my family, visiting me
Christmas 1978, but I could not discern any useful guidance. Most
of them badly wanted me home in a normal life with their mother;
on the other hand they feared to see me in jail. The kids showed
great distress at the idea of having their father in jail. None,
including my wife, wanted to face either of the harsh alternatives.

Projecting it I said to Muriel; "The way it is, it means we will
die separately. Either I will die down here alone or you will die in
Canada. Then for sure I'd be up there to see you if you were
terminally ill, or to be with the kids. The cops would be waiting.
Wouldn't that be a fine mess? Their mother dead and their dad
in jail?"

It was a horrible thought. I decided that no matter the cost,
I would have to exert every effort, take whatever necessary risk to
remedy this situation by now just about unbearable. My lawyer
had obtained the commitment from the government that they
would not oppose leave to appeal, so a few days after New Year's
1979 I drove to Calgary, spent the night at home. The next
morning my daughter Norma delivered me into the hands of the
RCMP. When she left she was crying.

I was moved quickly to the high security Remand Center, a temporary stop-over where accused are held, pending their trials. Here the doors were made of iron and were remote controlled. The guards never entered the individual cell blocks. Our block of eight prisoners was served meals on trays pushed through an opening in the iron gate. On visiting occasions I spoke with my family and friends one at a time, facing me through heavy plate-glass, connected by telephone. Conversations were limited to about ten minutes. Guards remained present.

Through my attorney Jack Marshall, I was now aware of the news that the Justice Department had backed out of its deal that if I came back voluntarily they would not oppose our request for appeal, as stated in page 290 of the last section. Now Marshall became enthusiastic about a *Habeas Corpus* petition which he had filed on the grounds that my sentence had not been one of the options for the judge, as outlined in the Canadian law books. If the sentence wasn't legal I was a free man. It was just too much to expect.

I will never understand how judges can hand down law contrary to the stated and written laws of the country and make it stick. But they do. Now the judge said that we should take this petition to the appeal court. We were afraid of that. Maybe they would simply add a huge fine to my already maximum sentence. My two-year sentence was left standing and I was soon hustled off to the Bowden Penitentiary about eighty miles north of Calgary.

A penitentiary is not called a penitentiary. When you get there it is an institution, or a correctional center. Prisoners are inmates. There is very little discussion about what they are convicted of. If the subject does come up, all prisoners are innocent. I also found out that eighty to ninety percent of the inmates are repeaters, some of them two or three times or more.

I was given the job of cleaning up the card room, a recreation hall filled with card tables where the inmates played, drank pop and smoked cigarettes every evening. I had to sweep it, wash it, move all the tables and chairs back in order, to stand inspection. The asphalt tile floor was literally covered with cigarette burns.

One day a guard came in and ordered me to clean up those burns. I protested that they wouldn't come off. He said, "You bet they'll come off. I'll show you how to get them off," whereupon he brought steel wool and some very soapy water and proceeded to rub vigorously at one or two burns, in which he was successful. "That's how they come off," he said. "Here you are."

I got down on my hands and knees and started in; there must have been a thousand burns, and here I learned very realistically of the amount of support that had developed for me among the inmates.

A black inmate from Montreal, who had been involved in obtaining a hit-man for a murder, and who was in charge of a large amount of cleaning down our halls, passed the card room, saw me. He came over, "What in the hell are you doing down there?"

"I'm taking off the burns," I said.

He said, "Get up, you can't do that."

I said, "I have to do it, the guard ordered me to do it."

"Well, stop it," he said and left.

I continued at my work. I didn't know when I would ever get done. A while later he suddenly reappeared. "You crazy old man, will you stop that! I'll be back in a minute."

Very shortly he returned with a round electric machine that would take the very top of the surface off the tile. He brought two or three helpers with him. They moved out all the book cases, chairs and tables, treated the entire area of the floor with the machine, removing all cigarette burns, and followed up with an electric polisher. Then they put everything back in order. My card room was a model to look at.

Generally, the prisoners were disgusted that I should be in jail. After their first wave of resentment came sympathy. Many of them told me, "You shouldn't be here. You have no business here." My living unit officer also was furious.

One day I heard him talking to his immediate superior. "This man has no business here. What's being served? What's the good of all this? He should be out, and he should be out soon."

My mornings were nightmares. Soon after sentencing I started having uncontrollable morning depressions. Things in my mind were as black as they could be in the blackest hole in the universe. My mouth and throat were dry. Once or twice I got sick to my stomach in the hallway. A nurse told me that the L.U. (living unit officer) had exclaimed, "This is enough! Something has to be done!," as he marched off to office headquarters.

But nothing was done. I learned that the warden wanted me out. It seemed like everyone wanted me out, but there was a blockage at the highest quarters. Obviously **Revenue Canada** called the shots for the parole board, as established in the previous section of this account. A parole officer told me personally, "Whatever settlement you make with Revenue Canada will be all right with the board, and there is no doubt that Revenue Canada stepped far beyond its authority in the matter of your parole." (page 300).

I think only my newsletter saved me from a complete breakdown. The nurses were giving me valium in the mornings to help and I had capitalized on the one leniency of the Bowden Institution; visiting privileges every afternoon. Through my visitors I was able to contact a competent secretary at Innisfail about twenty miles away and arrange for her to visit me frequently. Every couple of days she would bring me mail and in the visiting hour I would dictate to her directions and some correspondence. She was paid from my office in Spokane.

After I had been in jail about four months I obtained the privilege of having my compact dictating machine delivered to me. They couldn't stop mail from coming in or mail from going out. It was all censored but unless there was objectionable material they had to let it go through. I received all my mail, newsletters, and correspondence as if I had been in my office, only later. Between the mail and the dictating machine they made my letter a lot easier. Whereas before I had to write it out very **carefully** because I have atrocious long hand, now I could put it on the machine and hope to God my dictation was worded carefully enough to pass without major error. The extensive reading and the work of doing the letter vastly improved my days. Gold was going up phenomenally, the energy crisis was on; I had a lot of thinking to do. One time my thinking got me in trouble.

I couldn't use the dictating machine in my cell because my voice through the cardboard walls would upset my adjoining cell-mates. I found a little broom closet on our floor, housing the pipes as they ran vertically up through the several floors. It was a cubby-hole about two and a half feet square. There I could sit on a narrow ledge inside the cupboard, spread out some of my papers and talk into my machine. I had to be careful not to get carried away in my work to the extent where I would miss a roll call.

Before each meal they had what they called "count." You had to be standing in the doorway of your cell as the officer walked by and every prisoner in the institution had to be accounted for before they could release the herd for dinner. One morning I entered my "office," steamed up about an involved story I was going to write for the newsletter, I looked at my watch, noted it was eleven o'clock and told myself severely I'd better be out of there and standing in my doorway for count at twelve sharp. But twelve sharp came and I wasn't in my doorway and at 12:15 I wasn't in my doorway.

Totally oblivious to the exhaustive search that was in progress throughout the jail, I kept on working. All of the prisoners were lined up in the halls ready to be released to thunder down to the dining room. With every passing minute the guards became more excited, they looked in the gym, the downstairs, the upstairs, the johns, the yard. They were beginning to think I must've escaped. I simply wasn't around.

However, they did not want to report me as an escapee until they knew. Maybe I'd had a heart attack, or something similar. Finally one of the inmates, friendly to me who knew my habits and figured he knew where I was, relented. He suggested to the guard that if he went into that closet there might be a chance I'd be there. Suddenly the door flew open; a most incensed guard confronted a most startled inmate.

They didn't do anything to me, but I sure did get some stern warnings about what would happen if I pulled that trick again.

My behavior in prison was exemplary. I determined before I went in that I would obey every instruction without protest. I would quell my dislike of regimentation, adhere religiously to the rules and the discipline, remain cooperative and obedient.

All of this was highly corrosive to my personality. I was failing in both mind and body. Friends who visited me were sometimes shocked and occasionally showed it. A prison picture of me with my convict number on my uniform is appalling. You wouldn't want to see it.

As my parole date approached tension increased. I found I was having a hard time staying calm in the face of stupid orders. One day I flew off at a guard. I simply lost control. I challenged him, "Put me in the 'hole' - if you like. I dare you to put me in the 'hole'." (The hole in the prison is the ultimate in punishment. It means complete isolation in a dark place, with only subsistence food, not even a guard to talk to.)

So challenged, the guard responded, "All right, I'll put you in the hole!"

I was ready. He strode into the office where apparently a higher authority overruled him.

It was a shaking incident for me. Now I feared for my eventual sanity. I feared I would lose control, that this might give them an excuse to send me to the psycho ward in Saskatoon, Saskatchewan about five hundred miles away. If I got in there I might never get out. At that distance I would be pretty well cut off from all visitation except rarely by members of my family. I was scared to my very center and core. I felt I was breaking down. I was sure that if I didn't get parole my very survival would be in danger because of the things I would do or of what might happen. I began to hatch a plan.

I was eligible for a forty-eight hour unescorted temporary absence July 7 (page 293). This decision is made at the institution. It is predicated on the attitude of the prisoner under incarceration, cooperative behavior, and whether or not he might pose any danger to society while absent. On these counts I passed easily and my July 7 date was settled.

Since under the terms of the absence I would be leaving at dinner time Friday and would not have to return until dinner time Sunday, I began to envision a plan which would bring me across the border into the United States that very Friday night.

Meanwhile, I had to have the answer to an extremely important question. Was escape from prison an extraditable offense? Income tax wasn't, but escape might be.

I had to be careful how I found out the legal answer. I couldn't implicate my attorneys and I didn't want them to know what I had in mind. I was lucky to be able to arrange a visit by an attorney other than Marshall, because of his absence from the office. I met with the attorney in the yard which was used in summer by inmates and visitors sitting around outside tables. I couldn't take any chance that my conversation would be bugged. It was something you always had to guard against. I found a remote table and before my visitor left I posed to him the question, quite impersonally. Under the law is a failure to return from a "temporary absence" extraditable? He said; "I'm going to Edmonton. I'll find out and on my way back I'll stop in and let you know."

Three days later I had the answer. It was not extraditable.

I was now ready to execute my plan. In order to involve as few people as possible in a guilty knowledge, I would not at first go home at all. I would be driven from Bowden to meet my family for dinner at the Palacer Hotel, all of them. I think there must've been more than fifteen at a large table in the Palacer Dining Room. When the main course was served, I would get up to go to the men's room. Meanwhile, one other of the party would have already departed for the men's room. Then we would proceed to the elevators leading to the parking lot on the fifth floor, but we would stand apart and when unobserved take elevators separately and meet on the fifth floor where the car was parked.

That's the way it went.

It felt very good after all this time, and after these tribulations to be sitting down to dinner with my own family in Calgary. Nevertheless, my enjoyment was slight. I was very tense. When the main course had been nearly consumed my accomplice left. A few minutes later I left. On the fifth floor, being unnoticed and unwatched, I got in the car with him. Although there was no prohibition against such an act, I wanted to make sure we were not followed.

My accomplice drove me to an appointed place on the west side of Calgary where he let me off on a residential street corner. After he had departed I walked up and down the street, waiting for my second accomplice and making sure no followers were around. Very soon the second car drove up and I got in. In less than two hours we were at the American border.

I was not afraid of the border crossing, although my driver was. On passing from Canada into the United States you do not stop at the Canadian border. My accomplice was petrified that we would be flagged down at the Canadian station and apprehended. I reasoned there was not much danger here because even if we were apprehended what could they do about it? I had a legal absence until Sunday evening. There was nothing in my permit confining me to any certain limited distance outside Calgary. The intention to escape is not escaping, even if they wanted to infer the intention. We passed safely through to the American side. I had the green card which I had picked up in Helena, Montana in April 1977. I'd had a tense moment in getting it out of the jail.

When I went to jail January 1979 I had had the card in my briefcase. They took the briefcase into custody. I had to get that card before I started out on my absence and the execution of my plan. I went down to the property containment room where inmates' personal belongings are kept. I asked for my briefcase on the pretext of getting out a gold pen that I had left there. I knew exactly where the card was and while I was searching the briefcase with the attendant on the other side of the counter I slipped the card quickly into my pocket and returned the briefcase apologizing because I couldn't find the pen.

So at the border I was armed with the card in case I should be questioned. The U.S. Immigration officer asked me if I was a citizen of the United States. I replied I was a resident. I was reaching for my green card but he didn't ask to see it. We sailed on through and suddenly, all at once, I was free of Canadian authority. Now I knew I could **never** go back!

We stopped at the town of Shelby about forty miles inside the United States, the same Shelby we had stopped at fifty-two years earlier when Jack Dempsey had staged a heavy-weight title bout. I had so looked forward to a peaceful night's sleep, arising maybe after ten o'clock. It was already two o'clock. I went to sleep soon enough, but at five o'clock in the morning I found myself up and walking around the vacant lot outside the motel. This first day of freedom wasn't like I'd thought at all.

And the many days, three thousand days, and for nearly full nine years following, my peaceful sleep did not return. Always I awoke disturbed, sometimes frantic. The depression would not go away. The future loomed out ahead exactly as I had pictured it to my wife earlier unless something was done to solve our situation. Now all of the horror and the sacrifice of the past seven months had come to naught. Back again at square one, unable to return to Canada.

Actually things were worse than before. My wife's health had been failing. It didn't look now like she would ever feel able to join me in the United States. We didn't want any divorce. And soon the United States Immigration bureaucracy would enter the picture to press for my deportation. If they succeeded, and if I were deported, back in Canada I could expect an additional jail sentence for having escaped. No one had a good idea of how long that might be.

Back in my house at Graves Road in Spokane I couldn't find the sense of relief I had so hoped for. I went on with my newsletter, facing the morning depressions which, even under the most advanced anti-depressants, would not go away. Often I awoke to the worst of the nightmares still present.

One dream that kept recurring was especially frightening. I was driving up a long ramp in a parking lot. I had six horses, three teams in tandem on a loaded wagon of grain. We were making the curves until we came to the very top, two hundred feet above ground level. On the top curve the planking had been removed, and my lead team instead of making the turn tumbled over the edge of the planking. There my dream ended. In another dream I might be driving a huge motor home and at that very point at the top of the ramp the front wheel would go over the edge. The dream ended.

Beyond that I was sick about another thing that had happened while I was in prison. In Canada I'd accumulated a cache of gold coins including 750 one ounce Krugerrands and other coins. I'd had them moved and had buried them alongside a shed at my Spokane home.

One evening, some weeks after my return, I asked my two sons Brian and John to go down and dig up the cache. After a while when they didn't return to the house I went down to see what was wrong. By this time they were deep in the ground all along the shed, shoveling with urgency. When I saw the hole I knew the gold was gone. The gold I'd had the foresight to buy at $35 an ounce when very few others did, now belonged to someone else. I was loser by about half a million dollars. Who took it remains a mystery.

The loss of the money was great but not as painful as the fact that it had been stolen while I was locked up. I felt discouraged, used up and beat up. Of course, had I been a conformist I'd have put my money in the bank in the first place. But as a conformist I wouldn't have invested in gold at all and would, as a consequence, have missed the investment opportunity of the century.

Still, I hadn't seen the last of my misery. The U.S. Immigration bureaucracy was about to play its hand. The BIG SQUEEZE was coming.

Chapter Thirty

SUING THE QUEEN

The assault on my U.S. residency was very serious.

In Canada, I had pulled the lion's whiskers and then hurled invectives from the safety of my U.S. haven. Now if I should be delivered into their hands the consequences wouldn't be nice.

They might be worse if I brought a lawsuit against the Parole Board and lost. And still worse if I brought a lawsuit against the Queen (the government) and lost that as well.

Still, if I won I would be home free. Was there justice or not? I decided to take the risk and find out.

My lawyers asked the court to issue an injunction against the National Parole Board to restrain it from making arrangements with Revenue Canada, as a condition of the granting of parole. Our motion was dated December 30, 1980. I was suing via long distance.

Since the Parole Board was a national body the action was brought to the court in Toronto, Ontario with a request for the hearing to take place in Alberta. The judgement was handed down by Judge Patrick M. Mahoney February 5, 1981.

Firstly, the judgement recounted the fact that I was released on temporary absence of forty-eight hours July 28, 1979, that I did not return, and that I remained at large outside Canada.

The judgement said in part:

> "The **attitude** of any convict, to the satisfac-
> tion of the civil liability incidental to his offense, is
> clearly among the factors to be weighed in deciding

*whether the inmate has derived the maximum bene-
fit from his imprisonment.*

*"The tax evader is in no different position than
any other cheater whose actions are deemed criminal
at law.*

*"The attitude toward satisfaction of the inci-
dental debt is properly to be taken into account by
the Board in the exercise of its discretion.*

*"The Board clearly, and properly, had in mind
Myers' efforts to reach a settlement. It may also have
had in mind the conclusion of such a settlement as
a relevant factor in itself, rather than as evidence of
his efforts; if so, it was wrong. Should another
application come before it, the Board should not
regard failure to reach a settlement as being material
in itself but should look to the reasons for that
failure, insofar as they may reasonably be ascribed to
Myers."*

We had argued in court that it was virtually impossible for me,
while incarcerated, to raise the assets necessary for a settlement.
My assets were in Switzerland. I was allowed only two phone calls
a month and in any case Revenue Canada had refused to negotiate
with me. They simply demanded the full assessment which I could
not raise.

But Judge Patrick Mahoney said:

*"In any event, it (incarceration), is no excuse for not negotiating.
"The application is dismissed with costs."*

I was not satisfied with the judgement of the lower court so
I instructed my lawyers to launch an appeal where our case would
be heard and decided by a panel of three judges.

Among the numerous arguments, the heart of the case was
still as follows:

(1) The Tax Department has powers under the Income Tax
Act to collect its assessments; it doesn't need assistance from
another agency.

(2) The courts have abolished imprisonment for debt, leaving
the civil remedies for recovery as the basis for recovery for debt.

(3) The parole system should not be used as a means for

threatening continued imprisonment for the purposes of collecting tax debt.

The learned judges of the Appeal Court agreed with the lower court. They found the Parole Board free of fault in refusing my parole on the grounds that I had made only minimal effort to settle with Revenue Canada, and that therefore it was proper for them to withhold parole because my **attitude** toward settlement was found wanting.

It seemed to us that the honorable judges were relying on a very faint line between attitude toward payment and actual payment.

It is generally well known that the thief is not asked to repay what he stole before he can be paroled from prison. The embezzler is not asked to make restitution to those he embezzled before he is paroled. Nor are either of them badgered about it. An embezzler of a sum of $300,000 with a sentence of two years had immediately proceeded me on parole, after six months in jail.

Apparently only when the prisoner owes the **government** is it fitting for the Parole Board to use its powers to help enforce settlement.

The Parole Board's report says:

> *"Until he makes a sincere effort to begin a settlement with Revenue Canada his offense of evading payment of taxes appears to be continuing."*

The judgement of the Federal Court of Appeal essentially approved the verdict of the lower court. The appeal judgement said:

> *"There is no reason to believe that the National Parole Board has exceeded or will exceed its jurisdiction by requiring the appellant to pay or settle his tax indebtedness before granting the appellant Parole.*
>
> *"Moreover, the Board is entitled to take into account what the appellant has done since his incarceration to make amends for the evasion of taxation in respect of which he was sentenced to imprisonment.*
>
> *"The appeal is dismissed with costs."*

335

I was still not satisfied that justice in Canada was anything more than a whitewash job, with the verdicts often predictable in advance, and in favor of the government and the agencies, regardless of the statutes.

I had long felt certain that the Income Tax Act, as it was administered, was *ultra vires,* that the federal government was violating the Constitution of Canada by collecting taxes from the individual provinces for use in the provinces on programs of strictly provincial jurisdiction. Based on the information related via Norman L. Stone (Pages 314-315) I decided to take the plunge against the highest authority in the country - the government.

Right away I ran into a roadblock. My lawyers advised that being outside the country I would have no status to bring such a suit in Canada.

But my daughter Norma had been loyal and supportive of my beliefs all along. She had a company in Canada by the name of Winterhaven Stables Limited. That company had status to challenge the Canadian Income Tax Act. Since I could not do this myself it was her desire to pick up the fight where I had left off. And that is what happened in the Statement of Claim delivered against the Ministers of Canada November 14, 1983.

SUING THE GOVERNMENT

In part the statement said:

> *"The income tax is ultra vires the Parliament of Canada as it constitutes 'direct taxation within a province in order to the raising of a revenue for provincial purposes', which is within the exclusive legislative jurisdiction of the provinces by reason of section 92(2) of the Constitution Act, 1867.*
>
> *"The direct taxation revenues, or a portion thereof, raised by the Income Tax Act, fund programs established and administered under the following statutes:*
>
> *(i) The Federal Provincial Fiscal Arrangements and Established Programs Financing Act 1977, R.S.C. 1976-77, c.10, as amended;*

> (ii)   *The Hospital Insurance and Diagnostic Services Act, R.S.C. 1970 c.H-8, as amended;*
>
> (iii) *The Medical Care Act R.S.C. 1970, c.M-8, as amended;*
>
> (iv) *The Canada Assistance Plan Act, R.S.C. 1970, C.C-1, as amended;*
>
> (v) *The Blind Persons Act, R.S.C. 1970, c.B-7, as amended;*
>
> (vi) *The Disabled Persons Act, R.S.C. 1970, c. D-6, as amended;*
>
> *which are the vehicles the federal government uses to apply direct taxation within the province to fulfill exclusively provincial purposes."*

The Statement of Claim asked the court for "an order declaring that the Income Tax Act" is *ultra vires* the parliament of Canada. We had two capable, learned and experienced attorneys. Their opinion of the validity of our action coincided up to a point. They agreed without question that the federal government was violating the British North America Act, collecting via income tax large sums of money from the various provinces which the government then used to fund provincial programs with strings attached, quite illegally.

Our attorneys agreed that these statutes had been put in place originally largely to protect the rights of the provinces against an undesirable concentration of power in the central government. They agreed, and they knew, and they had the proof, of what the federal government was doing and that the sums of money collected were very large. At this point they parted company. One of the attorneys, resting on the fact that our position was fundamentally sound, was optimistic that our case would command a serious hearing by the Supreme Court with a reasonable chance of success. The other attorney believed that our case was sound, but he did not believe that we would ever get a Canadian court to rule in our favor simply because of the adverse results of such a ruling on the central government.

Both felt that this case would surely go as far as the Supreme Court of Canada simply as the result of the initiative of whichever side lost in the lower courts.

I will not say which attorney was which but I will let you guess which one turned out to be right.

This was a very large case, one of the biggest Constitutional cases in the history of the country. The arguments were long, sometimes complicated, sometimes amazingly simple. The biggest arguments were the simplest, and I shall deal with only a few of them in the nature of a brief review.

As far back as 1887, a case was referred right up to the Privy Council in England whose findings reversed the lower courts and even the Supreme Court of Canada as follows:

> *"Their Lordships adhere to the view, and hold that, as regards direct taxation within the province to raise revenue for provincial purposes, that subject falls* **wholly within the jurisdiction of the provincial legislatures.***"*

Well, as a result of subsequent agreements between Canada and England there is no longer an appeal to the Privy Council. The supreme authority is the Supreme Court of Canada consisting of nine judges in Ottawa.

Our witness, a renowned economist Dr. Bird, testified in essence: *"The Government of Canada intended through these programs* **to shape and indirectly control provincial spending** *in these important fields and to a considerable extent, it has succeeded in its purpose."*

The chief witness for the government, Dr. Norrie, testified in essence: *"The choice came down either to abandoning the welfare measures for the time being or* **finding ways to circumvent the strict legalism of the Constitution.***"*

Later on Dr. Norrie developed his testimony to conclude: *"The system was* **sufficiently innovative to be able to circumvent the strict legalism of the Constitution** *at a time when there was great popular demand for broad-ranging welfare measures."*

Our counsel in this case, Jack Marshall, said of the government's chief witness: *"Dr. Norrie admitted that such measures were intended to circumvent what the federal government saw as the strict legalism of the Constitution as it had been interpreted by the Privy Council."*

Another specialist witness of the government, Dr. Broadway, is paraphrased by Marshall's statement; *"The reason why the federal government has determined that it can't leave decisions as to the development of programs in spending up to the provinces (is) because **if it were to do so the provinces would act differently than the federal government wants them to.** To prevent the provinces from establishing the types of programs they want, and to spend on them as they determine advisable, the federal government establishes conditional grants. **Their purpose, as we clearly see from Dr. Broadway's evidence, is to change the behavior of the provinces so that they fall in line with the federal government's wishes."***

"These programs are all clearly programs within the exclusive jurisdiction of the provinces under the Constitution. The inescapable conclusion is that federal income tax had been used to fund such programs and that it continues to do so in provinces which have not opted-out.

*"We have witnessed the creation of a scheme of federal-provincial fiscal measures established by economists rather than by constitutional lawyers. When faced with clear indications from the courts that provincial rights were inviolate, and when proposals for constitutional amendment were rejected by the provinces, the ingenuity of the federal economists created the world of tax rentals, tax collection agreement and conditional grants. These programs are in their words **designed to circumvent the strict legalism of the Constitution."***

In general, Marshall sums up; *"The sole issue in my submission is whether the people of Canada are entitled to insist that if their governments, both federal and provincial, wish to alter the distribution of powers established by the Constitution, that they do so by way of constitutional amendment rather than by circumvention."*

Marshall calls the whole thing, ***"a federal scheme to regulate and thereby indirectly legislate within areas of provincial jurisdiction."***

That is a very brief summary but it contains the main thrust of the argument.

The response of the defendants - the various ministers of Canada - pointedly failed to address the real issue which was in the first instance the prevention of the complete concentration of power in one central government. They pleaded that since all of the monies collected by the federal government, including duties and taxes, under the Constitution of 1867, was placed in the **CONSOLIDATED REVENUE FUND,** and since appropriations are made from this fund, the spending from this fund cannot be said to come from any particular source, and that therefore the funding of the provincial programs was perfectly legitimate.

Yes, the Constitution had been circumvented, they admitted that, but they had taken the necessary steps to make their unconstitutional act **seem to conform** to the Constitution.

This is the type of reasoning which is common today in government, in finance, in banking, in the bureaucratic world. Black can be defined as white and white under certain circumstances can be defined as black.

The name for this kind of sense is nonsense. It's quite popular these days.

* * * *

The Court agreed with the government. In judgement the Honorable Mr. Justice Medhurst puts it in fairly plain language:

> *"The monies then are first collected and paid into the* **Consolidated Revenue Fund.** *The accounts are structured so that the source of all revenue cannot be distinguished. It is therefore not possible to trace the payments made by the federal government to the provinces for provincial purposes to any specific source.*
>
> *"The monies received under the Income Tax Act are intrinsically mixed with other monies and some of theses funds are transferred to the provinces. They are undoubtedly then used for provincial purposes. It is, however, clear that the main object of the Income Tax Act is not to raise money by direct taxation for provincial purposes. It is concerned with raising money by taxation.*
>
> *"In my view the impugned legislation is simply carrying out objects that the federal government is authorized to undertake.*
>
> *"Accordingly the plaintiff's action is dismissed with costs."*

* * * *

In the next court before a panel of three judges Mr. Mervin C. Leitch Q.C. presented basically the same arguments and evidence and received basically the same reaction.

Our case against the government ministers was dismissed October 17, 1988.

We then sought our last avenue of justice, the Supreme Court of Canada. In that case we had to ask for **leave** to be heard.

The court summarily declined to hear us. And that was that.

The Trial Court and the Appeal Court condoned the subterfuge. The Supreme Court evaded the issue by simply refusing to hear about it.

The unmistakable **TRUTH** was this: *The government of Canada knows and admits that it cannot legally collect income tax in the province, to be spent in serving the people of the province. To do it within the law they would have to get a constitutional amendment. They have tried that unsuccessfully. So they have in their own words "circumvented the constitution."* That is **"to make a circuit around."** That's the **truth.** And it cost $150,000 to find it out.

The net result of the case in the end served to fortify and consolidate the growing power of the central government over the purse strings of the provinces. Now an overbalanced Canada heavily populated in Ontario and Quebec could override the west, from Manitoba to the sea, where the land is broad but the votes are sparse.

An inherent weakness in the whole system of justice is that all the servants work for the same boss; the judges, Revenue Canada, the Parole Board all work for the government of Canada. Most are political appointees, sometimes understandably loathe to bite the hand that chose them.

Chapter Thirty-one

BUREAUCRACIES JOIN HANDS

Those two lawsuits have taken us ahead of our story, since they dragged out for some years beyond 1979. Basically we are still back in the fall of 1979.

A few months after my escape I received a letter from one of the inmates at Bowden, now on parole, an intelligent man but a jail repeater most of his life. He had been in touch with a certain Calgary lawyer who frequently did parole work for inmates with enough money to pay for it. This lawyer had told my friend that a high-standing bureaucrat in Ottawa had recently declared, "Myers seems to have quite a knack for making every bad situation worse. He's done that again, and he'll be finding out about it soon."

That was ominous because it was typical of the vengeful mentality of Revenue Canada.

I think it was no coincidence that soon thereafter I received a summons from the United States Immigration Department to attend a deportation hearing (trial) in Seattle on a certain January day of 1980. The complaint was that I was an excludable person and that I had entered the United States as an excludable person. I was excludable because I had been convicted of a crime in Canada, notwithstanding the fact that tax evasion in Canada, as I have explained earlier, is not rated as either an extraditable offense or a crime of moral turpitude. If they could establish to the immigration judge, however, that I was an excludable person when I entered, I would be out on my ear in short order back in the clutches of the Canadians.

Once again my heretofore unknown friend Congressman Larry McDonald in Washington came to my aid. As we were entering the courtroom to face the immigration judge a wire was received from Larry McDonald's office. It advised the Immigration Court and the prosecutor that a bill had just been entered in the **House**, and a companion bill in the **Senate** which could establish my right to permanent residency in the United States. The wire was delivered apparently a few minutes before ten, just as the judge and the prosecutor were getting ready to come into court. The session was somewhat subdued.

The Immigration Department had to be careful with this. A vote by the Congress reversing an immigration ruling could not be questioned. If this should come to a vote immigration would have a red face with the Congress. Immigration gets all the money for its budget from the Congress. A confrontation with the Congress was not a good idea for the Immigration Department.

Just before the hearing came to order the prosecuting attorney showed us a letter from an immigration bureaucrat in Washington. It was without doubt the most vengeful, personally destructive, the meanest letter, I have ever read. It was so bad in fact that the prosecutor did not enter it in his batch of evidence against me.

My own feeling was that such a letter could not have originated without strong agitation from the Canadian side. It's not beyond reasonable speculation in their rage of having lost their prey in their moment of triumph, they had now asked the U.S. bureaucrats to return the favor of coming down on me on the gold question in the first place. Of course that's speculation, but it's very strange that a U.S. Immigration official in Washington should suddenly of his own volition, and without any outside motivation, pounce on any unknown person with such a venom.

The hearing was not very exciting. The Immigration Judge Jones took it under advisement. That was in January 1980. In January 1987 he still had it under advisement. Apparently the

Immigration Department, particularly the judge, was reluctant to rule against me, and for damn sure he wasn't going to rule for me. So once again we had the bureaucratic answer. Nothing. Nearly seven years under the threat of deportation. Seven years of lost citizenship. Seven years of existence hanging only from a thread. Seven years and still subject to a new outbreak of deportation.

Indeed, that's what happened.

Larry McDonald lost his life when Soviets shot down the Korean passenger jet in the Western Pacific September 1, 1983.

Bills in the House and the Senate die if they are not renewed with every new Congress, which is every two years. The threat from a Congressional vote had disappeared.

In July 1987 I received an order from the Immigration Department to present myself for a deportation hearing in September. At the trial my lawyers contended that the proceeding was without purpose since I was an American citizen carrying a passport issued by the Department of State dated July 7, 1986.

Judge William F. Nail gave that argument short shrift on the contention that the passport should not have been issued and was being recalled by the Department of State. I was not a citizen, he declared. I was an excludable person in the U.S. because I had been convicted of a crime in Canada.

The judge issued an order for my deportation effective January 20, 1988. Thus a matter that had been under procrastination for seven years was suddenly crystallized. But the fact remained that I was still in **possession** of a passport bearing a declaration of citizenship by no less authority than the Department of State. If that stood up the judge had flushed a bird that would not fly.

Unknown to the judge, but not willfully withheld, was the fact that, after all of these years under threat, I decided that I wanted to take a trip to Europe and, with Magnuson's evidence from Oklahoma on my father's U.S. citizenship in hand, we made an application to the Department of State for a passport. The Department of State had never been involved in any of this and to them it was easy to act objectively. They resisted at first, but finally found the evidence of my dad's citizenship feasible enough.

We had evidence that records from Hawley, Oklahoma had been lost. My grandmother's naturalization paper was missing but we knew she had to be a citizen in order to have filed on her homestead. It was very likely that my grandfather and my father had also become citizens. Since the State had lost the records we were entitled to liberal consideration. Even if they hadn't been citizens my dad would have become one by virtue of Oklahoma getting statehood in 1907. The State Department agreed with us and issued me a passport.

When the Immigration Department was asked to rescind their order on the basis that they could not deport an American citizen, the hounds of hell were loose. Under American law, tested many times, the power of the State Department and the Immigration Department to grant citizenship are equal. The passport itself states as follows:

The Secretary of State,
of the United States of America
Hereby requests all whom it may concern to permit this citizen national of the United States named herein to pass without delay or hindrance and in case of need to give all lawful aid and protection.

Under that appears my signature, my picture and the passport number and date of issue, the 7th of July, 1986.

I guess an army person would say we had outflanked them. However, that wasn't the purpose of applying for a passport. The purpose was simply to have the right after all these years to travel abroad.

Purpose or no, the Immigration Department was enraged and fired off a letter to the State Department, whereupon the State Department caved into the Immigration Department and sent me a letter March 23, 1987: demanding that I return the passport they renounced the passport issued by Paul Bigelow, an officer of the Department of State.

> *"A review of your file indicates that this passport was issued to you in error...*
>
> *"Therefore, the Department of State requests the return of U.S. passport 070404841 issued at Seattle, Washington on July 7, 1986. Your failure to do so immediately would be a violation of 18 U.S.C. 1544, which provides in relevant part that a person who willingly or knowingly uses a passport in violation of the rules regulating the issuance of passports shall be fined not more than $2,000 or imprisoned not more than five years or both... "*

We entered a lawsuit against George Schultz and the State Department July 28, 1987.

On July 19, 1988 Judge Robert J. McNichols of the District Court, Eastern District of Washington, passed judgement in part as follows on our case, against the Department of State:

> *"... It is clear from Mr. Bigelow's deposition testimony that he acted within the scope of his authority, that he had substantial experience in reviewing citizenship issues, that he examined the evidence in minute detail, that he engaged in research above and beyond the norm, and that notwithstanding the incomplete documentation in this case, he exercised conscious discretion in deeming the showing adequate...*
>
> *"Finally, and dispositive on the issue, the government candidly admitted during argument that it could not prove fraud, and consequently does not allege it.*
>
> *"The net result is that there are no regulatory grounds for re-opening Mr. Bigelow's determination, and thus under the rule... the Secretary has no authority to do so.*
>
> *"THEREFORE IT IS ORDERED that: ...*
>
> *...The purported "recall" of plaintiff's passport ... was without legal effect..."*

On September 18, 1988 we were notified that the State Department would register an appeal.

Although the attorney for the State Department opposed an appeal in this instance and in lieu of all the precedents of law, nevertheless Washington by now in full communication with the Immigration Department was adamant in their determination to appeal the completely lawful decision of Judge McNichols.

It seemed to me as if this whole crusade of "GET MYERS" starting with Revenue Canada had crusaded its way into the U.S. Immigration Department and finally infected the State Department itself. It seemed like this crook, Myers, had to be stopped by any means and every means in either country.

Bureaucracies die hard. They may be likened to the wild dogs of Africa which in great numbers will pursue any mighty beast of the veldt, yipping and ripping, constantly ripping and tearing until through loss of blood and exhaustion their prey tumbles and they close in.

Bureaucrats become so worked up over their mission that the law doesn't matter to them any more. The object is to expunge, destroy and virtually devour their prey. The forty-ninth parallel does not mark a distinction in the bureaucratic mentality. The pity is that regardless of what party or persons come to elected power, the bureaucrats remain forever. They are needed by their new bosses and soon the new bosses find that they are themselves superseded by the cancerous bureaucracies whose power seems never to diminish but always to grow.

My interpretation is that this whole problem started in the United States in the first place, firstly because I had infuriated the Securities and Exchange Commission by my defiance of their authority over me and by my insistence of immunity under the sovereignty of Canada, and secondly when I bought gold for American citizens, repressively prohibited from doing so in their own country.

I believe, and a lot of my readers believe, that U.S. bureaucrats appealed to their friendly Canadian counterparts in Revenue Canada for help. The knowledge that I was holding large amounts of secretly stored gold was just the kind of a Pavlovian stimulus to set the tax hounds salivating.

There are a lot of things we never get to know despite the

347

Freedom of Information Act. Private conversations, telephone calls and maybe some informal notes can quite unobtrusively start the bureaucratic balls rolling. One favor deserves another; if Revenue Canada went to the aid of their U.S. buddies on gold, why not U.S. Immigration deport Myers in return?

By Christmas 1987 the deportation date of January 20 still stood, and the State Department appeal still stood, both temporarily blunted by our own appeals.

Then something happened to upset everything.

It came in the form of a tragic development from a totally unexpected quarter.

Chapter Thirty-two

BACK IN THE FURNACE

As 1987 drew to a close I was ending my thirteenth year of turmoil, torment, torture. Unequally matched against two governments, it looked at last like I was beginning to hold my own. The penitentiary in Canada had nearly killed me, but by now it was clear that the tax hounds could not make good on their collections, although from an accounting standpoint they could still claim victory. My tax assessment of $1.2 million had by now, with interest, increased to over $2 million. No doubt this was and still is being carried in the books of Canada to the credit of the government.

In the United States the multi-billion dollar loans to the South American countries too are still being carried on the credit side of the U.S. banks; my alleged debt is probably an asset of about equal quality. Think of how much this will be worth by the year 2,000. Just as much as it's worth now.

In my fight with the U.S. bureaucrats I was by now carrying not only a green card which they had failed to take away from me in the course of a dozen years, but I also had tucked away a passport authorizing my citizenship. It's true that my opponents in City Hall on both sides of the forty-ninth still hadn't thrown in the towel. But they hadn't scored any victories either, that you could take a picture of. On the official scoreboard I seemed to be holding my own.

Under the surface, the division of my life remained unimproved. My daughter and her family had moved to Spokane and that had helped immensely, but on the larger purpose it had only served to split the family deeper. To make matters worse my wife's health was becoming increasingly worrisome.

She had been suffering from a chronic illness known as Crohn's Disease for several years. She had undergone two major operations. She was now becoming ill again. Now she was **afraid** to move to the United States. She knew her doctors, and they knew her. She felt another surgery looming. The dismal outlook for our future and the quality of our life had worsened. I tried my best to persuade Muriel to let me take her to Rochester, but by now she was insecure about that, generally insecure.

I couldn't get back to bolster her spirits. I could barely keep my own afloat. Living on a day-to-day basis I could get by. But whenever I tried to peer beyond the immediate present I became distressed, depressed, and sometimes nearly **possessed**. There was no way out of the trap. The jaws were closed.

Settlement with the Canadians was out of the question. I tried it early on with the offer of a quarter of a million dollars - which I didn't owe - and they rejected that. Later in the mid-1980s the torture became so intense that I could sometimes listen to myself talking late at night at the kitchen table. "I'll do anything; I'll pay any price. I'll pay a million dollars - even though I don't owe it - I can pay that. Anything to end this everlasting pain!"

And in fact I did ask my attorneys at one time to offer the government a million dollars for a full and complete resolution of the case. Revenue Canada flatly turned it down. They are the government's Pitbulls, charged with collecting money, but this time they were not interested in money. They wanted blood. They wanted me in jail. They wanted my hide and if they had to take my family's hide with it, they wanted that too.

Think of the vengeance I would face if I should ever cross the border and get picked up by the Mounted Police?

That turned out to be a very realistic question.

In the summer 1987, with my wife's health failing, I took on the risk of a trip on the sly into Canada with someone else driving a car not owned by me. While the risk of getting apprehended wasn't very great, the consequences of apprehension would be cataclysmic. Nevertheless I felt compelled to visit my wife and my home once more. I was concerned about her because her habit of visiting me in Spokane had tapered off almost completely.

I found her in good spirits, but not looking well. I think we all became apprehensive that she might be facing another surgery for Crohn's Disease. Meanwhile the doctors kept her on a steady diet of antibiotics, oblivious to the compounding effects of antibiotics on the system's immunity against a fatal yeast infection. Muriel seemed to lack the spirit as well as the initiative to travel. Rochester was out of the question. I returned to Spokane more apprehensive.

By October her condition had worsened and I got word that surgery for the Crohn condition was scheduled. Apparently now something was going to be done. I asked about the kidney stone which she was known to be carrying, but no one seemed concerned over that.

Muriel came through the operation, but she didn't recover. She was sent home and urged, ordered and badgered to walk around, take exercise, get going. She didn't have the strength.

In December, after seeing her mother through the operation, my daughter Norma with her family came down to visit me in Palm Springs. There we received a call of some urgency advising us that Muriel was back in intensive care. Norma flew to Calgary that night. I returned to Spokane the next day. Now we learned that the major surgery for Crohn's Disease had proved useless. There had been no further deterioration with the colon, only the formation of some harmless fibrous tissue around it. The operation needn't have been done at all. Tunnel vision on Crohn's Disease had been responsible for overlooking what was now confirmed to be a yeast infection, generated in a massive kidney stone, which had gone unchecked for quite some time.

In an atmosphere of urgency and a little bit of panic, a second major operation was scheduled. She had done well to withstand the first one showing a great deal more strength than had been expected. The second one was too much for her.

The surgery had taken place a few days before Christmas. I had flown back to Spokane for Christmas with members of my family. On Christmas Day we received word that Muriel was in critical condition and failing, and the suggestion that she might not live. By the end of the day word was that anybody that wanted to see her better do so at once.

At once means **AT ONCE**. I didn't have to think about what I was going to do. I didn't have to weigh any consequences, benefits or disadvantages.

On December 26, the morning following Christmas, I started on the four hundred and fifty mile trip to Calgary with some members of my family, proceeding immediately to the Foothills Hospital where my daughter Norma, my son Richard, my son Brian and my son John were huddled together. I was shown directly to Muriel's bedside. When I saw her, I knew I had arrived none too early.

When I arrived her heartbeat was weak, her pulse slow, her blood pressure very low as registered on the monitor. Upon my arrival she whipped back into consciousness, her heartbeat increased dramatically and so did her blood pressure and there was no doubt that she recognized me and heard me and understood all that I had to say. I said a great deal within those fifteen minutes that I wished I had said fifteen years before. It was too late now, but better said now than never. I praised the job she had done and the wonderful kids she had raised and I knew from her eyes she heard and understood me. It was obvious she wanted to speak, it was bitter medicine that with the tube down her throat, she couldn't utter a sound.

When the nurse asked Norma and I to leave for a few moments I went to the waiting room to make sure the road was still clear.

There had been an ominous complication. A woman had been burned to near death in Calgary. The gas jets had been opened, the flame extinguished. When she got up in the morning and lit a cigarette her house blew up completely and she was set afire, her body covered with third degree burns. She was in the intensive care concurrently with Muriel. This brought cops crowding day and night into the hospital waiting to lay a murder charge in case of the woman's death. At the same time my family was at the hospital visiting their mother. No doubt the police were well aware that Muriel was fatally ill and no doubt, as I know now, they hoped at last to pounce on me should I make an attempt to see my wife. The woman died and the police left, having apparently also left some ground work behind.

When we went to re-enter the curtained enclosure a Doctor Johnson stepped up and began to explain to me the ins and the outs of Muriel's sickness in tedious detail. I couldn't figure out the reason for it. I would suspect in about fifteen minutes that it was a delaying tactic. (They have up there a "CRIME STOPPERS" program featuring a reward system of up to $2,000 to anyone turning a convict over to the police, anonymity guaranteed.)

As Norma and I again approached my wife's bed, again her heartbeat and blood pressure increased and she was again aware but this time not for very long.

Inside ten minutes, I am told, police were swarming in the Foothills Hospital. Six uniformed policemen were counted in the main waiting room which I had just left and four more were at the back door. My son-in-law, Sam Jensen, personally saw Doctor Johnson padlock another door which my son-in-law presumed to be an exit. Norma, who had left as soon as I returned to the bedside, came back now and urgently whispered, "The cops are here, Dad. They've come for you!"

At about the same time, the lady hospital administrator appeared at the edge of the curtain and motioned me to come out. My daughter said to her; "You can't do that now. My mother is dying."

The administrator said, "It's either come out now. Or they're coming in to get him."

353

The jig was up.

I hope that Muriel did not know what was going on. I tried to bid her a casual and quiet good night. There was no way I could prolong this visit another moment. When I came out two of the policemen advanced toward me and led me to the elevator and down and out of the hospital.

I was driven at once to the Remand Center, familiar to me now from the days of 1979, eight years earlier. The same routine, prison clothes, clanging steel doors.

Not especially well myself, suffering from an ulcer, I was taken to the prison hospital ward, which is not much better than any other ward, but I was allowed to receive a call from my son. Richard, now a lawyer himself, was working with some other lawyers to prevail upon the Remand Center and the Royal Canadian Mounted Police to allow me to return once more to the hospital to talk to my dying wife. That was arranged finally. By one o'clock in the morning I was back again in the General Hospital.

But this time Muriel's response was much weaker. I don't believe she was fully conscious. I believe she said good-bye to me on my first visit, when I left her.

My kids were in a state of disarray. The dynamite that I had foreseen had exploded now in the midst of us. Mother dead and Dad in jail.

This time the cops didn't let me stay very long, perhaps ten minutes, but this time it didn't matter. I knew it was all over now. At noon the next day Muriel passed to the Great Beyond.

Chapter Thirty-three

TURNING UP THE HEAT

Two officers returned me to the Remand Center and by 2:00 A.M. I was in my prison cell and in my prison bed. It was quite a jarring change from my Spokane bed of the night before, Christmas night.

An exhausting and traumatic eighteen hours was behind me, but I was far from sleep. The worst of my nightmares had come to pass. I wondered how my kids were faring with their grief. I felt it was worse than mine and I wished that I could be near them to comfort them. This black hole was the blackest of the black. No dad this time to lift me out. Nobody in this world could lift me out. I expected the full wrath of Revenue Canada. My enemies had me at last.

I couldn't help but think back on my life, my austere childhood, but nevertheless a security, gone forever. I thought back too of the early days of my marriage with Muriel, the "Ralph Cramdon" bare apartment, the small gas stove and the icebox, the rapid development of my career, the earning power, the new house which I had extracted from the stock market, the big happy home on Mount Royal; in retrospect now, the near idyllic life in our new country home with our children a single family unit, the battle for *OILWEEK* survival, the great victory when the fledging *OILWEEK* had finally trounced its last competitor. And then, more than any time since it had happened, I regretted that sale.

When I had *OILWEEK*, I didn't worry about taxes; let my auditor figure it out, I signed whatever he told me to sign. I made the cradle for my troubles when I began to publish my investment letter. Now *Myers Finance and Energy* might be a legend in its field, but Myers himself was in the hands of the Philistines.

A man now seventy-five years of age would ask himself, "Where did I go wrong?" I didn't ask that question. I didn't go wrong. The law went wrong and the law was still wrong!

No way would I cave in now; my wife's death was a direct result of the unprovoked raid of 1974.

In the States my plight was often referred to in the context of "Canada's curious system of justice." It was widely known that my trial had been an example of double jeopardy. In no other country in the western world would an accused, tried and acquitted, have to stand trial again on the identically same charges and with the same evidence. It was a blot on the record of Canadian justice and therefore a blot on Canada. The longer it continued the bigger the blot would get.

I think by the time I went to sleep that night my mood had changed from grief, to anger, to defiance. I resolved, however, to keep my prison behavior beyond reproach. Their ammunition was pretty well used up; I would be careful not to hand them more.

In the Remand Center once again I visited my friends and family through thick plate-glass connected by telephone facing each other a few inches apart. In the week following I was allowed two or three so-called "open visits." An open visit was in a separate room with the visitor or visitors. I had one such visit with my attorneys, one with my son Richard, the lawyer, together with my daughter, Norma, and one other poignant visit. My sister in New York, the moment she heard the bad news boarded a plane for Calgary. Once in Calgary she immediately made arrangements with the Remand Center to visit me and they had okayed the visit, but when she got there the officers in charge refused to let her in on the grounds that she did not have the proper papers. My sister, now seventy years old, broke down in such grief that even cold-hearted men took pity on her. For once they bent the rules. They let her in.

A day or two after Muriel's death I had to get busy. I saw a new defense attorney, a specialist of some renown in criminal trials. Chris Evans discussed our defense primarily aimed at blunting an almost inevitable prosecution effort to exact the maximum punishment for the crime of escaping from jail. Also a newsletter would be due in about two weeks and I had to begin to think about that.

The funeral date was set for December 31, five days after my wife departed this world, never to suffer again the uncompromising stress, injustice, or any more pain. I was advised that I would be escorted to the funeral at 2:00 P.M. December 31.

When we were ready to leave the prison, one of the guards motioned for me to extend my arms whereupon he brought out the handcuffs. I begged, **"Please for this, don't make me . . .!"**

The officer spoke sternly, "It's either this way or not at all."

I extended my arms and the cuffs were clamped.

I was brought down early to the get-ready room where I exchanged my prison garb for some street clothes that had been obtained and delivered by my sons. We arrived a few minutes before two o'clock at the funeral parlor. I was led by two plain-clothes officers into the mourner's room which adjoined the funeral chapel, and from whence we could see the audience and the minister, but they could not see us.

In the mourner's room my small grandson, sensing the tragedy, wanted to sit on my lap. He did but I couldn't hold him because my hands were cuffed.

The funeral chapel was filled to capacity. My wife had myriads of friends and it seemed like they were all there. The eulogy by Jack Brown, one of my best friends and our next door neighbor on the Midnapore farm for twenty years, was a touching tribute to Muriel, her personality and her humanity. Then we were allowed to walk past the coffin to view the body. One plain-clothesman who had sat beside me throughout the ceremony moved aside to where he could keep me clearly in view . The other plain-clothesman who had been sitting behind us was observed by

357

a member of my family to have wept.

Muriel looked beautiful and young. Her countenance was never more benign. I could not reach out to touch her because my hands were bound. But now it didn't matter any more.

The plain-clothesman told me I would not be allowed to go to the burial ground. I would be returned immediately to the Remand Center. I didn't try to fight him. It would have been a useless provocation. Muriel would not have wanted me to create a commotion now.

They took me out to the enclosed garage, a part of the funeral home where the vehicle was parked. It was a station wagon. When they escorted me to it and motioned me to get in I noticed the letters on the side of the vehicle in silver or nickel. They read "Attorney General Dept."

I was returned to the jail.

It took an hour or more by the time we got through the red tape to complete the change from the street clothes back into the prison clothes.

That completed, another officer approached me carrying handcuffs. I asked with genuine curiosity, "What now?"

The officer replied, "You're going to Bowden."

I said, "When?"

"Right now."

Within a few moments I found myself under double escort seated in a prison vehicle on the road to Bowden, eighty to ninety miles north.

It was a bitterly cold day, December 31, 1987. My wife was in the ground. I arrived at the Bowden Penal Institution, was inducted and processed, fingerprinted and photographed, all in time to witness the new year, January 1, 1988.

Chapter Thirty-four

TO THE RESCUE

The Bowden Penitentiary of 1988 was a far cry from the penitentiary of 1979. Old buildings had been demolished and new ones had sprung up. The jail I had served in, with its cardboard walls between cells, had been destroyed. The prison population at Bowden was several times what it had been eleven years earlier. There were none of the same inmates, although there were several of the same guards.

The old guards generally were very friendly toward me. Most of them expressed regret that I had returned.

The rules of the prison hadn't changed much. A little more lenient perhaps, individual cells with private toilet and sink, a modest bookcase, and room for a personal TV set to any inmate who could afford to buy one. The inside of the building looked more like a conference hall than jail. The control center might have been a replica of the control center at NASA where they shoot up the rockets.

But a prison is a prison. The amenities are superficial. The basic thing about a prison is denial of liberty. The high fence, the gun turrets, the uniformed guards, the regimentation; they all are constant reminders that you are penned up. You will get out at **their** pleasure, when they let you out, **if** they let you out.

You were free to phone but they only had one phone and in the evenings this was at the disposal and use of about sixty inmates. You would find yourself in a line-up that could last a couple of hours in order to get a phone call away. If the number was busy you might have to get back in the end of the line again. Generally the atmosphere was good. The only thing wrong with it, really, was that it was a prison.

I knew almost right away that this was going to be a different go-around than I had in 1979. I hadn't been in prison much more than a week when I got a letter from the Parole Board stating the date of my parole hearing. Normally, you have to apply for your hearing about a month in advance and then if there is too big a case load you will have to wait until the Parole Board comes around for another visit the following month. This early notice of hearing without any initiative on my part told me a big story.

They didn't want me. I wasn't the only one getting heat. They were getting some too. A rash of human interest stories infected the press of Canada. One story, in the *Calgary Herald* I think, following the day of my arrest was headlined "LOVE OF DYING WIFE BRINGS FUGITIVE HOME." This was a story that seemed to catch the imagination of the media. It was on local radio one place or another nearly every day. Subscribers in the United States were firing off letters to the Minister of Justice. No doubt the Minister didn't relish the job of replying to all these irate correspondents. They used words like despicable, repressive, curious system of justice. I knew there was a rush on to get me the hell out of there.

But I was afraid the Parole hearing was coming too early. Charges had been laid against me for my escape in 1979. There was no way of knowing what penalty the judge would levy. After all, following my escape, I had rather sneered at my former jailers and tormenters. A few days after I left in 1979 I was invited to appear on the Merv Griffin show. The first question Merv asked me when I came on the stage was: "I hear you have just escaped from jail?" Before I had a chance to answer he said, "a Canadian jail." He was obviously very anxious to let the audience know that he was not talking to some American convict who had escaped an American jail. Getting out of a Canadian jail was okay. When he repeated a second time, "You've escaped from a Canadian jail?"

I said, "No. I was out on a pass and I just haven't got back yet." For some reason this brought a great laugh from the audience.

I could think of many bureaucrats in Canada who would be less than pleased to see their ex-con, their tax evader, the guy that had bilked the government out of a million dollars, so they said - to see this culprit as the instigator of ridicule, laughter at the Canadian justice system. When you're a criminal you're not supposed to get honored. You are supposed to go in hiding, remain penitent and try to keep your crime a secret.

Instead, the show *Fifth Estate*, a Canadian version of *60 Minutes* followed me to New Orleans, Louisiana, where I addressed an audience of five thousand people. The camera showed bands marching, showed me prominently as the tough news reporter sparring with California's Governor Brown, at that time a hopeful for the U.S. Presidency. The *Fifth Estate* took their camera crews to visit Congressman McDonald in Georgia who gave them a piece of his mind regarding Revenue Canada. He said, "It just seems to me like some pointy-headed bureaucrat up there has got the idea that he's going to punish Myers." He said, "Here we've got one of the most brilliant analytical minds in the country and they want to put him in jail." He said, "In the old days they used to burn them at the stake." He said, "Maybe they should've burned Myers at the stake. Might have been more kind to him."

The camera crew then went to Bowden Penitentiary. They photographed the cell where I had spent my time. They photographed Judge Holmes' court where the **double jeopardy** judgment had been handed down. They went out to my Spokane home on Graves Road with their camera crews. Adrian Clarkson who was leading the inquiry rode horseback with me on my property. They followed me out to Coeur d'Alene Lake and photographed me at the helm of my Bayliner cruiser. They even went to see Howard Ladd, overseer of the tax oligarchy in Alberta. Mr. Ladd did not come across very well in the interview. All in all it couldn't have been a worse public relations effort for Revenue

Canada. It didn't seem like they wanted a reoccurrence of 1979 now in 1988, and that was why I was fairly confident I would get out soon, except for the possibility of a stiff sentence for escaping jail.

My Calgary attorney Chris Evans was working hard on that. He visited me several times in the Bowden Pen. He engaged a well known criminal psychologist and also a psychiatrist. He had them interview me and proposed to use parts of their testimony. The psychiatrist, Dr. Thomas Dalby said,

"At the time of his departure he was clinically depressed, anxious and was terrified of two things: the possibility he might die in prison and the possibility he would go mad."

The trial was put off several times because of unavailability of guards to take me to Red Deer, about thirty miles away where the hearing was being held under Justice A.M. Lutz. Finally in the nick of time a few days before the Parole Board was to hear me, the trial did take place and the judgment was issued quite promptly after the second day. It was very light I thought. I expected anything up to three months and maybe double that time. The judge sentenced me to thirty days. Since I had already served over thirty days it didn't amount to any more time at all.

I found the court sympathetic. Revenue Canada men were there to observe and one would have thought that the prosecutor would have been pleased by a sentence condemning me to a dungeon for life. They were not pleased by Evans' defense summary as it was reported in the media:

"Calling Myers 'one of the world's last angry men' lawyer Chris Evans said his client felt he had been treated unjustly because he was convicted of tax evasion after being acquitted in an earlier trial. When the Crown appealed the decision a new trial was held and Myers was convicted in absentia.

"'He had in his mind been kept in something that hasn't been around for a couple hundred years, a debtor's prison.'"

But by this time the strain had taken a visible toll on my health and I guess on my appearance. Evans appealed to the court for a short recess while he asked if I wanted to continue for the rest of the day. We had been going several hours.

Evans said that it may be that Myers needs a recess. He said, "But my client is a tough old bird and he may want to go on."

Of course I wanted to go on. I wanted to get it over with. The judge kindly ordered an easy chair instead of the stiff-backed wooden chair I was sitting in.

Evans spoke most emphatically, dwelling on my tribulations and on the life-threatening conditions, in my opinion, from which I had felt I must escape for the sake of my survival. When he was through Evans was ready to deliver the final K.O. "To harshly treat this man," Evans said, "would be like beating up on Bambi."

I think it was a good defense. I think it was a good line. And I think it was an extra lenient sentence.

Evans came up to be with me at the Parole Board hearing. At my previous hearing in 1979 you will remember the Parole Board would not even let my attorney Marshall into the room. Now they listened patiently to Evans but even before Evans had a chance to speak the Board spokesman informed me that **the tax situation would not influence their decision.** He seemed to want to make that very clear. That would be between Revenue Canada and me from now on. Only a masochist could have summoned a pessimistic state of mind in the midst of such an approach.

The board seemed generally understanding and they offered me a choice of two different paroles. In the one case I could be paroled in Canada but for the term of my parole I could not leave the country. In the other case I could be paroled in the United States if the United States would take me, but it seemed I would not be able to come back to Canada.

This would have still left my life dissected, neither one thing nor the other. For the first time the situation lost its glitter. I didn't see how any of this - even parole - could now heal me. My wife was dead; Canada had lost its allure. Why would I want to live here on a permanent basis now, with my newsletter business centered in Spokane, Washington? I couldn't make any money in Canada because the tax department had about a two million dollar bill against me. That alternative didn't look good.

On the other hand if I went to the States I would have to live out my parole without recourse of visits to Canada to my old Canadian home. Now with a bleak looking stretch of life ahead of me a temporary despondency settled in.

But it seemed like I might have given up too fast. Evans got in touch with my lawyers in Spokane and the next thing I knew I was being visited by Les Weatherhead of the law firm of Witherspoon, Kelley, a firm who had served me well since 1977. Now, it seemed, all the brains available were going to work on a solution to this problem. And maybe nobody would be more anxious to see it mature than the Justice Minister of Canada, for all I know. Maybe even Revenue Canada, having failed to collect their money, having lost their prey, had also lost their appetite for me. I nearly felt sorry for them - but not quite.

In 1979 after I escaped I was quoted in the *Calgary Herald* as saying I was coming back to serve out my time. On my demise, the *Herald* stated, and in the interest of fairness, I would have my ashes sent to Revenue Canada to finish out my term at Bowden, on the understanding they would then return my ashes to my beneficiary. Apparently a lot of people thought this was funny but Revenue Canada was not among them.

No wonder they hated me. I relished it. I had paid a high price for their hate.

Now it looked like one way or another I'd be soon out of this jail.

I hoped for that for more than one reason. In all my years I never saw such a cold winter, at least since my pig operation had collapsed half a century earlier.

I had to walk each day, and return, a full three blocks to the so-called visiting headquarters. The snow crunched under my feet, a sure sign of below-zero temperatures. My face had to be totally covered against the breaking cold. If the winter wasn't the worst in all of my experience, it seemed like it. Maybe the addition of fifty years made it colder. My blood didn't run as fast as it did then and neither did I.

But that was the last thing I would complain about. My visits meant everything to me and I could count on them every day. My loyal sister and my equally loyal friend, Katy Lord, had actually taken up residence in a small motel in this small town to make sure no day would pass without their undaunting support. Katy had seen me through many debilitating crises during my exile, and, in the time of my first imprisonment, my sister had taken leave of absence from her job in New York to be with me. The two of them fought blizzards and frozen cars to be with me now.

Following is an ultimate expression of the paralyzing cold as I had described it in one of my poems a long time ago. This is a fair description of the winter of 1987-88;

WAY OUT IN THE GREAT NORTHWEST

When the wild wind whips round the corner's tips,
And the cold crisp air right smartly nips,
When the warm words freeze on the speaker's lips,
Then they know that they're caught in the winter's grips
Way out in the Great Northwest.

When the blizzards blow with the blinding snow,
And the eye can see the great drifts grow,
And the swiftest streams refuse to flow,
The shiv'ring traveller then may know
That he's out in the Great Northwest.

When the moon glares down, with a chill'd frown
On hill and valley, city, town,
And every step is a crunching sound,
It's sure that the winter's coming round
Way out in the Great Northwest.

Where your breath comes out like a smokestack spout,
And the air will freeze the shrillest shout,
Within itself like the swiftest trout
Is caught in the ice e'er it twirls about
Way out in the Great Northwest.

But the ways are free in that great country,
Free from the bonds of society.
All is atune with the harmony,
And that is the life, that's the life for me
Way out in the Great Northwest.

No more will I roam from that starset dome,
Though the frost may chill to the marrow-bone,
Though the snow may fall and the wind may moan,
Yet I'm going back to my native home
Way out in the Great Northwest.

I may have felt nostalgically about "going back to my home."
Well, I was there; now all I wanted was to get out.

Chapter Thirty-five

FULL PAROLE

Now that the situation was straightened out with the Canadians we were up against a blank wall with the American Immigration Department. True, I was carrying a passport. The Department of State had ordered me to return the passport on the basis that it had been issued in error. Justice R. J. McNichols, in the Eastern District Court of Washington, rebuffed that attempt and it was an order in the court that I could retain the passport.

However, the State Department had meanwhile registered an appeal against this decision.

The question now was: If once outside the United States, would the Immigration Department, in view of their rather severe attitude, let me back into the States? I might be on legally sound ground but if the Immigration Department were to refuse me entry, what would happen to my parole arrangements in Canada?

The Parole Board had agreed to parole me completely if they could be guaranteed that the United States would allow my re-entry into the country. In order to make sure of this my lawyers in Spokane, spearheaded by Les Weatherhead, obtained a temporary court injunction requiring the Immigration Department to admit me into the country, but this was a narrow window. If I failed to reach the border by the appointed time for entry I could be refused. If refused I would be back in Canada without the official parole. Les Weatherhead was walking a tightrope. Here is the account of how it was handled, as I related it later in my newsletter:

The Board spelled out the condition for being paroled to

Spokane. *They would need a U.S. guarantee that I would be allowed to enter and that I would be able to spend the full sixteen months of parole in the United States. Meanwhile the U.S. began erecting barriers against my entry.*

* * * *

My U.S. lawyers had learned that the Immigration Department had flagged my name at all entry points into the U.S. and that even my passport was to be invalidated by the claim that it had been erroneously issued by the State Department.

First off Friday morning, March 18, my Spokane lawyers hauled the State Department into court, and were successful in obtaining the following restraining order.

"The Secretary of State, George Shultz, his agents and employees are enjoined from denying, restricting, revoking, invalidating or otherwise adversely affecting the ability of Charles Vernon Myers to use his passport."

But I'd have to be back over the border by the following Friday.

The Immigration Department still had to be dealt with. Over the weekend the injunction case was prepared. First thing Monday morning March 21 we faced them in court with the application for an injunction against Immigration from hindering my re-entry. We got that Monday afternoon.

Now the necessity was to get the Canadian Parole Board to act with unusual and maybe unprecedented speed. At 10:30 next morning (Tuesday) March 22 Les Weatherhead of my Spokane law firm was sitting before the Parole Board a thousand miles north at Saskatoon, Saskatchewan. Setting up this meeting in such haste was a minor miracle but it had been arranged by Magnuson late Monday.

By afternoon Weatherhead had prevailed upon the Board to issue an Order for Parole to the United States and the parole was electronically transmitted to the prison. Next morning **(Wednesday)** *Weatherhead was waiting for me in the Bowden jail at about 10:30. The order from the Board allowing my* release the next day, Wednesday, had run into opposition in the jail. The local parole officer said such speed was impossible. The injunction order to Immigration would expire the following Monday and we felt we had to be across the border at least on Thursday to prevent a possible weekend foul-up.

A 48-hour delay in release might still blow up the whole arrangement. We would not likely be able to get a second injunction.

But unknown to me Weatherhead had not taken no for an answer yet, and by 2:00 P.M. Wednesday was back in contact with the Saskatoon Parole Board several hundred miles away. There by some miraculous process Weatherhead prevailed upon the Board to reverse the order of the Red Deer official. The official had changed the release day to Friday. The Board now electronically changed it back to Thursday.

Early Thursday morning I was roused and ordered to get over to the Administration Building at once. I had no idea why.

It usually takes me an hour in the morning before I can become mobile. I stumbled the three blocks up to the Administration Building by 8:40 and at this point I was told that I was leaving by noon. I faced a very brisk morning. I had to get releases signed by the hospital, library, the games room, the gym, mostly places I had never been in, and the Administration had to issue a check for the money I had on account. I was required to give my cell an immaculate cleaning and emptying. I didn't get to lunch but I did get up to the gate at the jail by 12:15.

My lawyer, and my son, who had accompanied him, had been sent off to lunch, being told that I could not be released in less than an hour. Our vital departure from Calgary by plane to a small town called Castlegar, a hundred miles north of the border, was at 2:10. At 1:15 I was still standing in the exit room when my son drove up. Our average speed to Calgary was a little more than 100 miles an hour. We made it.

Meanwhile in Spokane the lawyers, now assisted by Brian

369

Rekofke, were preparing all the ammunition that might be required to stop Immigration Officers from obstructing my entry; including preparations to again contact the Spokane court and get a U.S. Marshal if necessary to pull the door open at the border.

Our plane arrived in Castlegar about 3:15 and by appointment and with some excess speed, three of my Spokane lawyers plus secretary Lori Svoboda, who had been in the thick of all of it, picked up Weatherhead and me, in two cars. They had driven 160 miles up from Spokane so we could cross the border by car together. Prepared for a battle with the authorities we drew up to the border about 6:00 P.M. And so faced the moment of truth!

The Immigration Officer on duty asked us if we had brought anything into the States to which we replied, "cookies" which we were eating. She asked Bob Magnuson, driving the car, his citizenship to which he replied American and she looked to each of us as we nodded, yes.

"Proceed," she said, and we were in the United States.

One stop to express our euphoria; six large goblets of beer and a toast to all.

By 8:00 P.M. on that Thursday I was in my home in Spokane eating dinner with some of my family.

* * * *

And the parole was enlarged to include return to Canada at any time by merely announcing my intended entry date and notifying of my departure date. That's more than I could ever have hoped for.

Not the least of the elements that brought eventual success was an editorial in *Alberta Report* magazine by publisher Ted Byfield, which in the space of one page, narrated a story of stinging truth studded with crystal clear damning fact on damning fact. A masterpiece that spread a swath of stinging truth ranging far and wide beyond the normal operating range of *Alberta Report*.

* * * * * * * * * *

From the *Alberta Report*, January 18, 1988, by Ted Byfield:

If Myers Had Merely Raped And Murdered He'd Be Free

Among all the careers pursued by human beings, the job of collecting taxes does not rank high. From the detested publicans of biblical times to the lupine ledgerdredgers of the modern Revenue Canada, they have always suffered a certain odium. An accountant friend speaks of any C.A. employed as a taxman as having "joined the other side." Such, fairly or not, is their image, and an incident last month in Calgary did little to enhance it.

I suspect the shoguns of the Revenue Department literally hate the name Charles Vernon Myers. No single case has done more to damage their reputation, undermine their authority, destroy their morale and impugn their integrity than the one they brought 14 years ago against Vern Myers. Worse still, he owes them money they can't get him to pay. They have raided him, audited him, hounded him, grilled him, arrested him, jailed him, and spent hundreds of thousands of dollars prosecuting him, and still he won't pay. They have also watched helplessly for eight years as he sneered at them on national American television and poured contempt upon them in the press. If they have some sort of hit list, the name at the top of it must be Charles Vernon Myers.

Last month, true enough, they got him. But they still haven't got the money. Moreover, he makes a disappointing conquest. How do you crow about "nabbing" a man who is 75 years old, having caught him only because he visited his wife on her deathbed from which you dragged him away? And especially when it took an irregular trial, a Supreme Court ruling, and the use of laws that have since been repealed to prove that he did anything wrong in the first place. . .

. . .And the tax officers are probably good men, doing the

job we assigned them, and on our behalf. But more and more they are viewed in the West as the agents of a government in which we have no effective voice, a government that increasingly speaks a language we cannot understand and have no real opportunity to learn, a government that takes our money and pours it into stupidly wasteful programs that impoverish and demean us. Small wonder that people who defy the agents of this government become folk heroes, while the agents themselves become, as my accountant friend calls them, the representatives of "the other side."

Chapter Thirty-six

BACK HOME

For a short time after I returned to my home in Spokane I felt pretty well beat up. But I had a newsletter to turn out and if it was to come out on time, as every issue had since February 1967, I would have to get at it right away.

When the newsletter was out I felt that I could use a short rest in Palm Springs and accordingly departed there soon afterwards.

I didn't expect any surprises in Palm Springs, but I got one.

On about the second or third day when I was out riding my horse in the desert I came up short with a terrible stab in my back when I went into the canter. This was something brand new; I couldn't understand it. I started the horse on a canter again, and again the excruciating stab in the back. I let it go for two or three days and tried it again. The same thing. I was going to see a chiropractor about it, but at the last minute changed my mind in favor of a medical doctor.

Upon examination the doctor thought that my liver might be a little enlarged so he ordered an ultrasound test. The ultrasound showed up right away but not in the area of the liver, rather in the area of the kidney. There seemed to be a very large growth. The doctor suggested that I should have a CAT scan and probably should go home and see my own doctors in Spokane.

It kind of looked serious but I wasn't very worried about it. I couldn't see how a growth on my kidney could relate to a stab in the spinal column. The CAT scan explained it.

My kidney was encased in a huge cancer. This cancer was

373

so big that it was pressing against my spinal cord. It was also pushing against the vena-cava vein, the body's largest blood thoroughfare. I was told I would have to have surgery right away. They would have to remove the kidney.

I wasn't too scared of that. I knew that people could get along well with one kidney, and of course the removal of the kidney would get rid of the whole thing. Accordingly within about a week thereafter I went under the knife.

I made a deal with the doctors that I wanted to see the kidney after they took it out. They agreed to that, but after it was out they didn't want to show it to me. They said the pathology lab might not be very agreeable.

Well, a deal is a deal. I made that a condition ahead of the operation. I insisted that they live up to it. So they prevailed on the pathology lab. I can't say it was a pleasant sight. The best I can say is; good riddance.

During the operation there had been some tense moments I understand. The kidney was so hard against the vena-cava vein that they had to scrape the vein. That could be a little dangerous. I'm told I lost six pints of blood. I believe my operation consumed six hours. Anyway when I got out of there I was pretty weak for a day or two.

There was another strange thing about it. Somewhere a short distance away from that infected kidney there was a lymphoma or a cancer of lymphocytes. As far as I can learn no one had ever seen this in conjunction with a kidney cancer. Recently I asked about it but they have not yet come up with an explanation as to why or how it was there. Anyway, it's gone.

After a couple of days I realized that the newsletter was coming up again before too long and a lot of correspondence was piled, so I asked my secretary to come up. I sat up for some time giving her dictation. The nurse on duty did say that she had never before seen anyone giving dictation while in intensive care.

I got along quite well there, no problems except for one instance when a nurse tried to push some tubes at me and I called her a "Sergeant Bitch." But maybe I was a little delirious then and I could be excused for that.

I was out in a little over a week and feeling pretty good. In ten days I was swimming and shortly thereafter I began to ride my horse. This time no pains in the back.

Within a couple of weeks I took a trip to Calgary to test out my new parole. According to the instructions all I had to do was to inform them when I was coming and how long I intended to stay and to call on them by appointment when I arrived. This I did. It all went smoothly. No hitches. I was finally clear of the fifteen-year-old Canadian disaster.

After I got back I went in for an examination and they found out that I had a carotid artery that was ninety percent plugged. My doctors said that while there might be a danger of a stroke under surgery, there would be a very much greater danger without surgery. I agreed, everything went fine, I was released from the hospital by my surgeon on September 3, 1988, two days after the operation. I returned on the afternoon of September 4, 1988 of my own free will because my swollen jaw gave me the appearance of a walrus. I went to Emergency, I signed no papers of admission.

After some treatment I asked for my clothes to go home and they refused to give them to me. They said I was staying all night.

As you know, I don't like being pushed around. I don't mind taking orders from someone who has the authority. But I was damn sure that the hospital had no authority to detain me any more than fifty years earlier Bechtel, Price, Callahan had any right to detain me, the contesting of which led to my being branded a nonconformist and set off the whole mess from the early 1940s to the present as has been here related.

No way was I going to stay in the hospital overnight. I didn't enter the hospital with that understanding. The following is an account of what happened in this confrontation from MFE Quiet Corner September 23, 1988:

You might think that the absolute heighth of authority would be found in prisons. This is not the case. Prison authorities work inside clear guidelines. They are careful not to exceed them.

Who would you think then would take first place in the exercise of carte blanche authority?

Surely not the hospitals.

You're wrong. Let me tell you a little story, just off the griddle, about a hospital.

On September 1, 1988 I underwent a second surgery this summer, in this case for the cleaning of a carotid artery traveling up the neck to the right brain.

When two doctors ordered me detained I protested vocally. One of the sergeant nurses read me the riot act and told me what I would do and what I wouldn't do. And what I would do would be to stay in the hospital.

So I simply got out of bed and started to dress. Three nurses tried to put me back. Seeing they couldn't handle me they called in the big guns; two bruisers, one at least 6'6" must have weighed 280 pounds, the other well over 6' and built like a bear. The wrestling match that followed was brief. In a minute I found myself strapped on my back, restrained, strapped tightly around my middle, arms shackled thereto just above the hands. When I began to rebel at this treatment the sergeant nurse confronted me with a needle and syringe in one hand, a large pill in the other. She said the pill was an oral dose of 500 milligrams of valium and I could have either the injection or the pill. Choose!

So faced with an ultimatum and bound to my bed, I indicated the pill.

When she put it in my mouth I spat it out. (Shades of "The Cuckoos Nest.") She came to me again and this time I agreed to take the pill and I bit it in two. I had to swallow the one half but I fooled them on the other half.

Remember they're dealing with a 76-year-old man 72 hours away from arterial surgery, where there is danger of a blood clot that could cause a fatal stroke. A wrestling match would hardly seem to be the ticket. I strained at my bonds secretly. I am lucky in that I have a very small hand. After a lot of wriggling I got one out of the loop. I unstrapped myself, threw the covers aside, and jumped out of bed.

The nurses came fluttering back, three of them again. By some prearranged signal the goons immediately returned. We engaged then in a second wrestling match. I didn't last long either. I found myself flat on my back again with a straightjacket binding my upper body and my arms and a second one over my knees binding my lower body to the bed.

Meanwhile, I had demanded the use of a telephone but they refused; they did agree to phone my son. My son phoned my personal physician, Dr. G.M. Pavey, and asked him to intervene. Dr. Pavey agreed to give up his quiet Sunday evening and came to see me in the hospital at ten o'clock. I started to speak but I could see Pavey's reservations immediately. He said, "Do you know who I am?"

"Of course, I know who you are!" I'm afraid I showed indignation.

Dr. Pavey, apparently coached on my failing sanity; "All right, tell me who I am."

"You're Dr. Pavey, and you've been treating me for nine years and for God's sake I ought to know who you are!"

At that point the good doctor reached in and undid the leather buckles. I still had a few tests to pass; I had to touch my index fingers together at the top of my head and at the point of my nose, walk a straight line, and a few other things whereupon the doctor said he would release me. He said it would give him trouble but he would release me.

Whatever arguments there were I don't know. But I do know that I was given all my clothes and my son was authorized to take me out. Just as I was passing the main desk the sergeant nurse slapped down a form and a pen. "Sign this!"

I said, "Are you telling me, or are you asking me? If you're asking me, I may sign it. Which?"

For answer she gave me a sabre-toothed glare. For answer
I turned my back and strode out of the hospital.

* * * *

Why do I relate this personal experience?

Because I think it is one that elderly people should be
aware of. Hospitals apparently have more license for tyranny
than our prisons do. If you should have to enter the hospital
of your own free will be sure that your friend or relative who
takes you in makes it clear to the authorities that you are
surrendering no rights. You might not want to take a big shot
of Valium to quiet you down any more than I did.

This example of raw authority and brutal strength took
place in my case at Sacred Heart Hospital, the biggest and best
known in Spokane. I don't doubt that there are scores like it
in the U.S.

* * * * * * * * * *

As of the summer of 1989 things have settled down pretty
well. But sometimes I wake up with the feeling that all of this must
have been a bad dream. Then it occurs to me that perhaps after
all FANTASTIC DREAM was an allegorical prophecy. Let me
take you back to the ending of that dream and see whether it differs
much from this improbable tale.

When I awoke upon the floor
Three bumps upon my head I bore;
I did not have to look for more
For all my body'd seen the war;
And I was marked with blood and gore,
From head to foot all bruised and sore.

I rose and to my bed I went;
The sheets in tiny shreds were rent;
The frame was battered, smashed and bent,
From the wildest night I ever spent.

378

The sun was riding noonday high;
No single star was in the sky;
How thankful then to know was I
'Twas all a dream and all a lie.

For stranger things I've never seen;
I dread to think what they could mean.

Still not manifest as of yet is the verdict of an appeal by the State Department against a court judgment which said they could not take my passport away.

That outcome isn't known, but whatever happens, I guarantee it won't be the subject of another book.